THE HIGH-PERFORMANCE CULTURE PLAYBOOK: UNLOCKING THE SECRETS OF HIGHLY SUCCESSFUL GROUPS AND WINNING TEAMS

USING THE PARADOXICAL MANAGEMENT ASSESSMENT SYSTEM

(PMAS)

BY

SAM SCHREIM

CONTENTS

INTRODUCTION

These are unprecedented times, and traditional ways of achieving high performance and competitive advantage by adopting best practices, management tools, benchmarking, or scaling are no longer sufficient in doing so.

Technologies and assets that once cost millions to access are now accessible at a fraction of the cost to companies and organizations of all sizes. Previously pricey and complex enterprise tools are now becoming simpler, cheaper, and quicker to deploy across all kinds of businesses. This has enabled large, medium, and small organizations to compete in leveled playing fields, and has fueled the growth of status quo disruptors.

Market changes taking the form of global shocks, unprecedented events, and positive streams of innovation are blessings to those who can embrace them but are curses to those who are unable to cope with the pace of change happening all around them. This is especially the case considering the current reality, as economic unpredictability, technological disruption, globalization, and fierce competition have been altering the market for quite some time and will not cease in doing so. As such, a company must be able to address these new realities, adapt to changing conditions, and deliver bold change in order to gain a competitive advantage and sustain itself in the long-term.

Until such a time exists when robots and humanoids take over the planet, at least two things are certain: 1. We will continue to rely on organizations and their members to deliver the goods and services we require for our daily lives. 2. The market is changing at an alarmingly accelerated pace. Accordingly, the companies that adapt quickly to these changes will thrive, and the market will be dominated by a number of successful companies that have adopted the "winner takes all" mentality.

In addition to changes in external factors, your organization may be experiencing a shift in one of its most vital internal factors:

9

organization culture. If you have worked in a company going through accelerated growth, you would have noticed an organizational culture shift which made it harder to establish a status quo. For example, an organization that is initially established as a startup with a small team of founders and new-hires is likely to first adopt an entrepreneurial culture promoting leanness, agility, and flexibility. As the organization grows in size and survives each stage of growth, the original entrepreneurial culture that formed its foundation of success would be sustained in the long-term. This is because new measures and processes for ensuring sustainable growth would be implemented, and new hires would import previous workplace cultures into their recent units. As such, a new type of dominant culture would take shape and evolve into the company's status quo.

In summary, two main factors are constantly changing, one rooted in the complexity and unpredictability of the outside world, and the second emerging from within the organization and its subsequent, uncontrollable growth patterns. The combination of these two factors makes organizational culture change an ongoing concern. If your status quo does not change for adaptive purposes then, following Darwinian logic, you have a problem of "adapting to change" and your organization may not survive.

Albert Einstein once said, *"If I had an hour to solve a problem and my life depended on the solution, I would spend the first 55 minutes determining the proper question to ask, for once I know the proper question, I could solve the problem in less than five minutes."*

In this context, what do you think would be the right question to ask? The main issues I tackle in this book do not only discuss how organizations can successfully achieve permanent and lasting change, but also how organizations experiencing constant changes in their environments should be set up in order to achieve dynamic adaptability at an accelerated pace, and how organizations can determine the right questions to ask when priority objectives and goals are constantly moving targets.

IF you...		They will...
Give them a fish,		...eat for a day
Teach them how to fish,		...feed themselves until some change happens and there's no more fish for them to eat
Teach them how to think for themselves,		...rise up to any challenge and figure out how to feed themselves indefinitely

Whatever your organization's culture may be, it might not be the one that is best suited for the current strategies adopted by your company. As such, you need to keep your organization in check when it comes to the culture it has adopted, and your organization needs to dynamically adjust to the ever-changing internal (from within) and external (environment) conditions. This is the main purpose of the Paradoxical Management Assessment System (PMAS).

Proven System

The methodological basis for the PMAS design was not developed from scratch. Its foundations combine research and applications from several fields and areas into a single, comprehensive system that spares you from trying multiple methods, techniques, and frameworks that can only address a small subset of issues regarding leadership, culture, and change management within an organization.

Furthermore, the PMAS system is the only system that can be internally administered with ease and permanently put in place with no need for outside experts or major investment. Its simplicity and its impact and results speak for themselves, as thousands of business organizations have experienced successful transformations

11

after utilizing the approaches, frameworks, tools, and methods that make up the PMAS. Moreover, the PMAS provides work collectives a.k.a. organizations, ranging from small departments to whole enterprises, with a comprehensive toolkit that delves into system thinking, organization culture, leadership, management skills, management tools, and behavioral science.

This toolset was designed and developed by combining research and evidence from selected scholarly sources (see Bibliography) and from real life applications by utilizing Business Model Hackers' collective experience, as this includes over 1.5 million hours of real-life engagement in more than 10,000 organizational units over the past two decades. As such, this is primarily where our discussion of organizational culture archetypes—and their undeniably vital impact on organizational performance and long-term efficiency—comes from.

If you have managed a company or a team before but you were to disagree with all the research, empirical evidence, and studies highlighting the importance of organizational culture, you would still agree that a dominant organizational culture can destroy a company if it is incongruent with the leadership vision and goals. It's undeniable that organizational cultures can have a positive or negative impact on an organization's performance or bottom line. For example, if you think of the newspaper industry in the last decade, the United States automotive industry in the 1980s, and the Steel Industry before that, you would notice that many of these organizations and conglomerates went bust when their internal culture and resistance to change prevented them from adapting to the real world and its industry-altering market trends. This alone should prove that dominant culture archetypes, brought forth by individual and organizational values, are important factors for you to continuously monitor and assess when considering company performance.

Finally, it is important to mention that a "System Thinking" process was adopted in the development and application of the PMAS toolkit, and this process utilizes analogies from "Power Laws" and "Fractals" (defined later). For example, as will be explained in subsequent sections of this book, the value map (a map reflecting how the brain works by means of different terminologies leading to the same paradoxical mental mapping) that applies to the entire organization and its culture exhibits "Self-Similar" properties (similar to the case of Fractals) in any direction, whether it be an inward trajectory that moves from teams, to individuals, and all the way down to brain neurons, or whether it be an outward trajectory that considers individual interactions.

Who's This For?

This system might have caught your attention because your organization is currently undergoing a merger, or because your organizational culture is suffering from misalignments due to M&A or a high number of new recruits. While investing in this book is a great first step, the PMAS is not a one-time fix; it's a permanent process that will not only fix such problems but will also foster adaptability and work on maintaining stability and consistency in the long-term. This system is for you whether you own, control, or run any kind of organization, no matter the size or industry. Whether you are the head of a business that is losing money and needs a quick turnaround, or you are a market leader looking to grow, scale, and sustain your leadership, the PMAS will aid you in achieving both short-term and long-term business success. The non-exhaustive list below describes the types of entities that can benefit from the PMAS system:

- Business owners
- Executives and managers
- Businessmen and investors
- Entrepreneurs
- Decision-makers
- Department heads
- Venture capitalists
- Private Equity general partners
- Asset managers
- Hedge fund managers
- Portfolio managers with influence
- Shareholders with influence
- Institutional investors
- Members of the Board
- High Net Worth Individuals

- Any of the above in corporate offices
- Heads of business units
- Corporate accelerators
- Startups
- Small and medium enterprises
- Family offices
- All of the above in any industry or sector
- Private or public sectors
- Large enterprises
- For-profit and not-for-profit organizations
- Independent professional services advisors
- All of the above in any industry or sector

How This Book Is Organized

You can think of the book as comprehensive toolset. In fact, it's several books contained into one single comprehensive book and toolset. It's the book version of the exact same pro-version online where nothing was held back and which can be found on the web under pmas.us or website: https://pmas.us

The first book is the main book and it starts with the theory and background titled The Paradoxical Management Assessment System a.k.a. PMAS. All books and workbooks that follow the main book, are individual components of the toolset. They consist of quizzes and assessment workbooks that explain how the toolset works and how results can be interpreted and acted on.

At a high level, PMAS is a comprehensive system that can be implemented in 5 consecutive steps:

1. Diagnose the organization and human resources.
2. Set desired targets and key performance indicators.
3. Develop a set of initiatives which can be combined into an organization transformation program.
4. Design and build monitoring, tracking and measurement capabilities.
5. Launch programs, track progress and take corrective actions along the way.

Once the system is put in place, steps 2-5 can be set to repeat can iteratively run indefinitely. Step 4 in particular is designed to regularly administer the quizzes and collect and analyze results.

THE TOOLSET

The PMAS toolset consists of four quizzes, four assessment workbooks and two handbooks designed for actions and initiatives management should take in order to nudge organizations towards their desired state.

Each quiz has its own assessment workbook for grading as shown below:

Quizzes	Assessment Workbooks
Leadership Archetype Quiz	Leadership Archetype Assessment Workbook
Organizational Culture Quiz	Organizational Culture Assessment Workbook
Aspired Organizational Culture Quiz	Aspired Organizational Culture Workbook
Aspired Organizational Culture Quiz - Leader version	Aspired Organizational Culture Workbook – Leader Version

The initiatives that can be taken to nudge the organization and the leadership in the direction of a particular archetype are contained in the two handbooks:
- Leadership Archetype Nudging Handbook
- Organization Culture Archetype Nudging Handbook

It's important to mention that the toolset is available as a "Pro" Version and can be purchased online to administer to teams, organizations and companies of any size. To access the online "Pro Version" toolset, you can go simply to pmas.us or:

https://pmas.us

Now with that out of the way, let's dive into the detail of the system.

BACKGROUND

Management Skills

While these are unprecedented and changing times, some things have remained constant throughout history: **our Values**. Values such as freedom, respect, survival, dignity, trust, love, and honesty, have been the driving force of human behavior, as they produce effective, satisfying, and evolving human relationships.

The same principles that brought about those outcomes in the tenth century still bring them about in the twenty-first century. Our values shape everything we do in life under any circumstance. In other words, and despite the expansive use and availability of technological resources, the same basic human relationship skills lay at the heart of effective human interaction and behavior. However, as technology continues to consume more of our daily lives, we experience very little human-to-human interaction. As such, it is important to remember how vital behavioral and physical interactions are and, subsequently, focus on the development of relationship and management skills. This is why making Values explicit is a part of creating a shared understanding of the system we belong to.

Management skills and relationships with others have remained effective and relevant over thousands of years, despite the changing and complex nature of the world. Numerous studies have shown that skillful management contributes to personal, interpersonal, and organizational performance across several dimensions: profitability, innovation, growth, shareholder value appreciation, productivity, etc... As such, the PMAS encourages organizational transformation via an improvement of management skills and organization management. What is reassuring is that despite requiring cognitive work, management skills can be easily taught. This is because they:

16

- Are able to be developed and improved upon with the right training and practice. Unlike analytical skills, IQ, or certain personality attributes that can only be developed over a very long period of time (or sometimes never), managerial skills can be enhanced through practice and feedback.
- Are behavioral and not personality attributes. As such, they consist of identifiable sets of actions that individuals perform in order to reach certain outcomes. These behaviors can be observed by others, unlike mental or personality-based attributes. Although managers may have different styles and, subsequently, different skill set applications, the core of these skills is common across all styles.
- Are controlled by managers and can be consciously demonstrated, practiced, improved upon, or restrained when non-managers are engaged.

As detailed in later sections, successful skills require managers to have a paradoxical mindset, despite the fact that these skills may be interrelated. Just like systems (discussed later), you have to consider skills holistically, as they all represent non-repetitive behaviors with complex responses. As such, successful managers rely on combinations of skills to achieve desired results. For example, management skills are neither entirely soft nor entirely hard. They cannot lean entirely towards one end of the spectrum; therefore, successful leaders typically strive to achieve balance in their skills.

Management Tools

It is important to discuss management tools that are deployed across organizations. The world is filled with methods, techniques, behaviors, orientations, and frameworks that claim to achieve successful performance. We refer to the most widely adopted management tools as compiled by Bain & Co's in the list found below. This list is updated periodically, as thousands of companies are continuously surveyed regarding the tools they utilize.

While management tools are necessary when implementing and sustaining organizational structure, there are major issues and drawbacks when it comes to why, when, and how these tools are used.

Top 25

Advanced Analytics	Complexity Reduction	Digital Transformation.	Scenario and Contingency Planning
• Business Analytics	• Decision Rights Tools	• Digital Disruption	• Crisis Management
• Business Intelligence	• Focused Strategy	• Digitization	• Disaster Recovery
• Data Mining	• Repeatable Models	• Internet of Things	• Groupthink
• Predictive Analytics	• Spans and Layers	• Digital Innovation	• Real-Options Analysis
Agile Management	**Core Competencies**	**Employee Engagement Systems.**	• Simulation Models
• Iterative Innovation	• Key Success Factors	• Employee Satisfaction	**Strategic Alliances**
• Lean Development	• Core Capabilities	• Organizational Commitment	• Corporate Venturing
• DevOps	**Customer Journey Analysis**	• Empowerment	• Joint Ventures
• Test and Learn	• Advanced Analytics	• Human Resource Management	• Value-Managed Relationships
Balanced Scorecard	• Customer Retention	**Internet of Things**	• Virtual Organizations
• Management by Objectives	• Customer Experience Mapping	• Digital Disruption	**Strategic Planning**
• Mission and Vision Statements	**Customer Relationship Management**	• Machine Learning	• Core Competencies
• Pay for Performance	• Collaborative Commerce	• Smart Devices	• Mission and Vision Statements
• Strategic Balance Sheet	• Customer Retention	• Internet-Connected Devices	• Scenario and Contingency Planning
Benchmarking	• Customer Segmentation	**Mergers and Acquisitions**	**Supply Chain Management**
• Best Demonstrated Practices	• Customer Surveys	• Merger Integration Teams	• Borderless Corporation
• Competitor Profiles	• Loyalty Management Tools	• Strategic Alliances	• Collaborative Commerce
Business Process Reengineering	**Customer Satisfaction Systems**	**Mission and Vision Statements.**	• Value-Chain Analysis
• Cycle-Time Reduction	• Customer and Employee Surveys	• Corporate Values Statements	**Total Quality Management**
• Horizontal Organizations	• Customer Loyalty and Retention	• Cultural Transformation	• Continuous Improvement
• Overhead-Value Analysis	• Customer Relationship Management	• Strategic Planning	• Quality Assurance
• Process Redesign	• Revenue Enhancement	**Organizational Time Management**	• Six Sigma
Change Management Programs	**Customer Segmentation**	• Productivity Benchmarking	**Zero-Based Budgeting**
• Cultural Transformation	• Customer Surveys	• Time Discipline	• Activity-Based Budgeting
• Organizational Change	• Market Segmentation	• Talent Management	• Complexity Reduction
• Process Redesign	• One-to-One Marketing	**Price Optimization Models**	• Cost-Benefit Analysis
		• Demand-Based Management	• Performance Budgeting
		• Pricing Strategy	
		• Revenue Enhancement	

Source: Adapted from Bain & Co. BMR research.

Considering the "Why" these tools are deployed, it is not uncommon for management tools to be deployed or selected based on the flavor of the month. If today's "it" topic happens to be about big data and artificial intelligence, then you will see a number of corporations redirecting their resources towards the implementation of these tools. This could be because of hype, because of FOMO, or because everyone else appears to be doing it.

The deployment of management tools across organizations is an important topic to discuss. While such tools are necessary for implementing and sustaining organizational structure, there are issues with why, when, and how they are used.

One issue is timing. Often, these tools are deployed as part of organizational transformation, but tool deployment may start before organizational culture is ready for such a shift. For example, when I

18

was in corporate management, we had to adapt to new tools like balanced scorecards and six-sigma without understanding their benefits. We felt that these tools only served to make us work longer hours to impress executives, shareholders, and the public. We ended up deploying these tools because we had to, not because they were beneficial. We even had to apply such tools in tasks where six-sigma blackbelt certification had little to contribute. The training was a waste of time.

Another issue with management tools is their deployment based on trends, or the "flavor of the month." If big data and artificial intelligence are trending, many companies redirect their resources to implementing these tools because of hype, FOMO, or peer pressure. This approach lacks a rationale for the selection and deployment of tools and may not lead to optimal results.

As such, deploying management tools at the wrong time and for the wrong reasons can lead to wasted time and resources, as well as a negative impact on organizational culture. It is important to carefully consider the benefits and drawbacks of each tool before deploying it and to ensure that organizational culture is ready for such a shift.

In the next chapter, I'll dive deeper into several observations about six-sigma. What I want to note here is that when fat-tail distributions exist, the errors are not proportional to the probability of events. In power law distribution, minute input variations such as the "Butterfly Effect" can underestimate the probability of events by 12 deviation standards, or by one trillion times. Therefore, when applying six-sigma and sensitivities to a five-year strategic plan, it may seem that all scenarios and contingencies have been accounted for. However, this process does not make it likely for contributors to consider the possible occurrence of extreme events. This point has been proven by Nobel Prize winner Daniel Kahneman in his work on Prospect Theory.

Prospect Theory studies the psychology of choice, and it is utilized in the fields of behavioral economics and behavioral finance. This theory puts forward two main arguments. Firstly, people are risk-averse and hate losing by a factor of 2 to 3 compared to how much they like winning. Secondly, people are highly overconfident, which works well in controlled environments where all data is available. However, in real-life situations where potential risks and losses are not quite evident, overconfidence does not play out well.

For example, when organizations go through the process of strategic planning and scenario modeling, major shocks and events that have a Fat Tail distribution are not obvious to managers and planners because they are hidden or unknown. As a result, they cannot be accounted for in a standard deviation, such as the case with six-sigma, because they follow a power law distribution.

Another issue in this same example relates to overconfidence, which stems from the fact we have the tendency to cling on to our old habits and old ways, especially when we have invested time and resources in perfectly developing strategic plans. As highlighted by prospect theory, the type of unease experienced when forgoing such plans is the same as that of losing. When we put so much effort into strategic planning efforts and commit to a 5-year strategic plan, we can lose sight of the bigger picture. Similarly, as we buy into our forecasts, we automatically become overconfident with our predictions and end up rigidly clinging to plans, even when our circumstances call for a radical change in approach and methodology.

When organizations are unable to provide sufficient justification as to why and when they adopt new tools, a majority of transformation programs fail to achieve target objectives. In such cases, companies tend to blame management tool implementation programs after investing and wasting big budgets in starting them. As such, these programs are abandoned before they even see the light of day.

When it comes to how these management tools are deployed, we will illustrate four limitations that, after years of observation, we deem relevant for this discussion:

1. Management tools are frequently statically deployed; they are usually implemented once, then forgotten. the results obtained from them, at best, additive. On the other hand, properly implemented tools, i.e. those that are used and

updated continuously, produce synergies that lead to compounded benefits.

2. Management tools tend to be deployed linearly and homogeneously, which means that their deployment benefits directly relates to the issue they set out to address. This creates linearity. The reason behind linear results, as opposed to those that are exponential or compounded, is reductionism (as earlier discussed). In other words, management tools are usually implemented one-at-a-time to address specific and isolated issues, gaps, or challenges. These tools are never applied holistically, and their selection is not always based on organizational needs (as discussed in the "Why" example earlier). For compounded benefits and exponential results when selecting and deploying management tools, the entire organization's needs should be viewed comprehensively.

3. Management tools are mostly internally isolated; they're neither directly nor indirectly connected to other management tools (or functions) within the organization (the system). This limits the effectiveness and the benefits that these tools have to offer and may lead to frequently wasted efforts and a decrease in productivity. As such, interconnected feedback loops may be beneficial when applying management tools, as these loops amplify the positive and placate the negative.

4. Management tools are deployed in an externally isolated manner, even when they are meant to take account of external factors. These tools utilize reports and paperwork, but they disregard feedback loops from the market. As such, this defeats the purpose of these tools, as they are meant to be updated in real-time and adjusted dynamically.

Hence, as highlighted in the first two limitations, typical management tool deployment is outdated when considering today's business world. Furthermore, considering the last two limitations of current management tool implementation, it would be fair to say that organizations have not been reaping key benefits that such management tools have to offer: providing an early warning system that responds to external and internal triggers, and implementing adequate hedging mechanisms (ex. choosing the right optionalities for perpetual growth).

For more detailed information on these limitations and for a more in-depth discussion on how management should be deployed, please refer to our Balance Score Cards and business process automation toolkit.

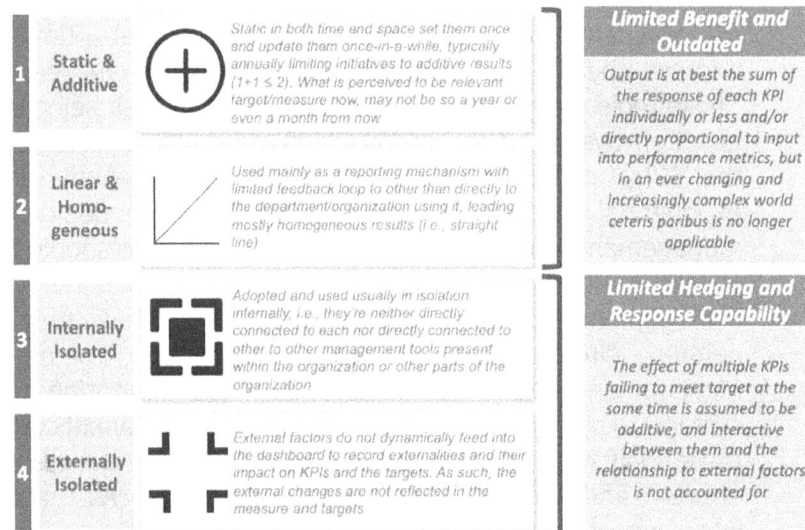

#			Description	
1	Static & Additive	⊕	Static in both time and space set them once and update them once-in-a-while, typically annually limiting initiatives to additive results (1+1 ≤ 2). What is perceived to be relevant target/measure now, may not be so a year or even a month from now	**Limited Benefit and Outdated** — Output is at best the sum of the response of each KPI individually or less and/or directly proportional to input into performance metrics, but in an ever changing and increasingly complex world ceteris paribus is no longer applicable
2	Linear & Homo-geneous		Used mainly as a reporting mechanism with limited feedback loop to other than directly to the department/organization using it, leading mostly homogeneous results (i.e., straight line)	
3	Internally Isolated		Adopted and used usually in isolation internally, i.e., they're neither directly connected to each nor directly connected to other to other management tools present within the organization or other parts of the organization	**Limited Hedging and Response Capability** — The effect of multiple KPIs failing to meet target at the same time is assumed to be additive, and interactive between them and the relationship to external factors is not accounted for
4	Externally Isolated		External factors do not dynamically feed into the dashboard to record externalities and their impact on KPIs and the targets. As such, the external changes are not reflected in the measure and targets	

In the next sections, I will introduce concepts such as system thinking and synergies, which are both necessary when considering and overcoming management-related problems and limitations.

System Thinking

What is system thinking, and why is it at the core of the PMAS design? In order to explore system thinking, I will begin by defining what a system is: A "System" is a set of things that perform a collective function. Whenever a set of interconnected entities—people, cells, molecules, etc.—produces its own behavioral pattern over time, a System emerges.

For example, think of the human body as a System that consists of many individual organs working together as a functioning whole. However, not everything is a System. If we put together a random collection of things, say an employee, a street and a tree, they won't make up a System unless they are interconnected for a specific purpose. They are simply a set of elements; they do not interconnectedly work towards the performance of a collective function.

A business, a governmental entity, a company, and a corporation are each an example of a System. Key elements in such Systems are the people or employees that make up these systems. In such spaces, the employees or individuals and departments' functions are interconnected to collectively generate some set of products and/or provide services. These systems are said to be greater than the sum of their parts because employees within such Systems perform collective functions (as with any System).

When considering the complexity of organizational systems, it is important to examine both organizational properties and organization structures. First, we must consider the number of employees within an organization (System): the more employees there are, the more complex the organization will be. A second driving force behind organization complexity is employee interconnectivity. The more interdependent team members are, the more intricately constructed the organization will be. To represent organizational structure on paper, one would draw a tree with a number of connections (branches) flowing top-down and bottom-up along the formal lines of reporting. As such, this would be a simple system with few connections between its elements and it would be relatively easy to understand the direct relations of cause and effect.

Direct lines can be drawn between single causes and single effects. However, real-life organizations don't work that way. Imagine you're working in an organization as an engineer, and you needed to talk to Accounting and/or HR. You cannot do so directly, as you have to follow reporting lines. So, every interaction would require you to first go to your CEO and then to accounting, which means that the flow would need to move upwards then downwards. If this were to occur every time there's a similar interaction, the node at the top end of the line— that of the CEO—would have a queue that grows exponentially relative to the number of requests. This would cripple the organization from functioning in its entirety. As such, you have to think of communication and interactions as multidirectional occurrences, which is why connections grow exponentially with the number of employees. Cause-and-effect relationships become more complex, as there can be multiple causes for a single effect or vice versa. As opposed to simple linear systems, we call these more complex organizations "nonlinear systems," and we consider that most organizations display nonlinearity in their functioning.

To summarize, we consider employees to be interconnected elements working within organizational systems in such a way as to produce their own behavioral patterns—"Culture Archetypes"—over time. Ultimately, this system exists to perform certain value-added functions. An example of this is currency and, more specifically, money in (i.e., investment and expenditure) and money out (i.e., share value, revenues, ratios). Let's now consider how these interactions between elements can result in more or less value out of the systems as they impact the culture of the organization.

Synergies and Interference in Organizations

When assessing an organization from a system's perspective, you need to consider the relationships between its employees. A relation is a simple but abstract concept; it is a connection or interaction between two or more employees. Through this connection, there is an exchange of information and/or ideas that binds the elements into a state of interdependency, where the total gains and losses of any component are correlated with those of others in the relationship. Relationships between employees can be fundamental of two different kinds, constructive or destructive. Constructive relations are referred to as "synergies," and destructive relations are called "interference".

Synergy is an interaction between two or more elements producing a combined effect greater than the sum of their separate effects. An example of synergy is the interaction between honeybees and flowers–their natural reliance on one another for survival is analogous with inter-party synergies. Bees need plants for pollen collection and subsequent nectar production, and plants need bees for reproduction, as bees distribute plant seeds when moving from

24

one flower to another. This type of interaction produces more output than the input it requires. Thus, the added value of the joint interaction is worth more than the simple combination of each in isolation.

Now, let's apply this to the classic example of mergers in organizations. Why do mergers happen in the first place? The key driver behind mergers and acquisitions (M&As) is the cost-saving and/or growth potential that the merger between two or more organizations can achieve from synergies. For example, think of the internal cost savings that can be achieved through economies of scale when merging accounting and payroll departments. Another example of synergies could be volume purchasing and the subsequent savings it generates. Other synergies from M&As can result in revenue and growth changes through, for example, expanded market reach/access, competitor elimination, shared knowledge, intellectual property, shared technology, etc. On paper, mergers often seem like a straightforward way to achieve cost savings and growth, which is why the total value of M&A transactions over the past decade has exceeded $30 trillion.

However, empirical evidence and countless studies of past mergers and acquisitions show that 3 out of 4 M&A cases fail to meet set goals and expectations, and more than half of M&A-related transactions end up achieving negative returns. A recent study by BCG shows that "cultural fit" is a leading reason behind post-merger integration failure, as the majority of mergers produce negative synergies—i.e. "interference".

Interference consists of destructive inter-elemental interactions that reduce combined system output to less than the sum of its parts. This is due to conflicts between elements that prevent processes or activities within the system from being carried out properly. An example of this would be the interference between a drug and an incompatible substance negatively affecting drug efficiency. For instance, simultaneous ingestion of antibiotics and dairy products dampens the effect of antibiotics, thereby reducing the overall positive effect.

In this book, we focus on destructive interference as it occurs in organizational settings— through culture clashes. As highlighted later in this book, culture clashes happen all the time in the real world, and they are driven by conflicts in values. Some real-world examples of culture clashes stemming from conflicting values are wars, civil rights movements, abortion debates, etc.

In the next section, we will discuss Emergence, which is the outcome of synergies leading to something new.

Emergence

Emergence is made possible as a result of synergies (and nonlinearity) when interactions between elements create something new. It describes a developmental process whereby many parts interact in a nonlinear fashion to create something worth more than their sum. It usually results in unpredictable and unexpected phenomena. Some examples include the emergence of the social networks we have today, i.e., 21st-century internet. If you used the internet in the 1990s, you would not have imagined the interconnectedness it would come to provide in the coming decades, as tools like app economies and cloud computing (and all its subsequent innovation) are truly technological forces to be reckoned with.

Cultural evolution within organizations occurs, for example, when a company transitions from a startup (e.g., a founder's garage) to a successful global enterprise (e.g., Apple). This evolution can only happen through synergies when the constructive forces of interference outweigh those that are destructive. This means that successful cultural evolution can occur only when cultural clashes are reduced and when emergence occurs.

Organizational Culture Emergence

As will be later illustrated through the concept of fractals, the emergence of organizational culture resembles the functioning of the brain. It's how every complex system works. Take our neural network as an example: trillions of neurons are interconnected in a manner that allows human beings to make decisions. However, it's impossible to study neuron interactions and their subsequent influence on the brain, which is why scientists study heuristics instead. This is also similar to the way ants and termites work together without a central command system.

Many factors causing changes in the status quo can lead to culture emergence in organizations: high growth in the number of employees and new hires, M&As, reorganizations, large-scale program transformations, external major events, etc. This being said, if you currently work in an organization, you will have noticed changes to the status quo, as global shocks and events are rife in today's world.

As such, if you have survived so far and continue to grow as an organization, it's likely because you've adapted to the reality around you. This is the result of the Emergence and synergies your organization has been able to achieve. Accordingly, the opposite is also true. Organizations whose cultures did not adapt to changing times either experienced interference, or stagnated, or ceased to exist. Examples of interference and its insidious consequences are illustrated in the next chapter.

In this book, I do not intend to discuss complexity theory or complex systems. Rather, I aim to provide a short introduction on the subject of system thinking—and its subsequent applications in our methods and thinking processes—by considering how organization structures should be viewed and tackled: as a complete system. This is because systems thinking expands the range of solutions available to us for problem-solving by broadening our thinking, helping us articulate problems in new ways, and emphasizing the fact that the choices we make have an impact on other parts of the system and, consequently, its entirety. By anticipating the impact of each trade-off, we can minimize interference and maximize synergies.

DEFINITIONS AND APPLICATIONS

Before we dive into the mechanics of the PMAS, I would like to use this section to introduce you to complex systems' tools, methods, concepts, and frameworks and how all of these are applied to leadership and organizational cultures. You can skip this section if you are already familiar with all these concepts or terms. However, I do recommend that you invest the next 30 minutes reading about our system's background and understanding it, as this will help you select the most effective and adequate initiatives for your case from the Nudging companion Handbooks.

This chapter is organized by the term, and I will introduce each term separately. Each section in the chapter describes how a specific concept, method, or framework is applied to organizational structure and culture within the PMAS context. While I did try to move cohesively from introduction to concept definition, it was difficult to achieve sequential flow when explaining certain ideas. This is because many ideas are interdependent, so explaining each one separately would be like explaining the "chicken or egg" paradox in its individual parts: an impossible feat. Therefore, you may want to consider reading this section twice if you are serious about developing a thorough understanding of how organizations work in the context of "complex systems".

Complex Systems and Systems Change

Complex system design principles were adopted in the development of the PMAS toolkit. As such, after applying the PMAS diagnostic toolset to an organization, you are likely to want to develop a long list of initiatives that aim to correct, maintain, or accelerate your organization's dynamic adaptability. In order to perform such a change, a system thinking approach is necessary, as it aids in selecting initiatives and designing holistic and successful transformation programs.

Systems Change proposes that we should first gain a deep understanding of a system's overall structure and workings before attempting any alterations. Narrow, analytical and partial vision will lead, at best, to partial results. If you want to achieve greater leverage, you'll need to take a step back and adopt a holistic view of the system. Only after developing a comprehensive view of the situation, will you be able to drive permanent and lasting change leading to complete results. Therefore, to achieve this, you'll need to develop a full understanding of the overall structure, features, and dynamics of the system.

Numerous studies conducted by BCG, Bain, and McKinsey show that the majority of major organization transformations fail because they are not tackled holistically. In fact, program managers propose partial solutions based upon a partial understanding of the system. For example, we may address cybersecurity problems by considering only computers and code and spending millions securing the information system itself. This approach does not properly account for human flaws such as problematic motives, behaviors, and habits. To avoid such pitfalls and achieve success in our systems change efforts, we need to account for the multi-dimensional nature of our organizations and map these dimensions out as best we can.

This is why we adopt the system change approach, as it forces organization managers and leaders to consider the many different dimensions of organizations including values, relationships, individual roles, informal and formal structures, metrics, performance management, goals, and policies.

When selecting the appropriate initiatives from the PMAS, you'll need to get a holistic view of the elements, relations, and networks regulating the organization (system). As such, the PMAS discusses a multitude of organizational dimensions, the first of which being the physical environment.

When thinking of organization transformation, one must consider the **physical environment,** as it regulates the form and frequency of interactions between organization entities. For example, during the pandemic of 2020, most offices stood empty, as office-based employees were asked to work from home. As such, this period had a substantial impact on a variety of culture archetypes, which led most of our clients to report challenges in their organizational cultures. While you may think this to be an extreme example, it is important to consider how microelements—such as the physical layout of an office, the structure of a building, the geographic spread of office locations, etc.—could regulate behavioral coordination and interactions. An example of this is the difference in functioning birds when birds are in a cage vs. when they are in the wild.

Another important factor of organization transformation is social structure in its many varieties. Examples of social structures include cultures, societies, families, nations, sports teams, etc. These communities enforce rules, incentives, and power dynamics that shape how people behave and communicate, both inside and outside the confines of the workplace. Every morning, billions of people get out of bed and go over their daily business in accordance with the rules, incentives, and power dynamics enforced by their respective institutional structures. It is necessary to consider these structures when developing your transformation program and selecting your subsequent initiatives and. For example, social norms may prevent you from implementing certain initiatives, as they may be taboo (or illegal) in certain countries or states.

Values and mental models are ultimately what shapes human behavior and outcomes, as will be shown in detail later on. Value mapping will be an important part of decision-making when selecting initiatives, as it helps in pinpointing alignments or misalignments. Subsequently, this can reveal points of conflict, resistance, and non-collaboration.

Scales and abstractions, as discussed in more detail below, are considerations of system scale from smallest to largest. As highlighted throughout this book, systems are subject to continuous change at all levels and across different dimensions ("abstractions"). This is characteristic of systems thinking which takes into consideration multilevel organizational functioning. For example, on the small scale, we may consider a newspaper editor whose job is threatened by the rise of digital publications and the subsequent transformation the organization must go through in order to keep up with the times. At a higher level, one could consider the global trends of the newspaper industry and how they're shaping its organizations. As such, by mitigating risks and leveraging their driving forces, we can align our initiatives with broader processes of change. In order to do this, we need to take different levels into consideration, or else we will not be able to harness the potential of the change happening at these different levels. Therefore, you should move across all directions when implementing an organizational transformation program.

Digital transformation and the Internet of Things (IoT) is the expansion of the industrial technology infrastructure and market systems around the world, otherwise known as the digital revolution. Running in parallel with the digital revolution is the change of pace around the world, as time seems to be accelerating. Consider this: when we entered the information revolution age, we immersed ourselves in a growing sea of data from numerous sources, including internet search histories, smart homes, social media, RFID tags, and GPS data. Companies and organizations are not well-prepared to handle this new era of digital transformation, as an unprecedented amount of multi-structured data—now known as "big data"— is continuously generated. On top of this, industrial companies are also in the process of going digital, and they are doing so by creating digital reflections of their assets and products. In fact, more recent times have seen the use of sensors and controllers that can pull a massive amount of real-time data from assets and products. This information is then input into a virtual model of the system that is unique to that product, asset, equipment, or machine. This digital reflection can be accessed on-demand, as it is located in the cloud and maintained throughout the asset's life cycle. For example, consider a new car entering today's market: the minute you start the vehicle's engine, thousands of data points are generated. Similarly, we generate data every time we make a call, exercise, watch a video, search the web, make a purchase, or even walk past a security camera. To give you an idea of the sheer amount of data that is generated nowadays, consider the following: in a single day, we collect more digital data than the entire world had available only a decade ago. Even though the majority of this data is not useful, most of the world's useful data remains untapped. This is because companies are not prepared to process the amount of data generated in this emerging paradigm.

In the corporate world, less than 5% of companies are successful at combining the right tools with the right people, to make use of important data and benefit from this new paradigm. For example, organizations that deploy management tools, such as Balanced Score Cards, Analytics, Strategic Planning, or any aforementioned tools, can only benefit from their use when their deployment involves the right type of real-time data. In the past, computing power was a scarce resource, and only large enterprises were able to afford and leverage technology as a competitive advantage. Small and medium enterprises had no such prerogative. This has now changed with the invention of global-scale cloud computing, which makes high-end computing power available to organizations of all sizes at a very low cost, on-demand. By using the right strategies, small companies and startups are now able to rapidly compete with large enterprises and scale up exponentially. This paradigm shift has turned the world into a winner-takes-all environment that is mediated and interlinked by increasingly complex systems. These emergent complex systems take the form of interconnected, self-similar networks that function like fractals, in that they are not confined by traditional domains and boundaries.

Yet, despite all this complexity, we continue to adopt reductionist approaches to problem-solving by basing hypotheses on flawed assumptions. We still plan with incremental, linear progress in mind, as we faultily assume that complex systems are predictable and controllable, but they aren't. Accordingly, we ignore feedback loops despite how necessary they actually are. As discussed in the next section of this book, the reductionist methodology focuses on individual parts, rather than how those parts are interrelated and integrated with the whole. While such an approach served us well in the past and helped us put a man on the moon, it's unfortunately, blinding as of recent, as a fresh approach is needed to tackle this new paradigm.

Therefore, we need to consider whole contexts instead of individual parts. Similarly, whenever we consider altering individual components for static change, we should stop, take a step back, and consider adopting a holistic approach that provides a better understanding of the dynamic processes shaping certain events.

The Reductionist Approach

Rooted in Physics, reductionism is the process of breaking down a large system to its constituent parts, then describing the entire system as the sum of its parts. When we analyze these individual components in isolation and put them back together, we ignore how they interact, and we neglect the impact of time and feedback loops.

The reductionist methodology is adopted by managers, business leaders, and management consultants who aim to tackle company problems. The method is based on incremental linear progress and is considered mono-dimensional in its structure. It's important to recognize that there's nothing wrong with the linear method, as it served its purpose during the industrial revolution and got us to where we are today. It is, however, limited and inadequate for today's more complex world.

A holistic approach suggests that there are different levels of interpretation, each with key properties that cannot be reduced to those of a lower level. For example, a physician trying to understand a patient's mental disorder uses a reductionist approach when they reduce the illness to a series of chemical imbalances in the brain and prescribes drugs. A holistic approach, on the other hand, would force the physician to consider factors that are not strictly related to brain chemistry. In such a case, the doctor would consider physiological, cognitive, and sociocultural factors.

One key drawback of reductionism is its core use of the "ceteris paribus"—other things equal"—concept. Ceteris Paribus holds variables within the environment constant in order to isolate and perceive other variables and track their changes in a linear fashion. Thus, the use of reductionism often involves an attempt to maintain variables within the environment constant so as to control a given system through a limited number of variables. In contrast, one of the guiding principles of holism is called "Panta Rhei," meaning "everything flows." The basic concept behind Panta Rhei is that everything changes, and it is derived from the Greek philosopher Heraclitus's observation that one cannot step into the same river twice. Where reductionism breaks processes down into static parts, holism focuses on maintaining whole processes and understanding the effects they have on certain variables.

Systems thinkers adopt synthesis (defined later) instead of reductionism. As will be later demonstrated, many organization aspects are not suitable for reductionist-approach analysis, as they bear the complexity of systems.

Power Law Distributions and Network Science in Complex Systems

Networks science is one more concept in system thinking that applies to organizations in two ways. The first is in the way organizations are structured, as companies can be viewed as networks of interconnected nodes. The second application of network science in organizations relates to employee growth, as interconnectivity between coworkers leads to exponential growth in organization complexity. Subsequently, this can give rise to power-law distributions, which are discussed in this section.

To recap from our earlier discussion, systems have a number of properties that make them complex. Firstly, the higher the number of elements–employees–within our system, the more complex our organization will be. Secondly, organization complexity also depends on employee connectivity: the more interconnected and interdependent employees are, the more complex organizations become. In a simple organization (less than 5 employees), there are few connections between employees, and it is relatively easy to understand the direct relations of cause and effect. We can draw a direct line between a single cause and a single effect; thus, we call these simple organizations "linear" systems. However, when the number of employees in an organization grows, cause-and-effect relationships within the organization increase. This makes the system exponentially more complex, i.e. more nonlinear.

Nonlinearity is a key property of complex systems. In an organization, the working relationship between two individuals can be represented by a network of nonlinear links. In the modern organization, these links do not simply move up and down reporting lines, they rather go in many directions across the entire organization. It is these relationships and interactions that shape organizational culture and drive its success or failure.

Organizational culture across nonlinear networks depends on employee autonomy. The more autonomous the network, the more robust and self-organizing it becomes. The trade-off between robustness and autonomy on one end is contrasted with control and vulnerability on the other.

Consider social networks where people highly value their autonomy: no one can control the networks that spawned out of YouTube, Instagram, Facebook, TikTok, or Twitter. They were self-organizing systems created from the actions and interactions of their users, so these systems will likely be less orderly. Consider this trade-off as you think of today's most innovative, dynamic, fast-growing businesses, as they have been creating platforms for technologies and people to interact, adapt, and self-organize.

This said the level of autonomy in organizations is rarely controllable, especially when it comes to successful organizations and their fast-growing environments. In fact, interfering with the autonomy of such a system could be detrimental to organization growth, as it could disrupt the very ecosystem that provided the organization with success in the first place. This is why an organization's growth will inevitably lead to the development of a complex network of decentralized, self-organized entities within the organization. This is because whenever 10 or more employees constitute a workplace, informal organization networks emerge within formal organizations. In the majority of cases, such informal relationships do not allow interventions —such as organization transformation programs, M&As, and others—to achieve their desired outcomes.

The second aspect of network science is applied here to illustrate power-law distributions. Simple networks have simple features and are characterized by bell-shaped distributions. As networks grow in complexity, power law distribution emerges. Where normal or Gaussian distributions have bell-shaped curves and averages, Power Law distributions have no averages and are said to have fat tails. As such, Power Law distributions are sometimes referred to as heavy-tailed distributions. They decay much slower than exponential distribution, and this is primarily what makes them so unpredictable.

Another method used to detect Power Law distribution is plotting. When Power Laws are plotted on a scattered log-log plot, the graph looks either as a downward-sloping curve or like a straight line, as shown below.

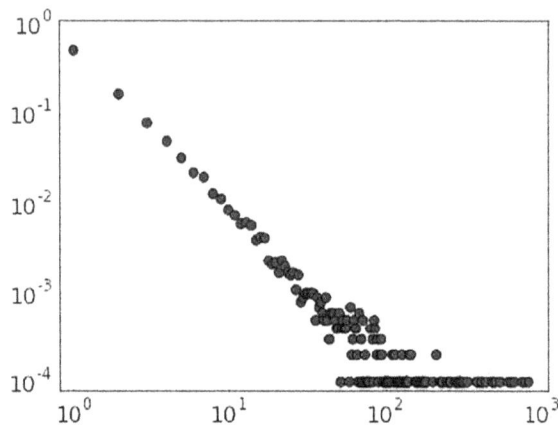

Real-World Examples of Power Law Distribution

Shown here are real-world examples of Power Law distributions that I think are interesting. Fat Tails, or Power Law distributions, highlight reactions to global shocks and events. In fact, an increase in global shocks and events stems from an increase in the complexity of our current world. Power Law, which is sometimes also referred to as Zipf-law, is a characteristic that applies to numerous events occurring in business, nature, wealth, and many other fields.

Below is a list of 40 examples where power law applies. We have also included reference papers for each distribution.

How does power-law distribution impact organizations? Before I get into this, I would like to introduce the concept of "Fractals", as it is key when considering how power laws have impacted organizations.

1. Cities	21. Size distributions in ecosystems; predators
2. Traffic Jams	22. Fractals
3. Coastlines	23. Punctuated equilibrium
4. Bush-fire damage	24. Mass extinctions
5. Water levels in the Nile	25. Brain functioning
6. Hurricanes & floods	26. Predicting premature births
7. Earthquakes	27. Laser technology evolution
8. Asteroid size shifts	28. Fractures of materials
9. Sunspots	29. Magnitude estimation of sensorial stimuli
10. Galactic structure	30. Willis' Law: number vs. size of plant genera
11. Sandpile avalanches	31. Fetal lamb breathing
12. Brownian motion	32. Bronchial structure
13. Music	33. Frequency of DNA base chemicals
14. Epidemics	34. Protein-protein interaction networks
15. Genetic circuitry	35. Genomic properties (DNA words)
16. Metabolism of cells	36. Heartbeat rates

17. Functional networks in the brain	37. Cellular substructures
18. Tumor growth	38. Phytoplankton
19. Biodiversity	39. Death from a heart attack
20. Circulation in plants and animals	40. Magma rising through earth's crust

1-(Estoup, 1916; Zipf, 1949); 2-(Nagel & Paczuski, 1995); 3-(Casti, 1994); 4-(Bak, 1996); 5-(Casti, 1994); 6-(Bak, 1996); 7-(Gutenberg & Richter, 1944); 8-(Hughes & Nathan, 1994; Marsili & Zhang, 1996); 9-(Hughes et al., 2003); 10-(Baryshev & Teerikorpi, 2002); 11-(Bak, 1996); 12-(West & Deering, 1995)Gardner, 1978); 13-(Gardner, 1978; Casti, 1994); 14-(Liljeros et al., 2001); 15-(Barabási, 2002); 16-(West et al., 1997); 17-(Shin & Kim, 2004); 18-(Brú et al., 2003); 19-(Haskell et al. 2002); 20-(West et al., 1997); 21-(Camacho & Solé, no date); 23-(Bak & Sneppen, 1993); 24-(Bak, 1996); 25-(Stassinopoulos & Bak, 1995); 26-(Sornette, 2002); 27-(Baum & Silverman, 2001); 28-(Sornette, 2002); 29-(Roberts, 1979); 30-(Willis, 1922); 31-(Szeto et al., 1992); 32-(Goldberger et al., 1990); 33-(Selvam, 2002); 34-(Song et al., 2005; Wuchty & Almaas, in press, no date2005a,b); 35-(Luscombe et al., 2002); 36-(Nahshoni et al., 1998); 37-(Wax et al., 2002); 38- Jenkinson, 2004); 39-(Bigger et al., 1996); 40-(Weinberg & Podladchikov, 1994).

Fractals

A fractal is a shape made out of parts that are similar to the whole in some way. Think of a fractal as an object that is "self-similar" or "scalable." A fractal is made out of both smaller and larger copies of itself. Classic examples of fractals which are found in nature include coastlines, trees, snowflakes, etc.

Fractals were first introduced by several German and French mathematicians over a century ago, including Felix Hausdorff, Paul Levy, Pierre Fatou, Waclaw Sierpinski, and Gaston Julia.

Then, in 1975, a mathematician named Benoit Mandelbrot introduced fractal geometry.

Landscape generated from a detail of the Mandelbrot set Picture by Wikimedia Commons by Prokofiev

Classic examples of Fractals are found in nature, coastlines, trees, snowflakes, etc.

Picture StockSnap By Lerkrat Tangsri

Real Life Snowflake Picture by Wikimedia Commons by Alexey Kijatov

Mandelbrot demonstrated how a simple formula with a feedback loop can lead to a complex system.

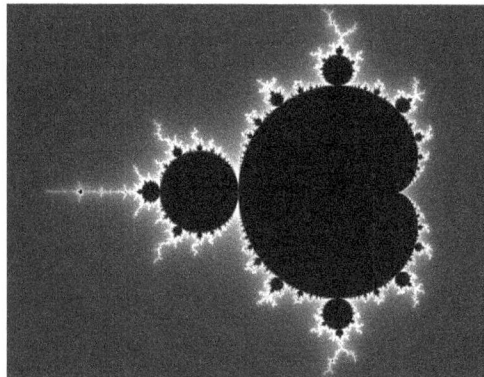

The Mandelbrot Set Picture by Wikimedia Commons by Wolfgang Beyer

Mandelbrot Set Simplified

$$Z_{n+1} = Z_n^2 + c$$

Simple Rule, Feedback Loop and
Non-Linear Equation
leads to a
Complex System

Self-similarity means that an object is made up of smaller copies of itself or looks the same at different scales. Moreover, the self-similarity continues across many scales. The main idea is that it repeats like a big shape that's made up of little shapes. That little shape is made up of little shapes of little shapes, etc.

Mathematically speaking, this kind of behavior continues indefinitely as you zoom in on a fractal shape.

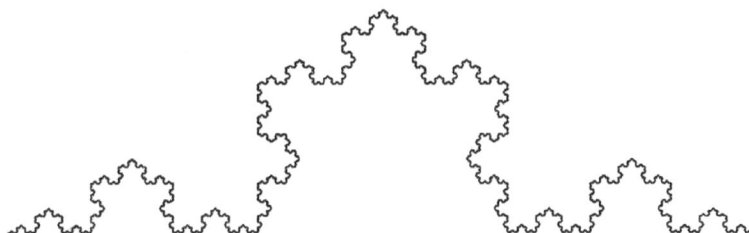

Figure 1. Koch Curve – Picture By Wikimedia Commons By Fibonacci

Fractal objects that are self-similar are said to be scale free. They don't have a sense of length or a typical scale or size that are associated with them. Geometrically speaking, it's counter-intuitive because in everyday life, we're used to a scale or size of objects we encounter.

Let me illustrate the concept with two different vegetables from nature. The first a zucchini and the second being a Romanesco, a type of cauliflower.

A zucchini has particular size, and you may have some that are larger or smaller than the one in the picture. You cannot image giant zucchinis that are heavier than say 10 lbs. There are smaller zucchinis or baby zucchinis, and these are about the smallest you can find. So there's a typical size associated with zucchinis, there's an average, and then there are smaller and larger zucchinis. We don't have microscopic tomatoes. That's why zucchinis are said to have a scale. If you statistically sampled zucchinis you'll get a bell shaped curve in terms of the size.

Picture By Pexels By Les Bourgeonniers

One final way to look at it is that if I snapped a picture of a zucchini, you can picture that size in your head.

In contrast, let's look at a picture of a Romanesco vegetable. The Romanesco does not have a characteristic size, and its spiral shapes come in a wide variety of sizes, making it difficult to determine the scale of the vegetable. If I were to show you the image below of the vegetable, would you be able to figure out its scale? You'll notice that it's much harder to see the scale of the Romanesco if zoom in and out because it doesn't have a characteristic size. What's the typical size of a they spiral-looking shapes in a Romanesco vegetable? Well, they're spirals of all different sizes. That's sort of the point as you've seen as we zoom in more and more we keep seeing more and more spirals and more Romanescos. And mathematically, that would go on forever. Compare that to the zucchini vegetable and it's a whole different situation. The zucchinis come in a pretty narrow range of sizes whether you zoom in on it or not and you'd be able to relate the scale of zucchini from its picture. While you may be off by a little bit, but you can get pretty close.

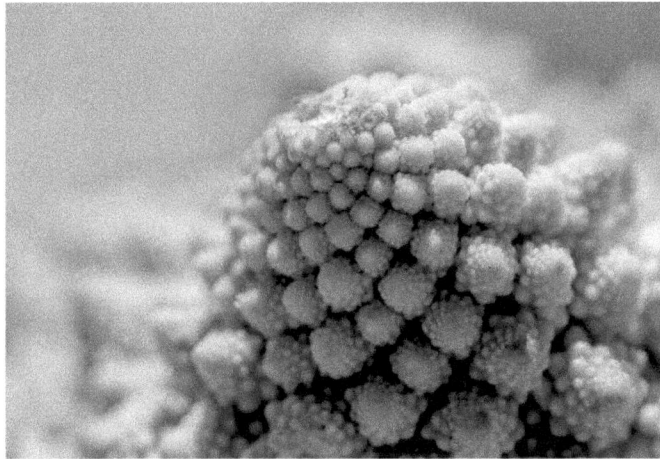

Picture by Pixabay By AlkeMade

Picture by Wikimedia Commons By Ivar Leidus

But imagine you live inside a fractal world of the Sierpinski triangle and not our world. So this world consists of triangles and triangles double size you get three times as many triangles so triangles within triangles within triangles. you wouldn't be able to tell, there is no sense of scale here. There is not typical with zucchinis. It's just the world of scale-free triangles.

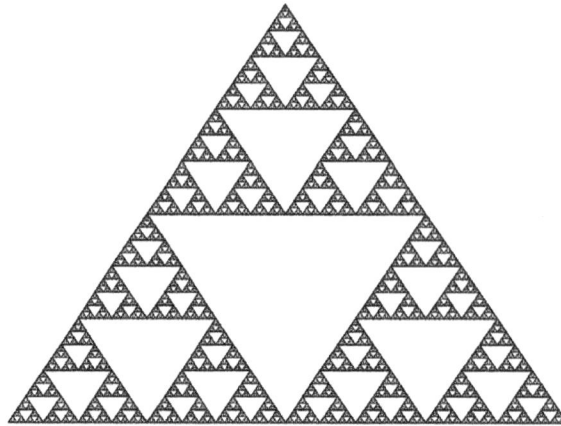

Picture by Wikimedia Commons by Sega Sei

Mathematical vs. Real-Life Fractals

Mathematically speaking, a fractal is an object that self-similar across all scales. If you keep zooming in forever, you continue to see the same shape.

A real-life fractal wouldn't have this theoretical property that you can zoom in forever, ultimately, as you keep zooming in say on snowflake, you'll will be looking individual molecules. So there's a cut off point. That's how real-life fractals are different from mathematical or theoretical fractals. That's why real-life fractals are said to be fractal-like.

In General, the notion of mathematical fractal is an abstraction, it's an ideal. That only exists in the world of math but doesn't really exist in the real physical world in which we live. Nonetheless, the important takeaway here is that the power law distribution feature of mathematical fractals still carries across to real-life fractals.

Stock Markets Fractals and Power Laws

Benoit Mandelbrot, the inventor of modern fractals, was the first to show how markets exhibited Power Law characteristics due to

44

fractal-like behavior. You can read all about it in his book *The Misbehavior of Markets*.

Applying the self-similarity principle of fractals to stock markets, this would mean individual stocks are also self-similar and exhibit. This concept can be taken down to companies, business unit, organizations, etc. which was studied and shown in Adriani & McKelvey 2007.

Implications on Business

By some amazing feature of unity of science, these scaling laws seem to work across from fractal geometry, to biology, to geophysics, to the spread of ideas, to the distribution of wealth and to artistic success.

This is no different in business. The fractal property of the stock market, individual stocks and many business dimensions, i.e., This is no different in the business world.

This is no small finding as the decisions that many business leaders make, e.g., 6 sigma, statistics, heuristics, etc. are based on normal distribution assumptions because our mind cannot grasp the scale-free concept of power laws.

As such, business leaders need to be aware of when a situation falls under normal vs. power law distribution to distinguish between garbage analysis and good analysis.

Item	Analysis Source
Structure of WWW	Albert et al., 1999
Structure of the Internet hardware	Faloutsos et al., 1999; Buchanan, 2004
Number of hits received from website per day	Adamic & Huberman, 2000
Blockbuster drugs	Buchanan, 2004
Distribution of Wealth	Pareto, 1897; Levy & Solomon, 1997
Publications and citations	Lotka, 1926; deSolla Price, 1965
Job vacancies	Gunz et al., 2001
Salaries	Buchanan, 20002
Firm size	Axtell, 2001
Supply chains	Scheinkman & Woodford, 1994
Growth rates & internal structure of firms	Stanley et al., 1996
Price movements on exchanges	Mandelbrot & Hudson, 2004
Delinquency rates	Cook et al., 2004
Movie profits	De Vany, 2004
Consumer products	Moss, 2002
Cotton prices	Mandelbrot, 1963
Economic fluctuations	Scheinkman & Woodford, 1994
Alliance networks among biotech firms	Barabási & Bonabeau, 2003, p. 207, building on Powell et al.
Entrepreneurship/innovation	Poole et al., 2000
Copies of books sold	Hackett, 1967
Number of telephone calls and emails	Aiello et al., 2000; Ebel et al., 2002
Macroeconomic effects of zero-rational agents	Ormerod et al., 2005
News website visitation decay patterns	Dezsı et al., 2005
Intra-firm decision events	Diatlov, 2005

Hierarchy and Abstraction of Organization Structures

The hierarchy of an organization can be illustrated by considering abstractions. If one were to compare a business to a computer, deployed management tools would be a 3rd layer abstraction, as is the case with computer applications. Moreover, 2nd layer processes and procedures would be comparable to a computer's Operating system. Finally, people and their organization's structure would constitute a 1st layer of abstraction, as would a computer's hardware and firmware.

Abstractions are processes often adopted in computer science and programming, and in engineering. For example, a building's

46

blueprint is one level of abstraction below the actual building, and it is designed to capture the essential features of the building. Another example is computer science, where machine code exists several layers below the application software and the algorithm. Every layer needs the below layers to function but can exist without the top layers.

So, with abstraction in mind, you can understand how organizations are, in fact, complex systems whose sum of parts outweighs the value of its individual parts added together.

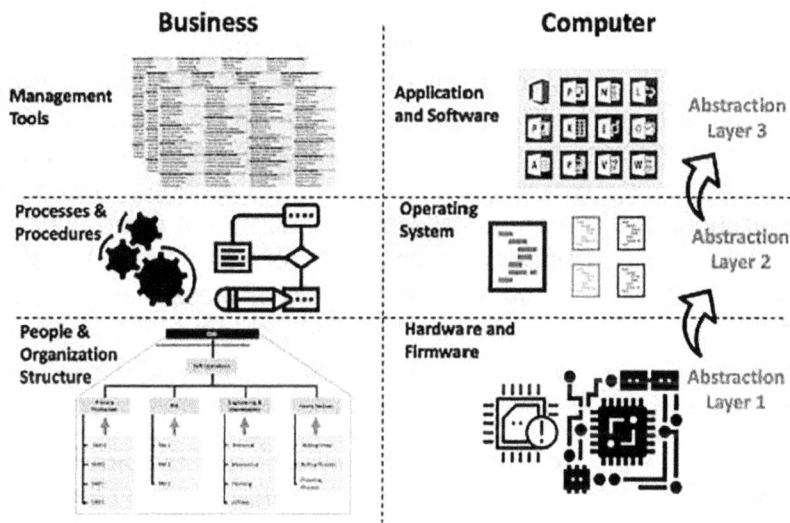

Organization Culture and Self-Organization Analogy

Consider groups of people in any setting—social clubs, scouts, sports teams, businesses, etc. It is factual that when we find ourselves in groups of just 10 individuals, we develop chains of command, acceptable codes of behavior, and unique language, that support and sustain our beliefs and attitudes. This behavior is also true of individuals gathering for the first time, for as brief a period as a few hours. This can be observed during large social gatherings or corporate team-building exercises. Dominant group behavior emerging out of such settings takes shape by itself and gravitates towards one of six archetypes. As highlighted in the following chapter, each of these archetypes is driven by the dominant aggregate values of its respective group.

This phenomenon—referred to by systems practitioners as self-organization—also depends on time and scale factors, because an organization matures as it grows (scale factor) over time (time factor). As an organization matures, an organizational culture with a unique identity and distinct properties emerges.

However, most business strategies that aim to mature and grow organizations fail to consider this emergence, and when management is faced with exponentially growing organizational complexity, only a few companies overcome this challenge into the next level of maturity. This is shown by our research and is backed by numerous studies conducted by the likes of McKinsey, Bain, and Goldman Sachs, which show that the challenges posed by organizational culture and a growing organizational complexity are one of the most significant reasons why, for example, only 1% of launches make it to 7-figures, and only 1% of these make it to the unicorn stage. Our research on both publicly-traded and private companies shows that traditional scaling methods and strategies only work in < 1% of situations.

The presence of emergence allows us to argue that organizational culture consists of uncontrollable, complex behaviors that one cannot alter except with a multitude of strategic and tactical initiatives. As mentioned, later on, successful programs need to be holistic in nature; they must utilize multidimensional initiatives related to vision, mission, values, training, management tools, and incentives in a process called "nudging," to achieve the desired outcome.

Another important factor of organization structure is employee diversity. When all the employees of an organization are similar or homogeneous (e.g. an assembly plant, a fast-food restaurant, a retail shop), it is much simpler to model and influence behavior. This is not the case when dealing with a heterogeneous organization composed of diverse individuals, each with their own unique sets of values and functions (e.g., multi-disciplinary organizations, multinational organizations). If heterogeneous organizations are

48

also highly autonomous and highly adaptable, then simple models and influence mechanisms become ineffective. This is because, in such cases, control is decentralized, driven by unit-level interactions, and motivated by informal homogeneous pockets within the organization. In contrast, as discussed earlier, organizations with low-level autonomy can be controlled centrally in a top-down fashion.

As such, this information allows us to consider the below two-dimensional framework highlighting the relationship between autonomy levels (x-axis) and homogeneity levels (y-axis).

This gives rise to another important feature of complex systems: self-organization. When elements have the autonomy to adapt locally, they can self-organize to form global patterns. This process is known as emergence. Thus, as opposed to simple linear systems with top-down, centralized order, complex systems exhibit bottom-up patterns of order. Self-organization will be another recurring theme in our exploration of complex systems design.

If, at some point in your life, you've managed a group of people of any kind, whether socially or at work, you will agree that the social structure that sets in with time (even after a short time), defines future team interactions, behaviors, and decisions. While these "emergent" group properties may slowly evolve with time (especially if the group count grows in size), changing these properties will become increasingly harder to alter by an outsider, or even by an insider of the group.

In nature, for example, it turns out that even a simple set of rules can define very complex characteristics, and changing one simple rule can lead to chaos and may send the group into disarray until a new emergent property sets in. This will be illustrated in the example of ant colonies below.

It may be surprising that the emergence resulting from ant colony synergies stems from a set of simple rules. Stanford University biologist Deborah Gordon conducted extensive research on the behaviors of ant colonies and discovered that ants exhibit self-organizing properties. Accordingly, the following section discusses task allocation–the process that adjusts the number of Harvester Ants engaged in each task in an appropriate manner.

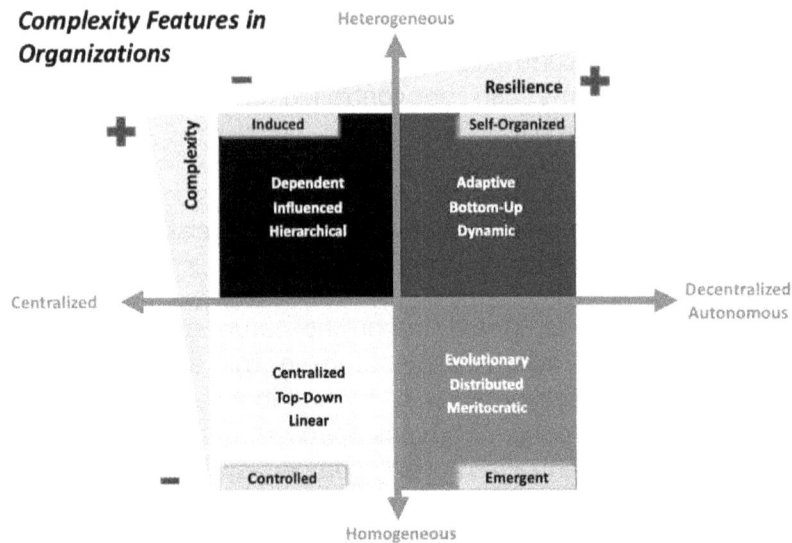

Complexity Features in Organizations

Contrary to your intuition, task allocation within ant colonies operates without central or hierarchical control. It's a self-organizing activity where a colony's harvester ants divide tasks–including nest maintenance, nest cleanup, and nest supervision–amongst themselves. The question is, how do ants decide on their tasks at any given time? Interestingly enough, tasks are carried out according to what needs to be done. Any task that needs immediate attention, or more attention than another task, will be taken on by the ants. For example, if an ant's nest has been tampered with, collective attention will go towards nest maintenance and repair, rather than nest cleanup or food search. Gordon carried out an experiment where she surrounded a nest with toothpicks and, as expected, the ants were attempting to remove the toothpicks and repair the nest.

It is important to consider how ants do this, as they rely on internal interactions and communication with one another. Individual ants do not know or understand the bigger pictures of their environments. Rather, they feed off of information from other ants. So, if an ant interacts with a toothpick, it will proceed to remove it. Another ant might have the same interaction, and this will result in the same action. However, if another ant interacts with an ant that is removing the toothpick, the first won't perform the same action because it recognizes that the action is already being carried out. Actions taken by ants depend on two factors: interactions with their environment and interactions with other ants.

Much like humans, ants seem to be influenced by the actions of those they come into contact with. This happens because when ants cross paths, they sense the presence of chemical residues on each other's antennae.

This phenomenon is also observed in fish and birds, where simple rules lead to complex structures and self-organization.

A starling formation is interpreted as a human-based systems thinking approach. Picture by MennoSchaefer from Depsitphotos.

In the 1980s, Craig Reynolds presented a very simple model of this phenomenon, known as Boid's model. His goal was to develop realistic computer graphics of flocking or schooling behavior. As a result, he wrote a well-known paper titled: Flocks, herds, and schools: A distributed behavioral model.

In that paper, he provides a simple model in which individuals obey three rules in order of importance.

The first rule is collision avoidance, which has only one purpose — to avoid collisions with their neighbors.

The second rule is velocity matching, which ensures that individuals are synchronized in speed and direction by matching their velocity to their neighbors.

The third and final rule is flock centering, a proximity rule to ensure that individuals remain close to their neighbors.

A group of fish collaborating to make a fish school, creating a complex system.
Picture by djmattaar from Depositphotos.

Reynolds and others who simulated this model found that these extremely simple rules produce surprisingly realistic results. It is an impressive demonstration of how complex behaviors and complex systems can be achieved from only three basic rules. Moreover, the model looks convincingly similar to real flocks except for the shape of the elements.

Knowing all of this, how can employees interact to create products and services in an organization?

In a nutshell, organizations are basically social reactors. They are spaces where employees come together and interact with each other. When things go well and the right technologies come into play, new ideas are sparked, and high productivity is achieved. But of course, the opposite is also true, as in the case of incongruence or culture clashes. In such situations, creativity, innovation, and productivity can be destroyed.

Gordon's ant study reveals an important finding of information flow and data accuracy. Her research showed that larger ant colonies were more deterministic and consistent in task allocation than were smaller colonies. The main reason for this is that ants from larger colonies are able to get better statistics on interaction rates because each ant experiences a higher number of interactions, on average. In organizations, internal and external data flow and data accuracy play a crucial role in the success of businesses. This leads us to our final two definitions.

The Iceberg Model

Before we dive deeper into the PMAS, let me introduce the Iceberg Model as another tool adopted by system thinkers when conducting root cause synthesis. The Iceberg Model occurs when you see the world as a series of events, like seeing the "tip of the iceberg", but you are only seeing the surface, and maybe slightly below the surface.

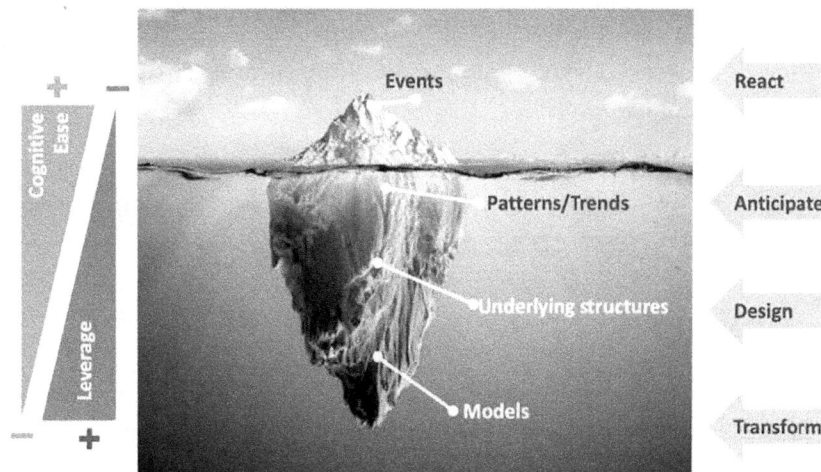

In level 2, you would consider underlying patterns, and this requires you to look a little below the surface of everyday events.

For example, we might determine that we are getting a cold every few months, usually during times when we aren't sleeping as much.

Imagine you get a cold; you might react to this event by taking some medicine. This is level 1.

Level 3 requires an even more in-depth consideration of circumstances, and this allows us to move past a simple cause-effect relationship, towards an understanding of a larger behavioral pattern. This does not only relate to physical structures like the human body, but also to cultural structures. As such, considering the example of a cold, lifestyle choices may be a level-3 determining factor in bi-monthly illnesses. Your lifestyle is essentially determined by the relationships between your work, leisure, income, diet, and health.

Finally, level 4 allows us to reach the root, i.e. the ultimate cause of the system. Here, we are able to grasp how things work in a way that allows us to understand our world and take action in it. In the lifestyle example, it is assumed that if you value happiness, you will choose the lifestyle that you think makes you happiest. However, people may have different models for what makes them happy. Some may view that health and leisure are more important than career development when it comes to reaching happiness and may, as a result, lead a totally different lifestyle than their more work-oriented peers. This lifestyle, in its ultimate pursuit of joy, may lead to fewer colds!

Similarly, when we have identified all these levels within our organization, we can tie them back to our objectives and goals and design initiatives accordingly.

Synthesis vs. Analysis

Synthesis is the process of taking a holistic view of things. We're telling you this because the first step you need to take is familiarizing yourself with synthesis, not analysis. You need to look at the problem as a whole and synthesize its parts in order to better understand how it all fits together. Once you've done this and you've identified all the challenges that are facing your current business, you can take the next steps.

Here, you need to conduct a deep, root-cause synthesis in order to develop an adequate list of initiatives addressing organizational gaps. This is very important, as root causes motivate your initiatives and programs. Most organizations work to conduct root-cause analysis below the surface, but they never go as deep as the levels in the iceberg model. As such, it's important that you identify every level of the root cause, not necessarily because you're going to propose initiatives at every level, but rather because you will be better able to decide the level at which you wish to take these initiatives.

THE PMAS

It's human nature that groups with less than a dozen members will develop chains of command, acceptable codes of behavior, and unique languages, that support and sustain their beliefs/ attitudes. In our context, these people are employees within an organization. Let's examine how Silicon Valley culture started. In the 1980s, a new craze came about with the computer industry and young engineers started to see themselves going places they never thought possible. They considered themselves to be young businessmen and started focusing on their talents and jobs. This flipped the hierarchy on its head, as engineers aren't usually top-level leaders. This is what created Silicon Valley culture.

One of the original companies behind this frenzy is Apple Computers. Apple started off much smaller, with an unusual branding and a not-so-healthy work life. Apple employees traded in expensive suits and black ties for a more casual look, opting for sneakers and jeans. They worked gruesome hours and ate junk food all the time. Co-founder and CEO Steve Jobs called his programmers "artists" and "pirates," and he rewarded their commitment with the promise of stock options and working retreats at cushy resorts. He had the most ambitious vision for his company and knew straight off the bat that Apple would be a head-turning and truly magical company. Finally, Jobs sold his products by giving customers an aura of complete superiority over other technological innovations.

We chose Apple as an example, in particular, to highlight how two aspects of cultural climate can impact an organization. Firstly, organizational culture during Apple's high-growth early years produced unintended consequences. At the time, the demanding work schedules fueled dysfunctional patterns when it came to health, family, and relationships. In extreme circumstances, this led to suicides. Consequently, overall company strategy and performance were negatively impacted, as many of Apple's early products flopped and stock prices plummeted. Aside from unexpected outcomes, the second aspect of organization cultures is their development over time. As organizations grow in size, their daily functioning is affected by the way the enterprise operates on a daily basis, and how it is perceived internally (by employees) and externally, outside of its walls.

This example is a perfect illustration of why a simple system like the PMAS toolkit can be highly effective, as it keeps your organization culture in check at all times. It also provides the tools and mechanisms necessary to navigate through the complexity of organization culture by enabling you to steer/nudge your organization culture and leadership at the first signs of incongruence. The toolkit is simple and consists of 5 steps:

1. Diagnose the organization and human resources.
2. Set desired targets and key performance indicators.
3. Create and prioritize initiatives that will make up the overall program.
4. Design and build monitoring, tracking and measurement capabilities.
5. Launch program, track progress and take corrective action along the way.

If you read the entire previous sections, you might be asking yourself, how can this be a dynamic system that will run continuously?

Once the system is in place, then steps 2-5 can be automated and can run indefinitely. In particular, getting to step 4 means you have implemented the necessary process to regularly administer diagnosis and gather required results. This allows you to fast-track adaptability via dynamic tracking and automation, as they help identify potential issues early on. This is similar to the cancer analogy: early detection provides higher success rates than does late detection. With early detection, you can implement corrective measures early-on, and you can utilize nudges that are simpler, quicker, and more impactful than those administered with late detection.

The Fractal Unit Challenge

As mentioned earlier, employees and leaders are what drive company performance and, subsequently, company earnings and value. As such, due to fractal-like behavior (self-similarity) across abstraction layers, all these factors motivate company stock value.

Inside an organization, subunits such as formal functional departments, product groups, hierarchical levels and teams may also produce their own unique cultures. Difficulties in coordinating and integrating processes or organizational activities, for example, are often a result of culture clashes among different subunits. This is a double-edged sword: it is necessary for each unit to develop its own values, despite different modes of operation across units. For example, manufacturing should be more internally-focused, as it is concerned with consistency, productivity, profitability, quality, and processes. Marketing, on the other hand, should be externally-focused, tailoring to the needs of the market. This leads to the concept of Paradox, as discussed in the next section. This is why it's common to have conflicts between organizational functions—for example, conflict between marketing, sales, engineering, and manufacturing departments. The main reason is that each of these units develops its own cultures from its set of goals, objectives, incentives and values. This will be discussed in the value mapping section below.

Individually, units and subunits have common elements that make them self-similar, i.e., structurally fractal-like. To illustrate this, imagine looking at an organization in a zoomed-out manner. You would be able to see the entire organizational structure, as well as how units and subunits interact. If you were to zoom in on the organization's lower levels, you would be looking at individual relationships between employees. As you zoom in further, you would be looking at individual behaviors, and further in would be the activities in the brain that lead to such behaviors.

Self-similarity (a characteristic of fractals) applies to certain cultural characteristics across the entire organization. As such, smaller units have cultural characteristics similar to those of the organization at large, and these self-similar characteristics shape organization culture as a whole and bind the entire organization together. In mapping out an organization's culture, therefore, you need to assess the organization as an entity (or System) consisting of self-similar individual subunits. Only then are you able to identify the common dominant attributes of subunit cultures and aggregate them. Such a combination can provide an understanding of both the cultural archetypes of the overall organization and those of individual units and subunits.

The Toolset

The PMAS Toolkit is a complete system comprising this book, the quizzes, the quiz assessments tool, and the actions/initiatives you can take to nudge an organization towards the desired state.

The quizzes consist of four assessment questionnaires to be used together in developing a comprehensive map of organization culture and leadership archetypes and aspirations. These maps constitute the system that will track, record, and guide organization transformation over time. The four quizzes are:

1. **Leadership Archetype Quiz**
2. **Organization Culture Archetype Quiz**
3. **Aspired Organization Culture Quiz**
4. **Aspired Organization Culture Quiz—Leader Version**

Each of these quizzes is supplemented with an assessment workbook that gives you step-by-step guidance on grading, as shown below:

Quiz	Assessment Workbook
1. Leadership Archetype Quiz	Leadership Archetype Assessment Workbook
2. Organizational Culture Quiz	Organizational Culture Assessment Workbook
3. Aspired Organizational Culture Quiz	Aspired Organizational Culture Workbook
4. Aspired Organizational Culture Quiz - Leader version	Aspired Organizational Culture Workbook

In addition, the toolset includes initiatives that can be taken to nudge the organization and its leadership towards a particular Archetype. This service is provided in the following booklets:

- **Leadership Archetype Nudging**
- **Organization Culture Archetype Nudging**

In the next few sections, I'll be guiding you step-by-step on how to deploy and interpret the PMAS Toolkit.

The Paradoxical Organization and Leadership Mindset

The PMAS describes two applications for the Paradoxical approach:

The first is a way to assess a paradox mindset as key to successful organizations. For example, how can a company like TESLA be innovative and flexible while also mass-producing cars, as manufacturing cars in mass is a process that requires automation, organization, precision and excellence in manufacturing, so consistency, structure, and defined processes and procedures are a must. How can Amazon be the "Earth's Most Customer-Centric" organization while also be managing a variety of internal business units requiring internal coordination and an internally focused approach towards holding the company together? These companies are able to balance the paradoxical opposites that emerge within a growing organization.

In the case of TESLA, manufacturing and marketing departments would have to work together, as per the analogy brought up earlier. How can manufacturing and marketing strategies produce competitive, high-innovation products, without getting crippling push-back from engineering and manufacturing departments, as these entities aim to design, prototype, launch, and deliver top-quality products, in mass, and on-schedule?

At an individual level, a paradox mindset indicates the extent to which individuals embrace and are energized by tensions. The adoption of a paradox mindset can help people leverage tensions and produce creative outputs. However, most people tend to have a preference for one direction over the other. Being simultaneously dragged in two different directions would result in cognitive tension and stress. However, counter-intuitive research suggests that these conflicts can often work in a person's favor. Several studies conducted by psychologists and organizational researchers on the topic of paradoxical thinking found that people who learn to embrace, rather than reject, opposing sides of a paradox tend n to be more creative, more flexible, and more productive. Hence, duality can lead to enhanced overall performance surpassing that of unilateral thinking.

You have undoubtedly experienced this phenomenon in your own job and even in your personal life. For example, you may have many contradictory goals that require paradoxical cognition. How did you behave when you were faced with such choices? If you cultivate the paradox mindset, you will have to consider ways to pursue both ends of a spectrum simultaneously, instead of fearing and avoiding potential conflicts. Furthermore, research shows that the very act of thinking about reconciling opposing ends of a paradox could train your mind for greater creative solutions in other areas.

The second application for the paradoxical approach was the development of both the quiz structure and the value-mapping. The quiz follows a framework presenting values in opposing axes across two key dimensions: Agility and Orientation. These lead to six sub-dimensions characterizing an organization's culture, and they are grouped into three pairs in a paradoxical representation along the two main axes, as shown below.

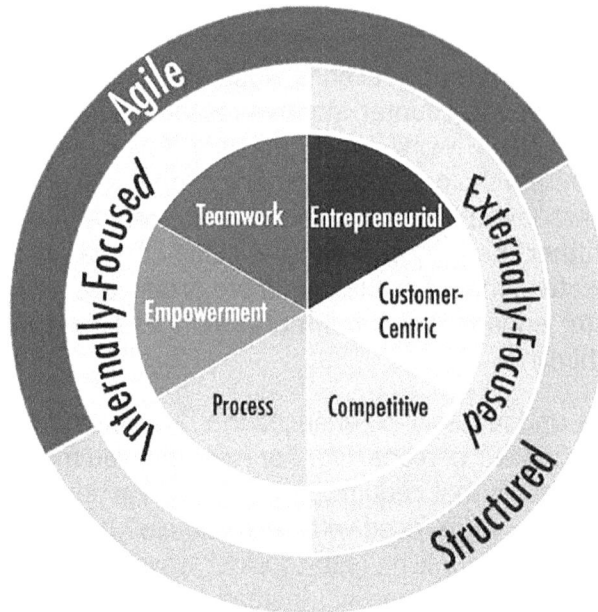

If the value dimension for organizations is fractal-like (self-similar), opposing paradoxes are key success factors for both organizational leadership and organizational performance as a whole. These same dimensions, named differently for leadership archetypes and individual behavior, would apply to both whole organizations and their leadership.

This is why a map of similar characteristics was developed for organization leaders. This is similar to influencer hubs within a social network, assuming leaders can influence their organizations.

The label for each archetype depicts the most notable leadership characteristics within each work culture. These archetypes were developed to form a set of mutually-exclusive and collectively-exhaustive maps derived from numerous, widely-used tools and frameworks. These techniques have been extensively researched, and you can refer to their corresponding publications in the bibliography section of the book. We represented these maps in a single framework that reflects the values underlying human behavior (discussed later).

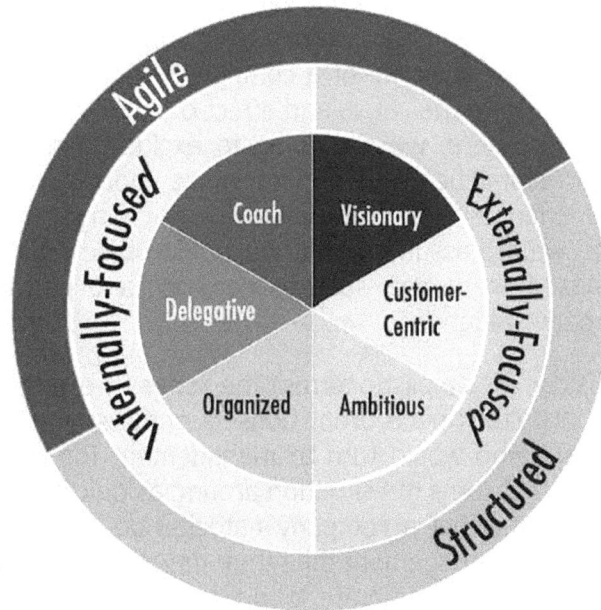

The Iceberg Model Analogy

Organization leaders often produce faulty judgments when they fail to consider the effects of individual values on whole organizations and their cultures. This is best illustrated via the "Iceberg" model, as it allows us to conceptualize how individual values affecting organizational leadership and culture can affect organizational outcome and strategic direction. We will do so by illustrating how cultures are shaped by external factors affecting employees' feelings, attitudes, and beliefs. We will also be discussing the internal factors affecting organizational culture—formal and informal policies and procedures, and informal work environments. These structures give rise to patterns of behavior and, ultimately, to specific events. Events are easily visible, while patterns and structures are usually hidden from sight. This is why we perform surface-level problem-solving when tackling organizational issues.

Let's consider a common scenario of company stock. Profitability, growth, and the ability to hit, miss, or exceed annual and quarterly target forecasts are all indicators that allow public shareholders in a public company to gauge the organization's success. Thus, the stock price appreciation or depreciation over time is typically the observable event or outcome of a company's performance. In this example, we illustrate the cause and effect of stock value relative to other companies. Here, we are going to exclude external market events and irrationalities that impact whole industries and stock markets—ex. changes in oil stock value due to changes in oil prices. Furthermore, we are assuming that we would objectively value the enterprise based on merits—such as earnings and performance—driving company valuation.

Let's consider (in simplistic terms) the series of events following a sudden, sharp stock price drop. Consequently, shareholders and board members who would turn to management for answers and demand a plan that turns the situation around as quickly as possible. Shareholders (owners of a company's stocks) do not usually have the patience to let management take their time in diving deeper into root causes, and cannot tolerate long-term measures that impact the valuation of their current holdings. As such, managers are expected to take the necessary short-term measures for boosting profitability and rectify performance within months and not years. This leaves management with very little time to delve beneath the surface and explore the fundamental factors that may have contributed to such an event. Events that follow typically include layoffs, changes in leadership, changes in short-term strategy, and incremental initiatives leading to short-term improvements.

By performing a more in-depth exploration of company issues, you would find that the aforementioned measures could only lead to temporary improvement, as the problem is chronic, with potentially irreversible implications, unless a long-term strategy was devised. For example, your investigation may identify why management has not acted sooner: there's a group of old-guard employees and managers who have intentionally ignored threats to the status quo brought on by the use of new trends and technology. If these technologies were considered sooner, the organization would have been in a much better financial position today. Accordingly, if management were to stick to a surface-level assessment, it would implement layoffs and replace the formal head of the "old guard" with external blood, or someone with experience in the new technology. Other measures possibly taken include M&As with more technologically-advanced companies. As discussed earlier, program transformations enforced during such scenarios will certainly lead to culture clashes and subsequently, high risk and high probability of failure.

Going one level deeper, you may find that the behavior of the old guard came out of fear of losing their jobs or having to reskill into something they may not understand. You may also find that both the culture and structure in place emphasized a strong sense of unison between team members, as they behaved much like an extended family. Moreover, you may determine that bringing in an external leader who falls into the Ambitious Leader Archetype (please refer to the assessment workbook for a definition of this archetype) may lead to clashes within the organization, as this type of leader promotes possibly unsuitable values, ex. internal competitiveness. Such an assessment would call for an entirely different approach to the transformation program when compared to each of the levels above.

By going in-depth, you would be able to understand multilevel challenges and issues, and you would be better equipped to make your case and prescribe the right initiatives for each level. Because you were able to develop a holistic map of the organization, you would be able to come up with short-term initiatives that satisfy shareholders, and long-term initiatives that provide long-lasting organizational change.

The above example is a simple illustration of a frequent pattern within organizational decision-making. As we will discuss in the next section, organizational performance depends primarily on human-based decisions and secondarily on data analysis, expert advice, strategic recommendations, or internal departments. Both the individual and collective values behind our beliefs are what drive our recommendations, actions, and decisions.

Baseline Mapping

As such, our values are foundational to our perception of how we see the world and to the actions we take and the environments we inhabit within this world. To get a deeper insight into an organization, we need a baseline that allows us to visualize the status quo by mapping out organizational values and beliefs. Everyone has different sets of ideas, aspirations, and perspectives as to how to deal with the world around us. Our values take shape over time through our lived experiences; they determine how we perceive new information and help us create new knowledge.

As is the case in real life, at work, values are the compass that directs our actions depending on what is of higher or lower value to us. Our values are what we subconsciously adopt in our decision-making when ranking what is good or bad and what is better or worse. As such, these rankings work to either motivate or demotivate us. Therefore, by learning how to work with values, we can begin to understand what is important to others and why they do what they do. In doing so, we can adopt the initiatives required to achieve target organizational transformation.

Initiatives designed to achieve organizational transformation represent interventions within a complex adaptive system. As such, these initiatives should be designed according to a solid understanding of the stakeholder's perspective. Most major organization transformation efforts and programs fail because they do not try to understand different perspectives present within the same system. Accordingly, the next section highlights why interventions should adopt a process of nudging.

First of all, a change in initiatives involves building a shared vision. This cannot take place without an understanding of how organization employees and stakeholders see things. Vision and mission statements are not just words; they are a reflection of the organization's common goals, objectives and values, i.e., should be the first steps in achieving alignment. Their wording can have very different meanings according to the background of those trying to grasp them. Without understanding personal contexts, misunderstanding and conflict will arise. We need to understand where people are coming from before we can learn to speak a common language. Unfortunately, we cannot simply look at other people and discern their mental models. We need to make them explicit by mapping them out, and this is the role of the four Quizzes in the PMAS Toolkit. These diagnostic tests provide insights about the organization and its employees and managers within the context of the work environment.

"If a factory is torn down but the rationality which produced it is left standing, then that rationality will simply produce another factory. If a revolution destroys a government, but the systematic patterns of thought that produced that government are left intact, then those patterns will repeat themselves." -Robert Pirsig, Zen and the Art of Motorcycle Maintenance

As such, value mapping helps us answer why employees in an organization do what they do, by enabling us to visualize the values embodied at work and in the wider organization. Because values are sometimes taken for granted, they're never actually articulated or written down. Revealing these values by baselining the current organization, however, is the first step in providing an understanding of the inner workings of this complex system.

Mapping values is not a new concept. One illustration of value mapping is The World Values Survey (shown below), a global research project that explores people's values and beliefs, how they change over time, and how those values affect their social and political reality. Similar to the PMAS value map, the global cultural map also takes a paradoxical approach when visualizing societies, as it represents society location along two key dimensions. Moving upward on this map reflects the shift from traditional values to those that are secular-rational while moving rightward reflects the shift from survival values to self-expression values. The World Values Survey project has been ongoing since the 1980s to measure and monitor support for democracy, tolerance, gender equality, the role of religion, attitudes toward the environment, work, family, and politics. This survey is adopted by policymakers seeking to build civil societies and democratic institutions in developing countries.

The Inglehart-Welzel World Cultural Map 2022

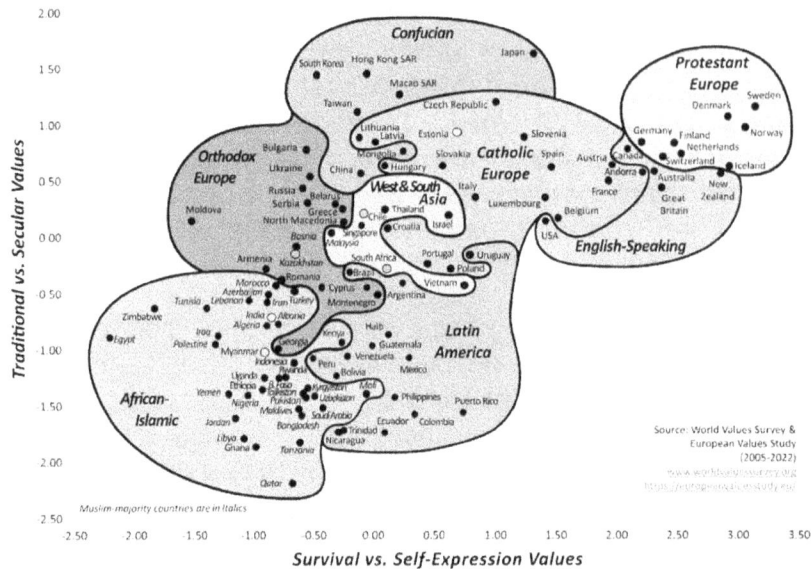

Inglehart–Welzel cultural map of the world. Wikimedia Commons by World Values Survey

Where Do You Start?

First, you need to draw a comprehensive picture of the organization starting with identifying both the formal and informal lines of reporting. This is because, more often than not, what's categorized as organization structure on paper does not always reflect reality. Accordingly, what usually appears as a formal line of reporting within organizational hierarchy is not what influences your organization.

As a first step, it would be more effective to identify non-formal organization lines and redraw organization structures in a manner that highlights influencers in the organization. You need to consider that hubs of influence within your network may improve your mapping by taking the leadership archetype quiz instead of the culture archetype quiz. That said, a decision can be taken on a case-by-case basis.

Formal and Informal Hierarchy and Power Mapping

In order to achieve a "System Change" you need to think of an organization like a complex dynamic system and develop a detailed map of power. This consists of all actors involved, including allies and opponents. You would need to ask the right questions and get their corresponding answers. You need to ask: Who's with and who's against the current vision or targets (if these already exist)? Who are your blockers? What are they in it for? Why might these unusual suspects be allies? An analysis of power will not only illuminate the factors holding a system in place but will also reveal key levers for transforming power and igniting system change.

Systemic change almost always involves changes in power dynamics, as it reveals new forms of power, and it challenges the status quo. In such a case, conflict may be a sign of progress and should be expected. Power can be defined in many ways; here, we will consider two definitions: 1. the ability to make decisions that will be implemented, and 2. the ability to influence people to believe in a set of values. Therefore, we need to identify where centers of power are and who has this power. Also, we need to consider what kind of power this is and who it's inaccessible to. We need to develop both abstract and practical understandings of power distributions. We need to be clear about the context of our discussion of power. For example, an employee who generally has a lot of systemic power and influence may not be as lucky when it comes to our specific issue.

Power mapping refers to the mapping processes that help us analyze power relationships and develop transformation strategies for influencing and achieving change. A power map is important, as it provides an understanding of who makes key decisions and who contributes to them. This is important when it comes to creating change and implementing and adapting strategies. Power mapping identifies the best individuals to target when promoting desired change. This mechanism also reveals available leverage points of influence and connections between these influences.

Power-mapping is the visualization process required to conceptualize spheres of influence around a person or a group. It should be conducted in a manner that is similar to crime investigation boards. When it comes to decision-making, we need to be able to clearly visualize links. As such, we need to pinpoint primary targets making key decisions and secondary targets influencing these decisions. It is important to remember that within any given system, there will be both formal and informal structures of influence and power. The formal dimension (structure) is not the only determinant of organizational functioning.

Once additional and informal levers of power are identified, they are then included in the leadership development initiatives. In addition, during organizational transformation, it may be necessary to consider hiring new employees. It is also recommended that new hires are screened for culture and leadership archetype alignment prior to joining the new taskforce. Failing to do so may disrupt any power map-based change initiatives and effort you have put in place.

Setting Targets Based on a Common Vision

As the very first step, you need to ensure and/or determine whether the current vision and mission of the organization reflect all stakeholders' aspirations and alignments. We advise you to refer to our book, "Vision Mission in Under One Hour" when trying to articulate your organization's vision and/or mission statement. Vision statements form the basis of your overall and top-level aspired organization culture archetype target (referred to below as the **"Target"** or **"Target State"**).

Articulating a compelling organizational vision and building commitment around it marks the beginning of the journey, not its end. The greater challenge that lies ahead is actualizing the vision in every aspect of organizational life. There needs to be a clear and coherent strategy for making the vision a reality at multiple levels of the organization, across all divisions, departments, and teams. In our book, "Vision Mission Under One Hour", we provide a method that allows the mission statement to be inclusive of individuals across all levels of the organization. The process of inclusion makes

70

change and alignment easier and faster to attain. Ultimately, visions must be real and meaningful to all those who adopt them in order to achieve success in organizational transformation.

Critical Gap Analysis Map

The next step in organizational transformation is developing a critical gap analysis map by comparing your current state or status quo to your desired state and assessing the gap size and criticality levels between the two.

The heat map (shown below) highlights dominant archetype characteristics; it also provides deep insights into the entire system down to the unit level, value level, and aggregate level. This reveals the specific attributes you are lacking and the areas where you are lagging. As mentioned earlier, unless you are a newly established startup company, your organization would likely consist of several teams and units, each with a different archetype and culture. For example, if you have an accounting department, you need to adopt a dominant process-oriented culture within this specific department, even if entrepreneurial culture dominates your organization as a whole. Therefore, you should consider the appropriate context when administering the quiz.

We recommend that you perform a diagnosis of all organizational levels in order to determine the most critical area, i.e. that which has the widest gap. In doing so, a simple heatmap similar to the one shown below is necessary, as it allows you to recognize the areas that should be accelerated and those that could have the highest impact on the program.

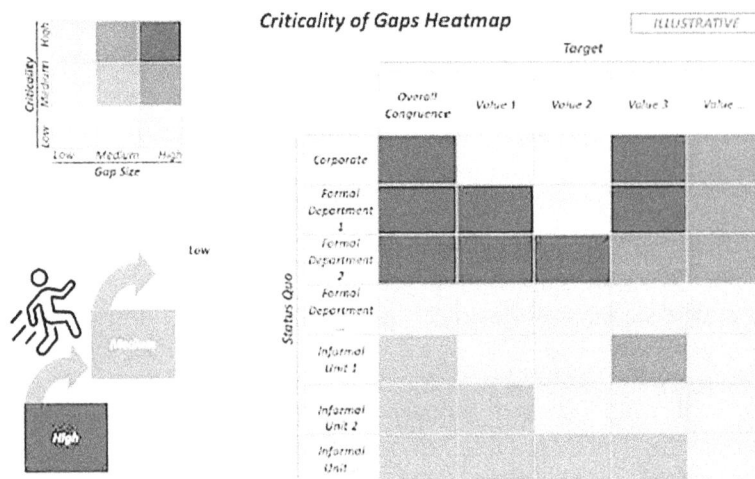

Picture by Sam Schreim by Business Model Hackers

Interpreting the Assessment and Transformation Program Plan Design

In the previous section, we discussed how individual units or departments within the organization can be viewed using a single Criticality Gap Heatmap. In this section, and in the interest of keeping the explanation simple, we will focus our discussion on result interpretations for single units. Because organizations are fractal-like, their individual, multiple, and aggregate parts behave similarly. As such, similar interpretations can be applied to fractions within organizations.

Stacking the four administered quizzes against each other will reveal insights and strategies in a prioritized sequence. Let's consider the results from the two quizzes and how they compare to the **Target** that was set in the earlier section. These results would provide indicators, insights, and an assessment of congruence and alignment among key stakeholders. This helps determine the initiatives required for organizational transformation, all while tracking progress every month. In addition, it enables the dynamic calibration of program initiatives, and it allows the organization to adapt to changing conditions and Targets, through a continuous feedback loop.

72

The following is a list of key indicator insights and an explanation of their significance towards achieving the desired Target. Moreover, these results will help you select the necessary initiatives from the nudging book to include in your **Transformation Program Plan**.

Culture Archetype (Status Quo) Vs. Target State

This indicator highlights the main culture gap your organization is currently experiencing between where it is at the moment and where it should be. Both indicator and gap size on their own are not sufficient in determining the difficulty in closing the current gap. You would need to combine this indicator with some of the indicators shown below in order to make such a determination. However, this is a good indicator of potential productivity-related issues and other structural issues and gaps within your current organization. As such, the higher the gap, the more severe the issues relating to organization culture, human resources, and/or management could be. Such issues could be hampering performance and preventing the organization from attaining its full potential.

Aspired Culture–Leaders Version Vs. Aspired Culture

This gap should be as small as possible, and aspirations should be as closely aligned as possible at the unit level (in the early stages of a company such as in a startup, this measure may not be indicative of a problem or gap). This measure can reveal several insights and should be considered in two stages:

The first stage should be used to determine the informal organization leaders. If these leaders have been correctly identified, and "Formal" Leaders have been excluded from this assessment, then the gap should be minimal. If on the other hand, the gap between informal leaders (only) and aspired culture is wide, then it is likely not all pockets of influence have been correctly identified. Moreover, a wide gap could signify the possible presence of multiple "clans" or units within the unit. This may require you to split the unit into congruent subdivisions and identify the influencers within these

73

subdivisions before selecting nudging initiatives. If this is not the case, then the organization's vision, mission, and/or values could be non-inclusive and/or badly-articulated.

If the gap in the first stage is small, then the second stage should include a comparison with only the "Formal" Leaders. A wide gap would mean that the high resistance to change would prevail if the state of the Formal Leaders' aspirations are aligned with those of the Target State (shown below).

A small gap in either stage would not reveal much, unless such a condition is compared to the target state, as per below.

Aspired Culture Vs. Target State

This comparison is a key indicator of the difficulty level of achieving organizational transformation. The greater this gap is, the more difficult it would be to achieve the desired state. The main reason is that this measure highlights the degree of congruence between aggregate employee values, and organizational vision and stakeholder objectives. Moreover, a wider gap means that it may be harder to align employees with the values that are in the organization's and the stakeholders' best interests. A wide gap may be the result of a clash of cultures between shareholders'/stakeholders' beliefs and those of an organization's employees. In such a case, resistance to change is very probable. Accordingly, an alignment program is necessary, as it would nudge the initiatives required for realigning employee beliefs and values with those of the Target State.

If a small gap occurs within an organization whose Target State and Status Quo are different, then simpler initiatives related to operations, managerial/leadership skills, and management tools should be sufficient in achieving congruence. This is because, in such a case, resistance to change is less likely to occur. Therefore, change becomes a strategic, operationally-driven program that includes initiatives such as reskilling and/or operational improvements.

74

Aspired Culture–Leaders Version Vs. Target State

If you were inclusive of organizational members when articulating your vision and mission statement, the gap levels between your organization's aspired state and the target would be small. You need to make sure this gap is as small as possible because the smaller the gap, the easier the change would be. Furthermore, in such a case, the buy-in would be happening from the inside, with little or almost no nudging required, and the emphasis would be on the rollout of required management tools that make change possible. If this indicator has a large gap, then solidifying the organization's vision and mission statements (along with company values and aspirations) is a priority. In order to fully bridge this gap, leadership archetype nudging initiatives need to be set in place.

Leaders Archetype Vs. Culture Archetype (Status Quo)

This indicator is similar to that of the 360 assessment of leaders, albeit it has the advantage of being unbiased and not as obvious and as biased as the 360 would be to subordinates. As such, this indicator provides a more accurate reflection of reality when compared to standard 360, as the latter type of assessment could be subject to biases. In standard 360 assessment, the ratings are usually based on a scale, and not a selection of options. As such, most leaders are likely to rate themselves higher than how much their peers and associates would rate them. However, the leadership archetype is structured in a way that determines the dominant archetype from a choice of options, so bias is eliminated on both sides of the equation. In such a case, it would be more relevant to draw out the congruence between culture archetype and leader archetype.

As discussed earlier, this indicator should be considered alongside the Target State, as congruence is more critical for Target States. However, even when this indicator is considered in isolation, a gap could reveal several insights and require the development of management skills in order to assist the manager/leader in improving managerial leadership competencies. The gaps help identify the most important competencies required for the long-term effectiveness of organizational culture adaptability objectives, an example of which is paradoxical mindset development.

The indicator discussed in the next section (Leader Archetype vs. Target State) serves two purposes: nudging the organization towards a new culture type, and developing the appropriate leadership skills.

It's important to note that this indicator is not for a replacement of 360 feedback. Its insights do not determine the most beneficial managerial skill gap for the development of a future culture (i.e., the Target State). This indicator reveals how accurate managers are in both their self-awareness and their self-assessment, and this is most likely to reveal a gap. If the leader's self-awareness competency is not the underlying issue here, then a gap in this indicator may mean that the organization's non-formal lines of reporting are stronger than their formal counterparts. This can and should be verified via the congruence between informal organization culture archetypes and formal archetype (status quo), assuming the informal organization has been mapped out correctly.

Because incongruence in this indicator may indicate a lack of self-awareness in management, and because self-awareness is a critical skill for leaders and managers to have, we will be detailing self-awareness in the next section.

The transformation program should include self-awareness development initiatives whose levels can be monitored via gaps between Leaders Archetype and Culture Archetype (Status Quo). These initiatives should also be added as a KPI for achieving PMAS objectives.

Leaders Archetype Vs. Target State

Interpreting the gap in this indicator depends on that of the Aspired State vs. Target State. If both Aspired State and Leaders Archetype vs. Target State have large gaps, then you would need to apply nudging initiatives to close the Aspired State vs. Target State gap before looking into rolling out management tools. If, on the other hand, the difference is only in the status quo of Leaders Archetype, then a lack of organizational software tools—such as management tools and processes—may be the root cause of such a gap, and incentives and management tools would be sufficient to close this gap.

Culture Archetype (Status Quo) Vs. Aspired Culture Archetype

Taken in isolation, this indicator is not insightful. It needs to be considered alongside the Target State. If the Status Quo vs. Target State gap is small, then a high gap in this indicator provides early signs of potential future problems. This means that while the Status Quo is where it is supposed to be, the organization may be heading in the wrong direction, as current values would not be congruent with employees' aspirations. If, on the other hand, the gap between Aspired State and Target State is small, then a high gap in this indicator is a positive sign, assuming the current plan is to move the status quo in the direction of Target State. In this case, this indicator would provide another indicative measure of progress towards achieving your Target State goal.

Aspired Culture–Leaders Version Vs. Status Quo

This indicator can be just as relevant as that of Target State Vs. Culture Archetype Status Quo if you assume that the "Formal" leader's aspirations are congruent with Target State. In such a case, this indicator would highlight the main cultural gap currently experienced by your organization. By themselves, the indicator and the gap size are not sufficient means of determining how difficult it would be to close the current gap. You would need to combine this indicator with some of the indicators shown below in order to make such determination. However, this is a good indicator of potential productivity-related and structural issues that may be affecting your current organization. As such, a higher gap means more severe issues related to organization culture, human resources, and management. Furthermore, higher gaps may mean that the aforementioned issues have been hampering performance and preventing the organization from attaining its full potential.

Aspired Culture–Leaders Version Vs. Leaders Archetype

A gap in this indicator is insignificant on its own and should be compared with that of the Status Quo vs. Leader Archetype. In the unlikely event that your "Formal" leader has aspirations different from those of your Target State, you would need to make sure that the current leader has the paradoxical skillset and the managerial ability to transition to a leadership style that is congruent with your Target State. If this is not the case, then you should consider one of two options. Option one involves the implementation of a management development program that emphasizes paradoxical thinking. This helps organizations achieve sustainable adaptability, but this may take a bit longer to accomplish than option two. The second method would be to consider hiring someone who already has the necessary skills to lead the organization forward.

Aspired Culture Vs. Leaders Archetype

A gap in this indicator reveals the organization's full picture, and it should be considered alongside the Target State. If your Target State aligns with the leader's archetype, you would understand the level of difficulty involved in achieving organizational transformation. You can refer to the above section—Aspired Culture vs. Target State—for an explanation. If Target State and Leader Archetype are not aligned, then you should determine why this is the case by referring to the Target State vs. Leader Archetype section above.

Informal Leaders Archetype Vs. Culture Archetype (Status Quo)-Optional Hack

This indicator depends on your ability to identify and map out the informal organization. Although doing so may raise questions, it's logical to administer the Leadership Archetype quiz to a non-formal leader, as a comparison with the Informal Leader's culture archetype quiz would be a good proxy for the Leadership quiz. Therefore, comparing informal leaders' congruence and quizzes with those of their "tribes" can reinforce the existence of influence hubs within informal networks. Such insights can help you understand the deeper values underlying your organization's culture, and they can provide you with more levers in order to use high-precision initiatives that could turbocharge your program.

PMAS in Recruitement and Human Resources Strategy

On a final note, when it comes to administering the quizzes, we think it would be a good recruiting practice to include the Aspire Culture Archetype quiz as part of the screening process for new candidates. This helps ensure cultural coherence among newly recruited, non-entry level employees. As such, when considering candidates for key positions, you need to make sure to account for quiz results in your selection process, and you need to be willing to reject candidates on the basis of results, even if they check all the right boxes. This is easier said than done, in particular when it comes to senior executives, as attracting strong candidates for senior positions is a costly, high-effort feat. However, if your organization is resistant to change, having an ongoing change management program allows you to adopt the quiz as a criterion for employee selection. As such, your new recruits would already fall in line with the organization's aspirations, and they would help accelerate the process of reaching your Target State.

Self-Awareness Personal Development

Improving management skills requires an initial assessment of current skills, capabilities, strengths, and weaknesses. On an individual level, self-awareness is key when improving and developing your own skills. Considerable empirical evidence proves that more self-aware individuals are healthier, higher-performing in managerial and leadership roles, and more productive at work.

However, to make sure we've explored both sides of the coin, it's important to note that self-knowledge is a paradox that may, at times, hinder progress and inhibit personal improvement. The more

79

people know about themselves, the more likely this will affect their self-esteem and self-respect. This is because they have become more knowledgeable about their weaknesses, and this may give rise to feelings of inferiority and shame, which may subsequently hinder progress and maybe even productivity. Subsequently, people may avoid exploring themselves and may prefer to have lower levels of self-knowledge. They may avoid personal growth due to these fears, as they assume that their current state is inadequate. Psychoanalyst Dr. Sigmund Freud stated that people need to be completely honest with themselves when exploring their potential, as this requires continuous improvement, which may be uncomfortable for some to follow through with.

The paradox of attaining self-knowledge comes with a lot of mystery, doubts and questions. This forces individuals to face obstacles they might be unable to overcome. Furthermore, self-knowledge is a prerequisite/motivator of growth and improvement, despite possibly inhibiting these two markers of progress. How, then, can improvement be accomplished? How can management skills be developed when self-knowledge faces resistance from participants?

One answer bases itself on the concept of the sensitive line, which states that individuals become defensive when faced with inconsistent or unflattering information about themselves. However, this is not the case when it comes to minor discrepancies, as they render the person more aware, but not more defensive. Small inconsistencies in conceptions of outer appearance, for example, will not radically affect someone's self-esteem.

However, the closer a discrepancy edges towards people's sensitive line, the more likely they will feel the need to act against it or defend themselves. For example, if someone faultily judges a manager to be incompetent or untrustworthy, a defensive argument would arise, and the manager would possibly re-examine their self-conceptualization.

This response is known as the threat-rigidity response. When individuals are threatened upon encountering uncomfortable information or uncertainty, they tend to become rigid. Their attitudes and self-conceptions change, and they tend to build metaphorical walls to protect themselves from further shock. They tend to redouble their efforts to protect what is comfortable and familiar to them. In such cases, their defense mechanisms are at an all-time high to make sure they feel emotionally and mentally stable and go back to their comfort zones. Hence, it can be said that crossing the sensitive line creates a domino effect of self-preservation.

So, when an individual can become this defensive, you may wonder how such a person can implement personal change and increase their self-knowledge. First, the manner by which this interaction occurs has to tick three boxes. It needs to be a valid statement that is accurate enough to be taken into consideration. Also, the statement shouldn't be unexpected. Finally, there should be some control over what, when, and how much information is received. If these three factors are taken into consideration when giving feedback to someone, the sensitive line is less likely to be crossed and, consequently, defense mechanisms are less likely to go up.

Another answer is more personal and goes back to the individual. This individual needs to be more interactive and ready to disclose more information about themselves to others. The more they open up to others, the more room they leave for personal growth. As such, it is less likely that a sensitive line will be crossed between one or more people.

The uncertainty of dealing with self-awareness can easily be managed, by ensuring control over the information received and the involvement of others in your pursuit of self-understanding. Accepting and allowing feedback from others is vital for building stronger connections and for defining the sensitive line a little bit more with each interaction.

For more concrete initiatives addressing this paradox, please refer to the Leadership Archetype Nudging handbook.

Nudging, Incentives, and Management Tools Considerations

If you have reached this stage, you must have developed your Target State, outlined your value map and chosen your desired outcome. I want to quickly restate what I mentioned at the beginning of the book: while the PMAS toolset will help you reach your Target State by achieving more accelerated change than any other tool on the market, the main objective of this book and the PMAS toolset is to help you implement a lasting change that drives your organization (at any level, whether it be a specific unit or the overall organization) to quickly adapt to continuously changing external and internal conditions. Furthermore, as your organization experiences accelerated growth, you're likely to achieve success when correctly implementing these tools.

To proceed, you need to quantitatively and qualitatively address your desired results by selecting mutually exclusive and collectively exhaustive KPIs over time, and these can be in the form of balanced scorecards (refer to the Balanced Scorecard Toolkit for more information). More importantly, you would need to achieve congruence between the Aspired State and the Target State over time and frequently measure the impact of your program to ensure that it is nudging you toward closing the gap. Having a feedback loop that feeds into KPIs and targets provides your organization with a dynamic self-correcting and self-learning process.

As discussed earlier, both employee diversity and organizational polarization drive creativity and complexity within companies. When all the elements within an organization are homogeneous, then it is simpler to design effective nudging programs. In fact, the less autonomous and heterogenous an organization is, the more linearly it functions. This makes top-down control over the company more likely to occur and, in such a case, designing initiatives towards Leaders' nudging may be sufficient to drive transformations.

With this in mind, in all cases, whether you're adopting PMAS for designing a transformation program for a complex self-organized culture archetype on the one extreme, or for a leaders' archetype, you'll need a combination of initiatives, incentives, management

82

skills development tools, and management tools to achieve your program results. We will consider behavioral science techniques when trying to change individual behaviors at multiple levels, giving priority to points of leverage identified through informal and formal organization hubs. At a macro-level, governments have been adopting behavioral science techniques to change individual behavior in pursuit of policy objectives for decades. Over the last two decades, such techniques have been combined with nudge interventions, such as tax incentives and other financial inducements, to improve changes. In this section, we will focus our discussion on how to combine these techniques for the most impactful and accelerated results.

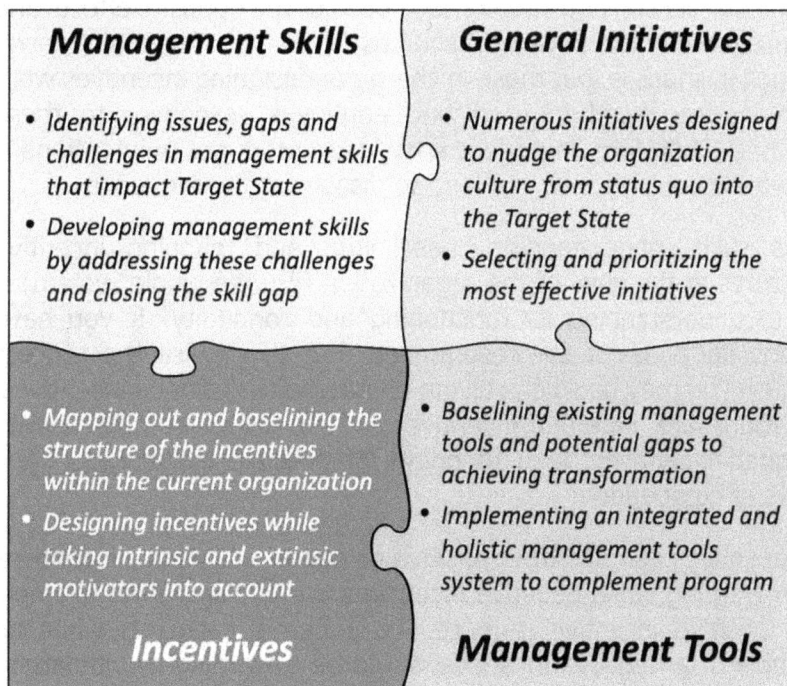

Management Skills	**General Initiatives**
• Identifying issues, gaps and challenges in management skills that impact Target State • Developing management skills by addressing these challenges and closing the skill gap	• Numerous initiatives designed to nudge the organization culture from status quo into the Target State • Selecting and prioritizing the most effective initiatives
• Mapping out and baselining the structure of the incentives within the current organization • Designing incentives while taking intrinsic and extrinsic motivators into account	• Baselining existing management tools and potential gaps to achieving transformation • Implementing an integrated and holistic management tools system to complement program
Incentives	**Management Tools**

Picture by Sam Schreim by Business Model Hackers

Incentives Scheme Design

Incentive design is one technique within the PMAS toolset that can be adopted to nudge archetypes in specific directions. The standard approach to influencing employees and peoples' choices towards desired outcomes is based on the principle that employee behavior is influenced by outside incentives. Therefore, by modifying the payoffs associated with different choices, we can alter their motivations.

Inversely, behavioral economics is built on the idea of agents as non-rational actors. It tries to understand how people act in the real world, looking more at internal motives and the environmental conditions influencing them.

Incentive systems have to be well-designed and aligned with employee interests and desired outcomes. However, real-life is full of examples of incentive schemes that were initially designed to accomplish certain objectives ended up with the opposite effects and a consequent waste in cash, resources, and effort. The main reason for such mishaps is that those in charge of designing incentives were often inexperienced in predicting employee responses to these schemes. Therefore, imperfect knowledge produces unintentionally distorted incentives that can lead to disastrous consequences.

As such, understanding, baselining, and mapping incentive structures at the level of the organization (i.e. the whole system) is key to understanding its functioning and continuity. If you have already done this, I still recommend that you revisit the process because you may be solely relying on internally-designed incentives. But there are inherent incentives which, when combined with designed incentives, lead to points of possible collaboration and points of competition.

Incentives can be either positive or negative: positive incentives are rewarding while negative incentives are punishing. An example of a positive incentive is more like a bonus payment, while an example of a negative incentive would be a warning or ultimatum. Man-made incentives are developed by organizational leadership to influence individuals, teams, and groups into behaving, acting, and performing in accordance with specific directions. The simplest example of a widely-used incentive in organizations is the sales commission, in which sales pay is linked to the sales, collections, and profits attributed to sales individuals or groups.

In this section, we will not discuss the pros and cons of one method over the other, as this would be reductive. All incentive schemes, whether based on intrinsic or extrinsic motivators, have an impact on nudging. The idea is to map out all possibilities, then adopt a combination of methods that will take intrinsic motivators, extrinsic motivators, and game theory into consideration when designing our incentive scheme.

Incentives Theory and Extrinsic Motivators

The theory of incentives is one of the key theories of motivation. It suggests that behavior is motivated by the desire to reinforce incentives, so we are pulled into action by outside incentives. According to this view, people gravitate towards behaviors that offer positive incentives and move away from behaviors associated with negative incentives. In other words, differences in behavior, from one person to another or from one situation to another, can be traced back to available incentives and the value people place on them.

The main objective we need to focus on here is: how do we create systems for aligning employees' behaviors with those of organization aspirations and targets? The most widely-adopted incentives are tangible and/or intangible rewards that are awarded for the occurrence of the action or behavior that one is trying to correct or cause to happen. Studies have shown that instant gratification is more effective when combined with frequent and repetitive actions and rewards that form habits. This model is well-suited for top-down management, as it explicitly attempts to alter employees' behaviors according to upper management instructions.

Extrinsic incentive systems work well with a clear set of steps and a well-defined expected outcome (e.g. sales, production). These systems function correctly only when the goal involves the use of rudimentary mechanic tasks, simple algorithmic operations, or predefined proven processes. Numerous studies have shown that as soon as tasks become more complex, involving creative skills or conceptual capabilities, extrinsic incentives are rendered ineffective and may lead to poorer performance.

Nudging, Choice Architecture, and Intrinsic Motivators

The incentives theory to management has been widely in use since the industrial age, serving as a motivational framework throughout the 19th and 20th centuries. However, this theory is no longer sufficient or effective as a multilevel blanket approach. This is because organization culture archetypes have changed since the time of top-down, hierarchical industrial companies, and new skill sets involving entrepreneurship, cognition, innovation, and self-awareness have become the norm. As of 2020, people's needs and motivation structures have become as increasingly complex as our world and environment. We live in an era where people are highly connected, as they use social media, collaborative consumption, co-creation, and peer production in order to foster a sense of belonging within broad networks. As such, it would be fair to say that one fact has remained unchanged throughout the centuries: motivation will always be driven by human needs.

Incentives and motivation are rooted in psychology. As such, I have decided to use Abraham Maslow's hierarchy of needs to discuss the effectiveness of motivation and incentives. Despite expert disagreements on the ranking/order of human needs, this model remains widely-adopted in sociology, management training, and psychology when researching human needs. We believe Maslow's model provides a good framework for systematic problem-solving, as this model allows us to consider an exhaustive list of relevant human needs:

- Basic needs such as clean air and oxygen, food and water, sleep, clothes, shelter, and overall health.
- Safety needs such as personal security.
- Emotional security and social belonging such as friendships, intimacy, family, financial security, health and well-being.
- Self-esteem needs such as recognition, status, importance, respect and ego.
- Self-actualization such as partner acquisition, parenting, talent use and development, talents and abilities, and pursuing goals.

- Transcendence, which involves reaching the most holistic levels of human consciousness by giving oneself to something beyond oneself.

We can categorize these into primary and secondary needs. Primary needs are physiological in nature and include elements such as food, water, shelter and sleep. Examples of secondary needs, on the other hand, include power, achievement, belonging, advancement opportunities, work relationships, etc. Moreover, needs change over time and, because of this, people focus on the desires important to them during a particular juncture in their lives.

Only by considering a wider spectrum of motives and values can we think about how the broader context affects employee choices. Let's take a simple example of how physical layout can impact choices. Experiments have shown that if we put healthy food at the entrance of a canteen, making it more accessible than other options, employees will end up eating healthier. This is what is called a nudge. In fact, any environmental factor that attracts our attention and influences our behavior is referred to as a nudge. Marketing has been using nudge theory for a long time, particularly when laying out shops and placing products. CPG companies pay premiums for their products to be placed in certain areas of grocery stores (e.g. next to the cashier), because product placement is a below-the-line marketing strategy that influences purchasing behavior.

Therefore, adopting a system thinking approach allows us to consider the physical, social and cultural networks where employee choices are made. This approach also makes us think about how different networks can alter employee motives, by either reinforcing them or diminishing them.

Another example of a powerful nudging method based on intrinsic motivators is the tool deployed by Alphabet Inc. which helped promote a culture of innovation and entrepreneurship within the workplace. By giving their employees one day off every week to explore their interests, Alphabet Inc. utilized intrinsic motivation instead of offering incentives for employees to come up with new ideas. Alphabet's approach is an example of how initiatives of this sort can nudge organizations in the direction of Entrepreneurship.

Choice Architecture is the process and impact of designing different ways in which choices are presented to the agents (employees of an organization) and the impact that such design can have on the organization's culture. In marketing and sales, the number of options offered and their arrangements play a key role in nudging. One such strategy is referred to as framing.

Framing is when a product is presented in the context of other related products. Choice Architecture leverages are built on our understanding of people as non-rational actors who use a variety of shortcuts to cope with decision-making. The most common and straightforward example is that of a car dealership. If you're in the market for a car and you happen to stop at a car dealership, the very first thing you would expect to see in the showroom is the most expensive, fully-loaded model of the particular car you're considering. Accordingly, you would expect to pay a high price. Afterwards, when you see the price of the lower-level option, you won't find it as expensive because you were "framed" in advance.

Many iterations of pricing and marketing strategies adopt choice architecture through framing. One such iteration is showing consumers three or four price options, as is the case with "super-sizing" at McDonald's. Another example of workplace nudging is the case of Virgin Atlantic. When the company wanted to cut its fuel consumption, it informed pilots that they would be part of a fuel consumption study. This simple nudge tactic ended up reducing carbon emissions by roughly 100,000 tons per year. However, nudges need to be carefully designed.

In this book, we focus on the context of organizational culture and leadership. How do we frame choices to nudge employees towards the actions we want them to take? The initiatives list in the Nudging Handbooks contains choice architecture nudges that you can implement once you have the organization baselined and mapped out, and have set your Target State. In order to make nudges successful, incentives must benefit the choice-maker. They must also be instantaneous and easy to spot because not all people are able to gather and process the information they need to make proper decisions. An example of making incentives visible is providing ongoing, real-time feedback on specific metrics, development needs, and KPIs, instead of waiting months for

88

performance reviews. To avoid backfiring and skepticism, employee-designed gamification and team leaderboards can be used to encourage inclusion and engagement. The British government's Behavioral Insights Team (also called the Nudge Unit) was created in 2010. By reaching out to people who were actively renewing their car insurance, the Behavioral Insights Team was able to enlist an added 100,000 organ donors in one year. However, Holland's attempt to increase its number of organ donors didn't go as planned. Following the policies of most European countries, the Netherlands imposed presumed consent, assuming this would cause numbers to spike. But, to the government's dismay, the invasive nature of this policy caused people to instantly reject it. It turns out, people preferred the previous policy of active election.

Game Theory

A basic understanding of game theory can help people perform more rigorous analyses of incentive structures. Incentive mapping is different from Value mapping, as discussed earlier, because it can be mostly designed and altered. Furthermore, developing such maps is useful, as it allows us to recognize how incentives motivate employees to act or behave in non-productive ways or in ways not initially intended by design. As such, game theory helps reveal possible areas of conflict, competition, and cooperation, as well as why these phenomena may arise. Also, game theory provides us with possible ways of altering "games" to realize new outcomes.

It's important to note that our discussion of Game Theory will not include classical game theory, such as solving for Nash equilibrium. The topic of Game Theory is vast, and there are numerous books and articles on the subject. However, this is not at all required for what we are trying to accomplish with the PMAS. The following will be a short description of the main concepts within Game Theory that are useful to the process of incentive design. If you're not familiar with how Game Theory is adopted, its applications span beyond business and include economy, psychology, and even biology. Whenever interdependence exists between adaptive agents, Game Theory can be applied to study the dynamics of cooperation and competition that emerge out of this relationship. For example, in business, it is used to design both customer-related initiatives (ex.

pricing mechanisms) and strategic initiatives against competing initiatives, such as pricing mechanisms. We will focus our discussion on the context of employee behavior, limiting our description to the four types of games discussed below.

The game theory works by considering interactions and organizations as games. A game tries to capture the dynamic of autonomous agents (employees), and how their own goals actively contribute towards a joint outcome. A game has three major elements: players, strategies, and payoffs. A player is a decision-maker, and a strategy is a decision specification for possible situations the player may find themselves in. Finally, a payoff is either a reward or a loss that players experience when following their respective strategies.

Games are played over some mutually desired pay-offs expressed in terms of resources currency. The resource is whatever is of value to the people in the organization (the agents in the game being played). The key consideration that shapes how the overall game plays out is whether the total value (pay-off) distributed to all agents remains constant irrespective of their actions, or whether it fluctuates based on player cooperation.

1. **Symmetry** reveals how games can be asymmetrical, meaning payoffs to individuals for different possible actions may not be the same. If the identities of the players can be changed without changing the payoff to the strategies, then a game is symmetrical. Many of the commonly studied 2 × 2 games are symmetrical. Moreover, games of coordination are typically symmetrical. This is the case when people choose which side of the road to drive on. Assume that two drivers meet on a narrow dirt road. Both have to swerve to avoid a head-on collision. They have to choose the way that will make them pass each other without colliding. In the payoff matrix, successful passing is represented by a payoff of 10, and a collision is represented by a payoff of 0. We can see how the payoff to each player is symmetrical. Symmetry can be adopted when designing incentives that promote teamwork and cooperation within a group, a unit, or an organization.

90

2. **Constant-sum games** are games in which the sum of the players' payoffs add up to the same number. This makes for games of pure competition: what one gains the other loses. There is only one winner. This is very common in sports games with strict competition and no cooperation (ex. basketball). Another example would be poker because the combined wealth of the players remains the same, but their distributed wealth is affected by who is winning or losing. Zero-sum games are a special case of constant-sum games, as players' choices can neither increase nor decrease available resources. In zero-sum games, the total benefit to all players in the game, for any combination of strategies, always amounts to zero. This is because the relationship between the agents' payoffs is negatively correlated, otherwise known as negative interdependence. In such cases, individuals can only achieve their goals via the failure of other agents, and this drives competition. For example, sales departments may structure their incentives to drive competitive archetypes via a winner-takes-all leaderboard payoff.

3. **Non-zero-sum** or **non-constant games** are ones in which the payoffs depend on the cooperation among actors. For example, if employees from separate departments in an organization cooperate, they could create more value than if they were to work separately. If there's some conflict that prevents them from working together, the payoffs would be negative. If you can create a situation in which group members are able to share common goals and to perceive cooperation as individually and collectively beneficial, this would create incentives for group members to work together. This concept helps us to envision the benefits of cooperation and incentives alignment across different departments, and across independent businesses.

4. A **cooperative game** or non-zero-sum game is one in which cooperation among players has the same payoff, and every player either wins or loses. A good example is when cooperation is achieved through peer-to-peer interaction and feedback mechanisms. The objective of this strategy is similar to that of non-zero-sum games. However, this strategy can also work top-down, such as through the

implementation of a 360-feedback mechanism, to help promote intradepartmental communication and open feedback. It will also force managers to consider their subordinates' best interests, as negative feedback can affect managerial promotions and bonus pay-offs.

In summary, the aim of this section was to discuss the choice of incentives within the Nudging Handbook. It's important to track your progress and layout your organization maps in front of you in order to monitor how your initiatives impact your progress towards your target state. With this in mind, we have developed the Nudging Handbooks containing a long list of initiatives that help you explore and achieve incremental nudges in complex organizations. Furthermore, combining initiatives with incentives and management tools can accelerate cultural change and adaptability. The nudging initiatives can be found in the Leadership Archetype Nudging book and Organization Archetype Nudging book. They each contain simple and straightforward lists that provide you with nudging methods in either direction. These initiatives are important when considering how to head towards your Target Archetype(s). As such, you can refer to the initiatives found in the Nudging books and select the ones most suited to your organization.

Management Tools

A comprehensive set of management tools is necessary for program transformation. These tools are provided individually under each archetype in the Nudging book. However, management tools on their own won't help you achieve Target Archetypes. To achieve PMAS objectives, you'll need to combine management tools with the right nudging initiatives and the right incentives.

For example, management tools such as Balanced Score Cards help implement and monitor programs designed to achieve nudging initiatives. However, using these tools in isolation won't achieve much. In order to, for example, drive the organization towards a "Customer-Centric" culture, Balanced Score Cards need to be combined with customer-related tools.

Leadership Archetype Nudging

On a final note, the nudging plan is designed to help managers improve their managerial leadership competencies and to identify the best competencies for short-term organizational culture change (i.e. nudging culture towards the Target State). However, for long-term change, two recommendations are made: 1. Leaders should understand and utilize the paradoxical mindset. 2. Leaders should work on developing weak Leadership Archetype dimensions. These recommendations ensure that leaders possess the skills necessary to adapt to new situations that call for changes in leadership direction or archetype. This allows organizations to achieve ultimate cultural adaptability and flexibility.

CONCLUSION

While the system is simple, it is not intelligent. It requires human interaction and manual interpretation to move in the right direction.

This book cannot possibly implement the system for you, because you have to set your own targets and develop the necessary initiatives to nudge the organization towards your desired cultural system. Furthermore, developing a more detailed map of secondary and tertiary values is difficult considering the limitations present when using the paper version of the quiz, as this version makes it impossible to use intelligent guiding or decision-based questions.

If you've gotten this far in reading, you should have no doubt that the PMAS is the only system in the market that allows you to administer quizzes yourself. However, you still need automated software to help you in this feat. This is why we developed an automated system that, when set up, will drive more precise diagnostics and more surgical initiatives, as these learn and improve with time and allow you to achieve your goal of cultural adaptability.

LEADERSHIP ARCHETYPE QUIZ

INSTRUCTIONS - READ CAREFULLY

The following quiz is designed to determine several key attributes of your leadership style. By being accurate and honest in completing the quiz, you will be self-assessing your key leadership skills and traits.

There is no right or wrong answer to any of these questions. In answering these questions, make sure that your answers reflect how you feel about your current leadership or your current organization, not how you felt in the past or how you aspire your leadership or organization to be in the future.

LEADERSHIP

Which these statements best describes your current leadership?

☐ I engage my team members' imagination and emotional commitment when speaking about my vision for the future. I motivate the team to pursue non-traditional ways of generating innovative products and services, and I recognize the efforts of all those who contribute towards this feat.

☐ I lead by placing my customers at the center of all decision-making processes, and I always make sure to exceed their needs and expectations by encouraging creative problem-solving and continuous improvement. These customer-focused interactions and dynamics allow me to better plan my organization's future.

☐ I foster a climate within which team members are energized and motivated to achieve excellence, pursue ambitious goals, and compete fiercely within the marketplace. As such, my team members are able to thrive throughout all aspects of their lives, not just their job-related activities.

☐ I clarify to my team exactly what's expected of them and establish ceremonies and rewards that reinforce the organization's values and culture. I foster an environment of stability to ensure team members feel secure and well-integrated into the organization's culture. I remind my team that consistency is the key to attaining desired results.

☐ I ensure constant cross-functional cooperation within the workplace, and I encourage team members to be actively involved in decision-making, so they can develop their skills and expertise and take responsibility for their actions. I facilitate information flow through the use of simplified data analysis for decision-making.

☐ I lead by mentoring my team, and not talking down to others. I strengthen my relationships with team members by helping them define their problems and by providing them with continuous feedback that encourages them to come up with their own solutions. I make sure that my team works as a cohesive unit heading towards a shared goal.

MANAGEMENT

Which of these statements best describes your management style in your organization?

☐ I encourage informed rule-breaking that leads to innovative and game-changing products/services, and I drive others in my organization to generate new trendsetting ideas and methods.

☐ I encourage my team to listen to customers, solicit their feedback, and take note of their needs and problems to ensure no stone is left unturned when it comes to day-to-day work and activities. I tackle customers' problems as creatively as possible.

☐ I insist on hard work, dedication, and high productivity by setting ambitious goals that challenge the status quo, and by using competitive benchmarks. I foster a sense of competitiveness that drives team members to consistently outperform competitors.

☐ I have well-established mechanisms and control systems in place that assure consistency in quality, service, cost, and productivity and that regularly report results. I closely monitor team performance and make sure that all employees are clear about objectives, policies and values. As such, I conduct regular assessments of employees' performance.

☐ I maintain an intelligent system for gathering information across the organization, and I extract and share the relevant information clearly, concisely, and consistently across the organization's functional boundaries. I facilitate coordination between these boundaries, and I empower everyone to contribute and participate in decision-making.

☐ I foster open communication, and I provide regular feedback regarding team member performance. I nurture teamwork, mentorship, and collaboration, in an environment where peers and subordinates learn from each other and where collective team results far outweigh the sum of individual results within the team.

PLANNING AND EXECUTION

Which of these statements best describes how you get things done when faced with a new challenge in your organization?

☐ I hold sprint-like workshops or meetings to identify solutions and either select or develop innovative methods, frameworks, approaches, and/or tools most suitable for the situation at hand. I am not afraid to adopt innovative methods even if the team is not familiar with such approaches or if such approaches have not been market-proven.

☐ I tackle issues by first brainstorming with my team in search of creative solutions, then by prioritizing the initiatives most-suited for the situation at hand and, finally, by adopting approaches and methods that have proved successful for either our company or for others.

☐ I prioritize the end goal and set targets challenging my team and me to swiftly address the issue at hand. As such, I recognize the efforts of team members who provide the most suitable solutions; then, I challenge everyone to execute tasks and achieve targets, knowing well that they will get rewarded for doing so.

☐ I am methodical when tackling new challenges and issues. I first identify and select best practices, proven methods, and/or commonly known solutions that have been of aid in similar situations; then, I develop time-phased plans with subsequent processes/procedures necessary for measuring and reporting results. Finally, I assign tasks/initiatives to the appropriate team or team members.

☐ I get things done by either researching the issue myself, or by assigning someone to investigate the problem at hand and develop a good understanding of challenges and organizational implications. I then identify the task and delegate its completion by empowering the most suitably-skilled individuals, teams, or units to take on such challenges.

☐ I get things done by consistently tackling the issue-at-hand as part of a team. As such, my team is expected to brainstorm appropriate solutions and initiatives for a variety of issues by working as a cohesive collective where everyone is heard and included in the problem-solving process. Accordingly, clear objectives and targets are defined, and selected tasks and initiatives are divided amongst team members so that they are able to tackle challenges as one team.

Which of the following statements best describes you as a leader?

☐ I encourage experimentation and creativity as means of innovation within the organization, as this allows the organization to be revolutionary and accomplish great feats. I foster agility, entrepreneurship, and risk-taking, and I'm always ready to adapt to unforeseen circumstances.

☐ I always listen to my customers' wants and needs, and I provide them with the products and services they desire by allowing their preferences to creatively guide my problem-solving endeavors and drive my initiatives and day-to-day priorities.

☐ I maintain competitiveness among team members and push them to provide products/services that meet competitive benchmarks by setting and achieving stretched goals and targets. I focus on building my strengths whilst continuously upgrading my skills and knowledge.

☐ I have a clearly-articulated vision with well-defined goals and objectives in place for my team, and I establish clearly defined processes and procedures before moving towards task-accomplishment. I ensure stability, productivity, quality, and consistency, and I regularly follow up with delegated tasks and try to maintain accountability for them.

☐ I recognize the importance of inclusivity in the workplace, and I empower my team and ensure that everyone is willing to participate consistently. Accordingly, I try to provide team members with autonomy, job training, and human capital development. I encourage cross-functions cooperation in order for the organization to work as one coherent unit. I emphasize the use of analytical processes and accurate data in decision-making.

☐ I foster trust and openness with others by being as honest as I can and by empathizing with those who come to me with their problems. I also provide them with the necessary support and regular feedback. I let teamwork and collaboration guide our processes and modes of action.

100

GUIDING PRINCIPLES

Which of these statements best describes the guiding principles of your organization?

☐ I develop and maintain an agile organization that fosters entrepreneurship, innovation, creativity, and ideation, and that rewards and recognizes experimentation and risk-taking.

☐ I create an environment that encourages creative problem-solving centered around customer's needs. I encourage all team members to continuously check and improve internal processes to ensure we are constantly keeping up with consumer demands and preferences.

☐ I create an environment where challenging tasks are continuously and vigorously sought out. Consequently, my team aims to achieve world-class recognition and higher levels of performance than both external and internal competition.

☐ I maintain an efficient organization by adopting policies and procedures that emphasize consistency and productivity. I ensure that for every problem, there are always a number of well-thought-out alternative solutions at hand.

☐ I create an environment where human capital is developed and empowered, where all departments are aligned, and where task-delegation is consistently embraced and well-coordinated. As such, collective involvement and participation are constantly sought out, encouraged, and rewarded.

☐ I create an environment of mutual trust and loyalty where self-worth and self-esteem are reinforced, where teamwork builds on cohesiveness and commitment, and where positive, constructive feedback is emphasized.

STRATEGY

Which of these statements best describes you?

☐ I articulate and reinforce a clear vision by emphasizing systemic and rapid innovation, transformation, and adaptation. As such, I constantly restate and reaffirm this vision when necessary. I have a clear strategy in place for challenging my team to steadily generate new ideas that help the organization achieve its vision of the future.

☐ I emphasize reaching out to customers and listening to their demands to ensure that all products and services exceed expectations and continuously improve. Feedback from customers is always our top priority, and it is what drives our future decisions and initiatives.

☐ I continuously monitor market trends and competition and use this information to set organizational strategies, goals, and objectives. Consequently, I use these market insights and intelligence as benchmarks to set time-bound, "stretch" performance targets designed to dominate the marketplace and beat the competition.

☐ I seek and adopt proven methods and best practices when dealing with complex issues. Then, I tackle these issues by breaking them down and adopting a process-oriented approach that utilizes the aforementioned methods. Our methods, values, goals and objectives, which are continuously controlled and monitored, are driven by quality, consistency, productivity, and efficiency.

☐ I establish cross-functional teams and/or task forces that work together to facilitate an integrated approach towards the strategic direction of the organization. As such, these teams gather and analyze as much information as possible before attempting to solve problems. Our laissez-faire approach encourages empowerment to drive our organization forward.

☐ I focus on building a strong and diversified team by forming a broad network of internal and external relationships. I encourage mentorship within the team, and I allow team interactions and teamwork to drive collective achievements that always amount to more than the sum of individual accomplishments.

KEY SUCCESS FACTORS

Which of these statements best articulates your current (not aspired) definition of success in your current organization?

☐ I define success as the continuous process of reinstating the organization's vision of the future and as the development of a culture of innovation, agility and constant change across the organization. I also foster an entrepreneurial culture of ideation within which my team members and I dynamically adapt our methods and ourselves as we march towards a new kind of future with endless possibilities and opportunities.

☐ I define success as the ability to meet and exceed customer demands and needs by both soliciting continuous feedback and anticipating customer requirements in advance. Moreover, by ensuring that the organization is always up-to-date with customer challenges and market trends, I am able to solve problems creatively and stimulate incremental product/service improvement.

☐ I define success as the ability to push my team towards world-class accomplishments by fostering a high-performance environment where internal and external competitiveness reign dominant. I am able to do so by setting ambitious performance goals and by implementing market-led differentiation in order to provide products and services that constantly outdo those of our competitors.

☐ I define success as having an organization that follows clearly defined procedures and processes, and as having systems and control measures in place that monitor, measure, report, and ensure the quality of service, cost-effectiveness, and high-level productivity. Moreover, I foster an environment where employees adhere to values, have well-defined roles and job functions, and feel stable and secure.

☐ I define success as having reliable teams with strong core competencies and expertise. I aim to expand these teams and empower them by means of cross-functional ties, cohesion and inclusion, continuous coordination, and idea-sharing driven by common goals. Moreover, I make sure that cooperation and collaboration occur across all departments and that information-sharing is based on meaningful analytical data that enables active participation in decision-making across the organization's functional boundaries.

☐ I define success as the ability to drive organizational performance by supporting and mentoring my entire team and by leveraging their core capabilities as a unit. Moreover, I emphasize that loyalty and teamwork are crucial to developing capabilities and producing results whose collective contributions far outweigh the sum of those of individual team members.

END OF Quiz

ORGANIZATION CULTURE ARCHETYPE QUIZ

INSTRUCTIONS - READ CAREFULLY

The following quiz is designed to evaluate seven elements present within your organization. By completing this quiz accurately and honestly, you'd be able to highlight how you personally and objectively view your organization.

Your answers will be aggregated with those of everyone in your group to provide a complete picture of your organization's culture and the values characterizing it.

There is no right or wrong answer to any of these questions. Every member of your team will most likely have a different take on each question. Therefore, be as accurate as you can in responding to the questions so that your resulting cultural diagnosis will be as precise as possible.

While answering these questions, make sure that your answers reflect how you currently feel about your organization — not how you felt in the past or how you aspire your organization to be in the future.

Which of these statements best describes the leadership within your organization?

☐ The leadership of our organization is visionary and highly entrepreneurial. It engages everyone's imagination while rewarding and encouraging adaptability, agility, innovation, and risk-taking. This leadership also drives everyone to set new trends and to constantly look for new ways of setting new trends and changing the world and the future.

☐ The leadership of our organization is customer-centric, as it is primarily driven by our customers' needs and wants. It encourages everyone to adopt creative means of providing customers with positive experiences, and it emphasizes surpassing customer expectations via the Introduction of incrementally innovative products and services to customers.

☐ The leadership of our organization enables a highly competitive environment that energizes people and keeps them on their toes, by setting aggressive targets driven by internal (departments) and external (markets) competition, all while recognizing and rewarding high achievers.

☐ The leadership of our organization is process-oriented and is, therefore, driven by efficiency, quality, smooth-running operation, stability, predictability and productivity. Everything is highly organized and systematic, as procedures dictate people's actions. Also, considering how central the organization's values and culture are to any steps taken forward, we regularly provide rewards and hold ceremonies to reinforce these two key factors.

☐ The leadership of our organization is delegative. Our leaders empower everyone, across functions (horizontal lines) and levels (vertical lines), to speak up while facilitating information flow in the form of simplified data analysis for decision-making. Under this leadership, everyone's thoughts and ideas are heard.

☐ The leadership of our organization bolsters team spirit, open communication, mentorship, and relationship-nurturing. Whenever there are problems, leaders guide their employees by coaching them and providing them with feedback that offers helpful solutions. Moreover, we cooperate and work as one team directed towards common objectives and accomplishments.

MANAGEMENT

Which of the following statements best describes how your organization is managed?

☐ Our organization can be compared to (or is) one that is entrepreneurially managed, i.e. one where risk-taking is encouraged and where contribution towards innovation is recognized and rewarded. Our organization encourages and rewards generating new ideas/methods as well as rule-breaking, as the latter can lead to creative solutions.

☐ Our management focus is centered around the customer, as key decisions, goals, and strategies are based on customer feedback. Through this feedback, we aim to improve our customers' experiences and to surpass their expectations, all while trying to improve products/services and work processes in creative and innovative ways.

☐ Our management focus is directed towards performance, dedication, and high achievements. As such, ambitious goals are set to challenge the status quo and to average benchmarks. There's a strong emphasis on competitiveness throughout the organization, as we are driven to consistently outperform competitors.

☐ Our management has clearly-defined processes and procedures in place whereby emphasis is placed on ensuring a predictable and secure work environment, and whereby activities are continuously monitored and measured against performance criteria designed to ensure quality, consistency, productivity, efficiency, and smooth-running operations, all while ensuring that all employees are clear about objectives, policies and values.

☐ Our management adopts decentralized decision-making through a "laissez-faire" hands-off approach that embraces autonomy and empowerment and that facilitates inclusion and collaboration across departments, in particular when it comes to information-sharing, communication, and cooperation. This ensures a clear and concise flow of information.

☐ Our organization values teamwork and continuous feedback, while making sure everyone feels like an integral part of the team by emphasizing self-worth and open communication. Attention is given to ensure the creation of an environment whereby peers and subordinates can learn from one another and whereby collective team results far outweigh the sum of individual results within the team.

107

Which of these statements best describes how your organization tackles problems emerging from a new challenge?

☐ We address new challenges by holding sprint-like workshops to identify solutions and select innovative methods, frameworks, approaches, or tools most suitable for the situation at hand. The organization is not afraid to adopt innovative methods, even if we're not familiar with such approaches or if such approaches have not been market-proven.

☐ We address new challenges by holding brainstorming sessions to develop creative solutions. Then, we prioritize the initiatives that, when used to address the situation at hand, will most likely lead to incremental results. We do all this while adopting solutions that utilize approaches and methods that we've either had experience with in the past or that have been adopted successfully elsewhere.

☐ We address new challenges by considering the issue-at-hand to be a potentially rewarding opportunity to shine and be recognized. Everyone is usually eager to propose the best ideas and come up with the most suitable solutions. We set ambitious targets and readily take on their execution, knowing that we will eventually be rewarded.

☐ We address new challenges by participating when we are asked, by adopting initiatives, and by creating new procedures, and/or changes to existing processes, that are based on best practices, proven methods, or widely known solutions that have been shown to work elsewhere. We then adopt a time-bound plan with clearly-defined and assigned tasks that have measurable results, and we report progress along the way.

☐ We address new challenges by thoroughly analyzing the issue-at-hand and developing a solid understanding of it. By having autonomy and being empowered, we are able to address challenges by either leveraging our own capabilities or by seeking external expertise and ensuring that we have the required resources to assign the most qualified people to handle the problem.

☐ We address new challenges by consistently tackling the issue-at-hand as a team. We come together as a team in a way where everyone is heard and is required to participate in generating a solution for the problem at hand. We then work together to prioritize initiatives and to divide tasks according to everyone's core competencies, and we set unified goals and targets to achieve.

DOMINANT CHARACTERISTICS

Which of these statements best describes your organization's culture?

☐ The organization is a dynamic, entrepreneurial space where risk-taking is encouraged and where emphasis is placed on generating new and futuristic ideas. The team is agile and highly adaptive to any new environment or unexpected situation that may arise.

☐ The organization is highly customer-centric, as customer demands, desires, and needs drive all key organizational decisions. Teams aim to continuously satisfy customers by providing creative products/solutions that go beyond customers' expectations.

☐ The organization is highly competitive and concerned with pushing everyone towards achieving world-class competitive performance. Competitors are closely monitored, and our performance targets are set and measured according to how well we do against the competition.

☐ The organization is well-structured and follows clearly-defined processes and procedures driven by a well-articulated vision. Importance is placed on stability, productivity, quality and consistency, and control measures are in place for monitoring and maintaining accountability on a regular basis.

☐ The organization is focused on empowerment and inclusivity. Our initiatives are the result of two factors: the flow of well-analyzed data and information, and active cooperation across departments. Delegation is practiced to a high degree, and it is supported by human capital development, job training, and autonomy.

☐ The organization is focused on practicing self-disclosing communication, and team leaders empathize with employees and provide them with regular feedback. We understand problems and respond to them as a team. There's a strong sense of support and mentorship, which makes the organization feel a lot like an extended family.

ORGANIZATION DYNAMICS

Which of these statements best describes your organization?

☐ The core of the organization is built on entrepreneurship, agility, adaptability, and innovation. The organization encourages, rewards, and recognizes experimentation that takes place by means of new methods and cutting-edge ideas.

☐ The core of the organization is built around continuous improvement, and it is centered around customer experience. Our team actively pursues means of generating creative products and services that meet and surpass customer expectations.

☐ The core of the organization is built around a high-performance culture, a win-to-succeed attitude, high achievements, and a constant drive to outdo (both internal and external) competitors.

☐ The core of the organization is built around formal policies, processes, and procedures that aim to ensure consistency in quality, service, cost, productivity, and adherence to rules and policies. For every problem, there is always a number of well-thought-out alternative solutions available.

☐ The core of the organization is built on empowerment, human capital development, and coordination across functional boundaries. The organization develops consensus through the flow of meaningful information and through inclusion.

☐ The core of the organization is built on mutual trust, loyalty, team spirit, and constructive feedback which ensures the development of mentor-mentee relationships. This allows team members to feel comfortable working with one another while simultaneously benefiting from each other.

STRATEGY

Which of these statements best describes your organization's strategy?

☐ The organization's strategy is grounded on a clear vision that emphasizes systemic and rapid innovation, transformation, and adaptation. Accordingly, the vision is reinstated and reinforced when required, as it allows us to be lean, agile, and innovative and it rewards experimentation, risk-taking and creativity. This ensures that the organization stays innovative and adaptive, no matter how uncertain the situation is.

☐ The organization is customer-centric, as its strategies depend on a consideration of market trends and customer feedback when planning. We also make sure to involve customers early-on when evaluating new products and services, all while making sure that we satisfy customers' needs and product/services gaps and that we continuously surpass customers' expectations.

☐ The strategy of the organization is driven by a careful, intelligent, and continuous benchmarking of the competition. Accordingly, this allows us to set ambitious, time-bound performance targets designed to outrank the competition and dominate markets. Consequently, achieving these targets sets us apart as market leaders via competitiveness and high achievements.

☐ The strategy of the organization is to maintain our competitive advantage by adopting best practices and proven methods that drive efficiency, quality, control, consistency, and stability while maintaining smoothly-running operations, job security, and permanence. This is achieved by having a complete system with well-defined job descriptions and clearly-defined tasks, policies, processes, and procedures in place, as well as with a clearly-articulated vision, mission, and values.

☐ The organization's strategy is designed in a way where decision-making is based on analytics, as well as on data collected and aggregated across functions and departments Then, this complex information is interpreted and simplified so that it makes sense to everyone. Our strength lies in practicing empowerment, inclusion, and autonomous decision-making while forming task forces that drive cross-functional cooperation and accountability across the organization.

☐ The organization's strategy emphasizes leveraging teamwork as a means of achieving excellence. Accordingly, this depends on inclusion and diversification, as different team member perspectives are brought together—through mentorship, coaching, training, communication openness, and continuous feedback— in order to yield strengths and capabilities that outweigh the sum of those of individual team members.

Which of these statements best articulates your current (not aspired) organization's key success factors?

☐ We measure success by continuously reinstating the vision of the organization's future and by driving a culture of innovation and constant adaptability across the organization. Moreover, our success depends on maintaining agility and on fostering an entrepreneurial culture of ideation and risk-taking, as the latter results in a new kind of future with endless possibilities and opportunities.

☐ We measure success by how well, and how often, we can exceed our customers' expectations when anticipating what they want and need in advance and providing them with it. Our success depends on our ability to remain customer-centric and staying on top in terms of understanding our customers' experience while continuously innovating and improving how we tackle the customers' pain points and in the way we deliver our products and services that exceed expectations.

☐ We measure success by outperforming competitors and by attaining world-class success in terms of market leadership. Moreover, we achieve success by fostering a high-achievement, performance-driven organization with an environment characterized by intense internal competition. We also set high-level, market-driven performance goals and distinguish ourselves from our competitors at all times.

☐ We measure success as having and complying with reliable systems, processes, and controls in place that continuously monitor, measure, report and ensure efficiency, quality of service, cost-effectiveness and high productivity. Moreover, adhering to the organization's policies, ethics, and values is essential to our success. Also, dependable delivery, smooth scheduling, and low cost are all indicators of high accomplishment within our organization.

☐ We measure success by considering how well we excel through empowerment, autonomy, cooperation, and inclusion occurring across functional and organizational boundaries. We also measure success by the strength and capabilities of our human capital, by our ability to enable information flow throughout the entire organization, and by our capacity to continuously analyze complex data sets to make information available clearly and concisely, all while maintaining strong cross-functional collaboration.

☐ We measure success by the degree of our team spirit and by our use of teamwork to leverage group members' core capabilities and to tackle problems and challenges as a single unit far more effectively than individually. Moreover, mentorship, coaching, on-the-job training, and the provision of continuous feedback among team members are all key to our long-term success.

END OF Quiz

ASPIRED ORGANIZATION CULTUE QUIZ

INSTRUCTIONS - READ CAREFULLY

The following quiz is designed to evaluate your aspirational state considering six elements within your organization.

Your answers will be compared to those of your group members in order to provide a complete picture of your organization's desired culture and the values you hope will characterize it.

There is no right or wrong answer to any of these questions, so be as accurate as possible in responding to them in order for your resulting aspirations to be as precise as possible.

IMPORTANT

When you answer these questions, make sure that your answer reflects how you desire your organization to be, **UNLESS** your status quo already reflects your aspiration in that particular question, in which case your aspiration would reflect your current state.

114

LEADERSHIP

Which of these statements best describes the Leadership you aspire to have for your organization?

☐ I would like the leadership to foster an environment that allows everyone to reach new heights of creativity without holding back on being innovative, taking risks, and being rewarded when coming up with new ideas.

☐ I would like the leadership to foster an environment where everyone is driven to continuously generate new and creative ways of solving customer problems. This would allow us to provide customers with exceedingly innovative products and services that surpass their expectations.

☐ I would like the leadership to foster an environment that supports a high-performance culture through competitiveness and high achievements. I would like everyone to be motivated by the prospect of constantly outranking our competition.

☐ I would like the leadership to foster a stable, secure, and structured environment where everyone knows their place and how they fit into the overall organization. I would like everyone to be clear about their goals, roles, and job descriptions, as this enables everyone to adhere to the organization's policies and values.

☐ I would like the leadership to foster an environment where everyone feels empowered, where all team members can contribute to problem-solving, and where subordinates are given the responsibility of handling important tasks and projects. Ideally, cross-communication would occur across all departments and functions of the organization.

☐ I would like the leadership to foster teamwork and an environment that nurtures relationships and camaraderie, that utilizes team-building and mentorship across all levels of the organization, and that allows everyone to give and receive feedback. Moreover, I would like us to cooperate and work as one team directed towards common objectives and accomplishments.

MANAGEMENT

Which of these statements best describes what you hope the emphasis of your organization's management to be on?

☐ I would like there to be an emphasis on innovation, agility, risk-taking, and initiative-taking. I hope to have an environment that encourages and rewards (positive) rule-breaking, in order to continuously challenge the status quo and consistently come up with innovative solutions.

☐ I would like there to be an emphasis on creative problem-solving when it comes to tackling our customers' issues. Moreover, all key decisions should depend on customers, and the organization should strive to meet and exceed customers' needs, wants, and expectations.

☐ I would like there to be an emphasis on sustaining an environment of hard work, dedication, productivity, and high achievement. I hope to see an organization that works well under pressure, that is ready to partake in healthy competition, and that works towards outperforming competitors.

☐ I would like there to be an emphasis on ensuring that stability and predictability are maintained throughout the organization. It would be ideal to have systems in place that ensure fairness and that set and monitor everyone's specific goals, objectives, targets, and achievements.

☐ I would like there to be an emphasis on empowerment and independence, as this allows employees to be involved in key decision-making. It would be ideal for everyone in the organization to participate in key projects and to seek consensus when tackling such endeavors.

☐ I would like there to be an emphasis on teamwork, on honest communication, and on the provision of continuous feedback. In addition, I think attention should be given to ensure that peers and subordinates can learn from one another. It is also important for teamwork and collaboration to be prioritized over individual work.

PLANNING AND EXECUTION

Which of these statements best describes how you hope how your organization would tackle problems when faced with a new challenge?

☐ I would like for the organization to frequently conduct sprint-like workshops aimed at identifying solutions and picking innovative methods, frameworks, approaches, or tools that are appropriate for tackling the situation at hand. I hope for the organization not to fear the use of innovative methods, regardless of our familiarity with such approaches or whether or not they've been market-proven.

☐ I would like for the organization to tackle problems, first through the use of creative solutions developed during brainstorming sessions, then through the prioritization of initiatives that produce incremental results. Ideally, the organization would implement the aforementioned tactics by utilizing solutions whose approaches and methods have been successfully adopted by either us (in the past) or by other organizations.

☐ I would like for the organization to look at the issue-at-hand as a means of achieving recognition, as it would be beneficial for everyone to be enthusiastic about proposing appropriate solutions and about coming up with superior ideas. Also, ideally, the organization would tackle issues by setting ambitious targets and by readily handling their execution, as the individuals responsible for successfully achieving these targets will eventually be rewarded.

☐ I would like for the organization to address new challenges by first having experts or skilled employees participate in problem-solving, then by having the organization implement initiatives and create new procedures, and/or changes to existing processes, that are based on proven methods, best practices, or well-known solutions. Then, ideally, the organization would implement a plan with well-defined designated tasks.

☐ I would like for the organization to delve into current issues by thoroughly dissecting them and understanding where they come from. Ideally, functions, units, teams, and/or team members would be empowered, and we would address challenges by either leveraging internal capabilities, or by seeking external expertise and ensuring the necessary resources are present when assigning the most qualified people to handle the problem.

☐ I would like for team members to commit to problem-solving as a cohesive unit, such that everyone plays their part and participates in finding solutions. Then, ideally, the organization's members would come together as a team in order to identify and set collective goals and targets, to divide tasks based on individual core competencies, and to prioritize initiatives.

117

Which of these statements best describes the Culture you aspire to have within your organization?

☐ I hope to be part of an organization that focuses on innovation and entrepreneurship. I would like our culture, as a whole, to be dynamic and agile, to encourage and reward the production of new ideas, and to advocate for the minimization of routine tasks.

☐ I hope to be part of an organization that places our customers at the center of every decision taken and every product/service provided to them. I would like my organization to be able to consistently exceed customer expectations by filling in the gaps that relate to customer demands, needs, and wishes.

☐ I hope to be part of an organization that aims to lead in the marketplace, beat the competition, and generate products and services that are able to achieve world-class status. I would like our culture to emphasize competitiveness, to drive performance, and, as a result, to reward goal-accomplishment.

☐ I hope to be part of an organization where everyone has clearly defined-tasks and job descriptions, and where a systematic follow-through of processes and procedures takes place. I would like our culture to encourage all team members to be organized and to carve out and follow a clear path that allows them to achieve the organization's common vision and goals.

☐ I hope to be part of an organization that focuses on the empowerment of its team members and that consistently practices inclusivity across any key ongoing initiatives or programs. I would like active cooperation to exist across all departments, and I want employees to autonomously take on the responsibility of completing tasks and projects.

☐ I hope to be part of an organization that focuses on team-building, self-disclosing communication, and supportive feedback. I like a culture where we're constantly supporting one another, where we're being provided with feedback for improvement, and where open communication exists between peers and subordinates.

118

GUIDING PRINCIPLES

Which of these statements best describes how you'd like your organization's guiding principles to be?

☐ I wish for my organization's guiding principles to be based on incorporating entrepreneurship, innovation, and cutting-edge ideas into the workspace, and on ensuring no one holds back when it comes to experimentation.

☐ I wish for my organization's guiding principles to be based on the active pursuit of means that allow our customers' experiences to be carried out to new and creative heights.

☐ I wish for my organization's guiding principles to be based on incorporating the following factors into our work: a winning attitude, meritocracy, ambitious goals, stretch (performance) targets, and high-intensity workload. These should be driven by a strong desire to out-perform the competition.

☐ I wish for my organization's guiding principles to be based on maintaining consistency and high standards of quality and service, without negatively impacting productivity and expenditures (or profitability). I would like my organization to be a leveled playing field where everyone follows procedures and adheres to formal rules and policies.

☐ I wish for my organization's guiding principles to be based on the following: a laissez-faire approach, a strong delegation of authority, strong collaboration and coordination among functions, departments, and teams/units, and the development of a strong and reliable human capital base.

☐ I wish for my organization's guiding principles to be based on mutual trust, loyalty, commitment and teamwork, on ensuring team members are willing and able to provide constructive feedback, and on developing mentor-mentee relationships within the workplace.

119

STRATEGY

Which of these statements best describes how you'd like your organization's strategic focus to be?

☐ To focus on continuously acquiring and experimenting with new methods and strategies designed to change the future and set new trends, all while maintaining agility, innovation, and entrepreneurship throughout the organization.

☐ To focus on creative problem-solving when it comes to tackling consumer needs. Also, to ensure customers are always involved and taken into consideration when it comes to producing and evaluating new products and services.

☐ To focus on market feedback and to set key performance indicators and goals in order to consistently outperform our competitors, dominate our markets, and maintain product and service leadership.

☐ To focus on having the necessary standardized controls, systems, processes and procedures in place to ensure long-term stability, employee retention, efficiency, consistency, quality of product/service, and reliability.

☐ To focus on empowering employees at all levels so that they participate and contribute to the company's strategic direction, all while practicing inclusivity and human capital development. Also, to maintain relevant information in a clear, concise, and organized manner, and to facilitate cross-functional coordination and collaboration.

☐ To focus on promoting openness and trust throughout the organization as a whole and on utilizing mentorship, coaching, training, and success to both leverage teamwork benefits and to reinforce team member capabilities across all initiatives.

KEY SUCCESS FACTORS

Which of these statements you think should be used in measuring your organization's success?

☐ Success should be measured by the levels of innovation, trend-setting, entrepreneurship, and agility across the organization. Success measures should also include the status of our current vision and how strongly it reflects a new kind of future rife with change, and our team's willingness to take risks and think outside the box in order to creatively solve and tackle problems.

☐ Success should be measured by how well we meet and exceed our customers' expectations while ensuring their involvement in every step of the decision-making process. Success should also be measured by how accurately we are able to anticipate customers' needs and by how creatively we are able to solve their problems.

☐ Success should be measured by how well we do in our markets when it comes to outperforming the competition, excelling in product/service leadership, and achieving world-class recognition. Success factors should also include the following: individual and collective measures against market-driven and key performance indicator stretch targets, internal motivation, and the number of exceptional achievements.

☐ Success should be measured by the levels of efficiency, productivity, stability, dependency, consistency, quality, compliance within the organization and by the degree of adherence to policies, values, processes, and procedures in place. Success should also be measured by our ability to quickly interpret results and by our capacity to continuously measure, monitor, and report the performance targets we set to drive efficiency and productivity.

☐ Success should be measured by the levels of empowerment, human capital development, inclusivity and cooperation while ensuring a smooth flow of information across the entire organization. Success should also be measured by how well everyone across the whole organization is able to take responsibilities and complete tasks.

☐ Success should be measured by considering levels of team-building, openness, employee resourcefulness, and teamwork across the organization. Success should also be measured by how the team performs, by how willing everyone is to provide continuous feedback, and by how possible/frequent it is to leverage collective expertise while ensuring individuals and the team members reach their full potential.

121

H ow strongly do you agree with the following statement across the three dimensions below?

"The CULTURE, VISION, AND LEADERSHIP ARE EXACTLY WHAT I ASPIRE THEM TO BE IN MY CURRENT ORGANIZATION."

Dimension	Strongly Agree	Agree	Neither Agree nor Disagree	Disagree	Strongly Disagree
Culture	☐	☐	☐	☐	☐
Vision/Mission	☐	☐	☐	☐	☐
Leadership	☐	☐	☐	☐	☐

H ow strongly do you feel about and/or do you agree with the following statement?

"THE ORGANIZATION'S VISION, MISSION, OBJECTIVES AND GOALS ARE WELL-DEFINED AND WELL-ARTICULATED, AND I AM WELL-AWARE OF HOW MY ROLE WITHIN THE ORGANIZATION CONTRIBUTES TO ACHIEVING THEM."

Strongly Agree	Agree	Neither Agree nor Disagree	Disagree	Strongly Disagree
☐	☐	☐	☐	☐

END OF Quiz

ASPIRED ORGANIZATION CULTURE QUIZ - LEADER VERSION

INSTRUCTIONS - READ CAREFULLY

The following quiz is designed to evaluate your aspirational state considering six elements of your organization.

Your answers will be compared to those of everyone in your group to provide a complete picture of your organization's desired culture and the values you hope will characterize it.

There is no right or wrong answer to any of these questions, so be as accurate as you can in responding to the questions in order for your resulting aspirations to be as precise as possible.

IMPORTANT

When you answer these questions, make sure that your answer reflects how you desire your organization to be, **UNLESS** your status quo already reflects your aspiration in that particular question, in which case your aspiration would reflect your current state.

LEADERSHIP

Which of these statements best reflects how you hope your leadership can impact your organization?

☐ I would like to lead by fostering an environment that allows everyone to reach new heights of creativity and to not hold back on innovation and risk-taking. I would like everyone to be inspired to continuously come up with new ways of solving problems and to feel rewarded and recognized when generating new ideas.

☐ I would like to lead by fostering an environment that focuses on our customers and makes them central to decision-making regarding our products and services. I would like everyone to rigorously go through customer feedback to make sure whatever is provided to our customers never falls short of exceeding their expectations.

☐ I would like to lead by fostering an environment that bolsters a high-performance culture through competitiveness and high achievements. I would like everyone to be motivated to constantly outdo our competitors and to set aggressive targets for themselves, and even higher ones for the organization.

☐ I would like to lead by fostering an environment that is stable, secure, structured and organized, where everyone knows their place and how they fit into the overall organization. I would like everyone to be clear on their goals, roles, and job descriptions, and I aim to have everyone adhere to the organization's policies and values.

☐ I would like to lead by fostering an environment where everyone can feel empowered and where all team members can contribute to problem-solving and can have their recommendations and suggestions heard and put into action. Ideally, cross-communication would occur across all departments and functions of the organization.

☐ I would like to lead by fostering an environment that nurtures relationships and camaraderie, that utilizes team-building and mentorship across all levels of the organization, and that allows everyone to give and receive feedback. Moreover, I would like team members to cooperate and work as one team directed towards common objectives and accomplishments.

MANAGEMENT

Which of these statements best describes the culture you hope would emerge as a result of your day-to-day management of the organization?

☐ I would like there to be a strong emphasis on innovation, agility, risk-taking, and adaptability. I would like to see an environment conducive to (positive) rule-breaking, where the status quo is constantly challenged and where everyone pushes the boundaries of creativity and innovation.

☐ I would like there to be a strong emphasis on creatively and constantly tackling any problems our customers face, and on making sure we provide them with an above par customer experience that satisfies every demand and exceeds every expectation.

☐ I would like there to be a strong emphasis on sustaining an environment of hard work, dedication, productivity, where employees steadily strive towards high achievement. I would like for the organization to engage in healthy competition, function well under pressure, and consistently strive to outrank competitors.

☐ I would like there to be a strong emphasis on sustaining stability, consistency, and predictability throughout the organization. I would like to have systems, processes and procedures in place that establish structure, that ensures fairness, and that set and monitor everyone's specific goals, objectives, targets, and achievements.

☐ I would like there to be an emphasis on empowerment and independence, as this allows employees to be involved in key decision-making. It would be ideal for everyone in the organization to participate in key projects and to seek consensus when tackling such endeavors.

☐ I would like there to be a strong emphasis on teamwork, open communication, and continuous feedback. It would be ideal to see peers/subordinates continuously collaborate and strive to build and maintain beneficial mentor-mentee relationships.

PLANNING AND EXECUTION

Which of these statements best describes how you hope your organization would tackle problems when faced with a new challenge?

☐ I would like for my organization to handle problems by holding sprint-like workshops whose aims are the identification of solutions and the selection of cutting-edge methods, frameworks, approaches, and/or tools that are suitable for tackling the situation at hand, regardless of how familiar we are with such approaches or the degree to which they've been market-proven.

☐ I would like for my organization to handle issues by first going through internal brainstorming sessions aimed at generating creative solutions, then by prioritizing initiatives that produce incremental results. Ideally, I would implement these initiatives by adopting proven approaches and methods.

☐ I would like for my organization to consider the issue-at-hand to be an opportunity by which recognition can be achieved. I would hope that my employees are excited about suggesting suitable solutions and about generating top-notch ideas. Ideally, I would tackle issues by setting stretch targets and rewarding individuals responsible for successfully achieving these targets.

☐ I would like for my organization to address new challenges by first having experts or skilled employees participate in problem-solving, then by creating new procedures, and/or changing existing processes, that are based on proven methods, best practices, or well-known solutions. Then, ideally, I would implement a plan and assign well-defined designated tasks to team members.

☐ I would like for my organization to tackle its issues through an in-depth analysis and understanding of them. Ideally, I would then delegate this responsibility to either a unit or to reliable team members who can be empowered to take on these challenges on their own.

☐ I would like for my organization to tackle its issues by having the team come together as one unit where all perspectives are considered and where everyone is expected to contribute towards generating solutions. Then, ideally, team members would collectively identify and set shared goals and targets, divide tasks according to each member's competencies, and prioritize initiatives.

DOMINANT CHARACTERISTICS

Which of these statements best describes the Culture you aspire your organization to have?

☐ I hope to have an organization that prioritizes innovation and entrepreneurship. I would like an agile, dynamic culture, that promotes and rewards the production of new ideas, and that enforces a reduction of routine tasks.

☐ I hope to have an organization that focuses on putting our customers first at all times and on ensuring that customer feedback, demands, desires, and needs drive our key decisions and organization goals. I would like to be able to consistently exceed customer expectations by filling in the gaps that relate to customer demands, needs, and wishes.

☐ I hope to have an organization whose primary driving forces are winning in the marketplace and achieving world-class status when it comes to our products and services. I would like our culture to be one that merits overachievers, that motivates performance, and that highlights the value of competitiveness.

☐ I hope to have an organization where everything is well-defined, including organizational structure, management systems, industry standards, operational processes and procedures. In such an environment, everyone has clearly defined-tasks, well-articulated job descriptions, and systematic means of following through and complying with processes and procedures.

☐ I hope to have an organization that focuses on delegation, empowerment, and on the development of its members. Ideally, the organization would emphasize the following practices: cross-functional collaboration, team member empowerment, communicational free-flow across organizational boundaries. The organization would also encourage everyone to participate and be included in key decision-making.

☐ I hope to have an organization that emphasizes teamwork, team-building, and supportive communication, all while constantly reinforcing self-worth and appreciation. I would like us to engage in a culture of constant support where honest communication between colleagues and employees is encouraged, and where feedback is always provided as a means of facilitating improvement.

GUIDING PRINCIPLES

Which of these statements best describes what you hope your organization's guiding principles to be?

☐ I hope for my organization's guiding principles to be based on entrepreneurship, innovation, and cutting-edge ideas, such that no one restrains themselves when it comes to experimentation and risk-taking.

☐ I hope for my organization's guiding principles to be based mainly on the prioritization of customers. I want the entire organization to focus on making sure customer satisfaction is always high, to ensure they are provided with the best experience, and to gain their loyalty for a lifetime.

☐ I hope for my organization's guiding principles to be based on the incorporation of the following factors into the organization: a winning attitude, aggressive performance achievements, and high-intensity. Employees should be driven by a strong desire to out-perform the competition and to continuously set high standards for themselves and the organization.

☐ I hope for my organization's guiding principles to be based on incorporating consistency in quality, service, cost-efficiency, productivity, into the company. I also wish for us to adhere to rules and policies. I want the entire organization to operate systematically and to follow clearly-defined processes and procedures, with the motivation to reach intended results.

☐ I hope for my organization's guiding principles to be based on a laissez-faire approach, a strong delegation of authority, strong collaboration and coordination among functions, departments, and teams/units, and the development of a strong and reliable human capital base.

☐ I hope for my organization's guiding principles to be based on mutual trust, loyalty, commitment and teamwork, on ensuring team members are willing and able to provide constructive feedback, and on developing mentor-mentee relationships within the workplace.

STRATEGY

Which of these statements best reflects the strategic focus you would rather (or like to) have your organization adopt?

☐ I would like to focus on continuously acquiring, creating, and experimenting with new methods and strategies designed to change the future and set new trends, all while maintaining agility, innovation, and entrepreneurship throughout the organization.

☐ I would like to focus on ensuring that customer input and feedback are key drivers of our organization's strategy and on adopting creative problem-solving, all while ensuring that we prioritize their feedback at all times and never fall short of meeting and surpassing their standards.

☐ I would like to focus on market feedback as a means of setting key performance indicators and goals, to consistently outperform our competitors, dominate our markets, and maintain product and service leadership.

☐ I would like to focus on maintaining our competitive advantage through the adoption of proven methods and best practices that drive our internal processes and procedures, all while having controls and systems in place to ensure long-term stability, employee retention, efficiency, consistency, quality of product/service, and reliability.

☐ I would like to focus on empowering employees at all levels to participate and contribute to the company's strategic direction wherein inclusion, autonomous decision-making, and cross-functional cooperation reign dominant, and wherein decision-making is based on analytics, and on data collected and aggregated across functions and departments.

☐ I would like to focus on leveraging teamwork as a means of achieving excellence. Accordingly, this requires inclusion and diversification, as different team member perspectives are brought together —through mentorship, coaching, training, communication openness, and continuous feedback— in order to yield strengths and capabilities that outweigh the sum of those of individual team members.

KEY SUCCESS FACTORS

Which of these statements do you think should reflect the organization's key success factors?

☐ I think success should be measured by the levels of innovation, trend-setting, entrepreneurship, and agility we exhibit across the organization. Success measures should also include the status of our current vision, how strongly it reflects a new kind of future full of change, our team's willingness to take risks, and our ability to adapt to change and think outside the box to be able to tackle and solve problems creatively.

☐ I think success should be measured by how well we value our customers and how often we are able to provide them with a product or service that truly surprises them. Success is to be measured by the following factors: our ability to remain customer-centric, our capacity to deliver products and services that surpass expectations, and our means of consistently understanding our customers' experience while continuously innovating and improving how we tackle customers' pain points.

☐ I think success should be measured according to how well we do in our markets in terms of outperforming the competition, product/service leadership, achieving world-class recognition, and having a performance-driven organization with an environment characterized by intense internal competition. Success measures should include internal motivation, high achievement, and individual and collective measures against market-driven and aggressive key performance indicator targets.

☐ I think success should be measured by the levels of efficiency, productivity, stability, dependency, consistency, quality, and compliance within the organization. It is also important to consider adherence to policies, values, processes, and procedures as well as the ability to have reliable systems, processes, and controls in place. Success measures should also include our ability to continuously measure, monitor, and report our performance targets which are set to drive dependable delivery, smooth scheduling, low cost, efficiency, productivity.

☐ I think success should be measured by how well we're able to rely on our employees and include them in key-decisions, by how much we can empower them and provide them with the autonomy they need to excel, and by the strength of collaboration across functional/organizational boundaries. Success is to be measured by the strength and capabilities of our human capital, by our ability to enable information flow throughout the entire organization, and by our capacity to continuously analyze complex data sets.

☐ I think success should be measured by the levels of teamwork, cooperation, team-building, openness, and employee resourcefulness within the organization. Success measures should also include mentorship, coaching, on-the-job training, and the provision of continuous feedback among team members as well as our ability to leverage group members' core capabilities and to tackle problems and challenges as a single unit far more effectively than individually.

131

How strongly do you feel about and/or do you agree with the following statement?

"THE CULTURE, VISION, AND LEADERSHIP ARE EXACTLY WHAT I ASPIRE THEM TO BE IN MY CURRENT ORGANIZATION."

Dimension	Strongly Agree	Agree	Neither Agree nor Disagree	Disagree	Strongly Disagree
Culture	☐	☐	☐	☐	☐
Vision/Mission	☐	☐	☐	☐	☐
Leadership	☐	☐	☐	☐	☐

How strongly do you feel about and/or do you agree with the following statement?

"THE ORGANIZATION'S VISION, MISSION, OBJECTIVES, AND GOALS ARE WELL-DEFINED AND ARTICULATED, AND I AM WELL-AWARE OF HOW MY ROLE WITHIN THE ORGANIZATION CONTRIBUTES TO ACHIEVINGTHEM."

Strongly Agree	Agree	Neither Agree nor Disagree	Disagree	Strongly Disagree
☐	☐	☐	☐	☐

END OF Quiz

LEADERSHIP ARCHETYPES
ASSESSMENT WORKBOOK

INTRODUCTION

In the last three decades, an abundance of research and evidence have proven that skillful managers and leaders—especially those that are competent in the management of people in organizations—are key determinants to the success of an organization. These studies have been conducted across all industry sectors, in many international settings and in every type of organization. The findings showed, with absolute certainty, that for organizations to succeed, they must have competent leaders and managers.

As such, there has been a noticeable rise in the number of research studies that aim to identify specific skills and characteristics required for truly effective leadership. We utilized this information as a foundation for further research and subsequently created an aggregate of traits present within multi-level managers at various organizations. Our combined research shows that such characteristics are all behavioral skills and not personality attributes or extensions of personality styles. The aforementioned skills have been added to the short quiz we compiled.

By using this workbook, leaders are given the chance to hone their skills and refine their assets through an in-depth exploration and understanding of different leadership styles. We hope to highlight the advantages of the various leadership styles we've researched in order to allow the readers of this workbook—whether they be leaders themselves or individuals who work with higher-ups—to become more emotionally and cognitively knowledgeable.

LIMITATIONS OF NON-PRO VERSION

The paper version of the quiz, despite containing the same questions as those of the "Pro" version, is more limited in its capacities. This is because the Pro quiz is designed in a manner that utilizes nested processing, as questions are continuously generated according to previous results. As such, unlike its pencil-paper counterpart, the Pro version contains built-in intelligence that allows for more thorough, complex analysis.

Within today's market, traditional employee surveys rarely have the built-in capacities that allow for complex business and managerial investigations to occur. This is why many of these surveys produce results that do not accurately reflect the reality of the situation. Consequently, these questionnaires seldom provide their users with a precise understanding of organizational gaps and challenges and, subsequently, hinder processes such as transformation and change management. Another drawback of conventional surveys is the number of complications that occur when administering and collecting information. These obstacles challenge surveys' ability to measure progress over a short period of time and to produce an accurate portrayal of the organization's reality.

Despite the aforementioned limitations of the non-Pro version, it still generates more information than most surveys out there and can, subsequently, identify the primary, secondary and tertiary dominant culture Archetypes. As discussed later and in the PMAS book, the quiz is structured in a manner that allows for any potential bias to be limited via the types of answer options in the multiple-choice section.

The Pro version, on the other hand, can reveal all primary, secondary and tertiary archetypes with more precision and can be easily administered with the click of a button. Furthermore, the Pro's results can be measured accurately and rapidly on a monthly basis. If you have not signed up for the Pro version, you can do so by following up with Business Model Hackers through the account generated alongside this book's purchase.

INTERPRETING RESULTS

The answer choices provided in the quiz were structured in such a way as to represent a wide array of leadership skills, strengths and behaviors. This was done in accordance with the concept of paradoxicality, as discussed in the PMAS book, in order to effectively reduce human bias. For more details and background information on how the quiz was structured please refer to the main PMAS book.

The assessment for each Archetype (whether primary, secondary or tertiary) is provided separately with each one divided into two sections: The Executive Summary and the Detailed Assessment. The Executive Summary displays a brief overview of the skills and strengths of each specific Archetype, whilst the Detailed Assessment delves into specific behavioral traits, common attributes and areas in which that leader naturally flourishes.

Characteristics of Leadership and Management Skills

Management skills have several defining attributes distinguishing them from other kinds of managerial characteristics and practices. Management skills are:

- *Contradictory or paradoxical:* The paradox mindset has been considered a key factor of a successful leader. Although paradoxes often throw us off guard, embracing contradictory ideas is the secret to creativity and leadership. For example, the core management skills are neither soft, nor hard-driven, and they are neither humanistic in orientation, nor directive in structure. They are oriented neither towards teamwork and interpersonal relations, nor towards individualism and technical entrepreneurship. In fact, effective leaders possess a variety of skills that may be incompatible with one another.
- *Interrelated and overlapping:* It's hard to demonstrate just one skill in isolation from others. Skills are not simplistic,

repetitive behaviors. Instead, they are integrated sets of complex responses. Successful leaders must rely on combinations of skills to achieve desired results. For example, to effectively motivate others, skills such as supportive communication, influence, empowerment, and self-awareness may be required. Effective leaders, in other words, develop a constellation of skills that overlap, support one another, and allow for flexibility in managing various situations.

- *Behavioral:* This consists of identifiable sets of actions that individuals perform in order to reach certain outcomes. Behavioral skills can be observed by others, whereas psychological or personality-driven attributes cannot. Therefore, people with different styles and personalities may apply their skills differently. A core set of observable attributes in effective skill performance is common across a range of individuals.

- *Controllable:* Unlike organizational practices such as "selective hiring," or cognitive activities such as "transcending fear," skills can be consciously demonstrated, practiced, improved upon, or limited by individuals themselves. Skills may certainly engage other people and require cognitive work, but they are still behaviors that people can control and improve upon.

- *Developable:* Skills can be improved upon, whereas personality traits and temperament attributes remain relatively constant throughout life. Individuals can improve their skill performance competencies through practice and feedback, progressing from less competent to more competent.

Therefore, it is clear that developing paradoxical and overlapping leadership skills is essential to achieving both individual and organizational success.

Fortunately, research shows that leaders who have been exposed to the process of refining and enhancing their skills succeed in developing their managerial capacities. For example, studies performed over several decades have shown that managers who were given the knowledge and ability to develop their skills showed improvement by more than 300% in social skills.

The Archetypes

A paradoxical mindset highlights the extent to which individuals embrace tensions and utilize them positively. This mindset can help with leveraging tension and producing creative outputs. However, most people tend to have a preference for one direction over the other and end up being simultaneously pulled in opposite directions, resulting in cognitive tension and stress. However, as counter-intuitive as it may seem, research actually suggests that these conflicts can often work in a person's favor. Several studies conducted by psychologists and organizational researchers investigating paradoxical thinking found that people who learn to embrace, rather than reject, opposing sides of a paradox tend to be more creative, flexible, and productive. This leads to enhanced overall performance when compared to that of individuals who lean strictly towards one direction.

The Archetype Assessment design utilizes two opposing axes: Agility and Orientation. These two dimensions branch out into six sub-dimensions, characterizing various Management and Leadership styles. The six sub-dimensions are grouped into three opposing pairs along the two main axes as shown below, leading to six Archetypes in total:

A. **Visionary:** Visionary Archetypes are entrepreneurial and innovative, and they manage their organizations with agility while fostering creativity, risk-taking, and innovation in the organization's strategic direction.
B. **Customer-Centric:** Customer-Centric Archetypes put the customer first and manage their organizations by letting customers heavily weigh in on and influence the organization's strategic direction.
C. **Ambitious**: Ambitious Archetypes are performance-oriented leaders who manage their organizations by monitoring their markets and having competitor benchmarks influence the organization's strategic direction.

D. **Organized**: Organized Archetypes are process-oriented and manage their organizations with clearly-defined processes and procedures that are designed to maintain efficiency, quality, consistency, structure, hierarchy, and order.

E. **Delegative**: Delegative Archetypes are empowerment-focused and manage their organizations with a "laissez-faire" approach that's designed to leverage their organization's capabilities and drive high cross-functional coordination.

F. **Coach**: Coach Archetypes are team-oriented and manage their organizations by emphasizing teamwork and team effort as means of getting the job done.

Each Archetype is explained in detail in the next section.

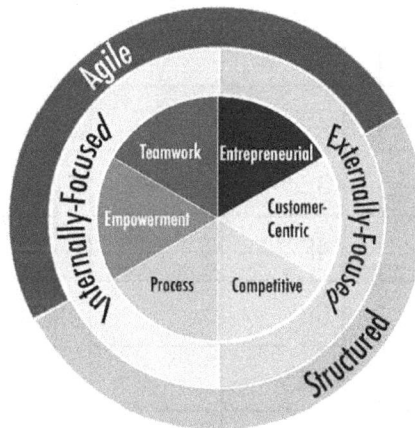

Scoring

Scoring the quiz is simple and requires you to add up the points from the seven different sections and then the total in each category (ranging from A-F). Accordingly, whichever category ranks the highest indicates the most dominant leadership archetype. Below, you'll find tables that you can use to help in the scoring process; you will also find 6 tables representing the 6 different categories (A-F).

Answers for questions 1-6 are each worth 14 points. Please note that question 7 is worth 16 points.

For example, if 'A' were chosen for questions 3, 5, and 7, 14 points would be placed in rows 3 and 5 in the first table, and 16 points would be placed in row 7 for that same table. Follow through with the tables according to the quiz answers. Any number-letter combination that does not have an answer is worth 0 points and, subsequently, has a score of "0."

Eventually, you will be able to add up the scores in each table, and the table containing the highest total indicates the primary leadership archetype.

A	Score		B	Score		C	Score
1A			1B			1C	
2A			2B			2C	
3A			3B			3C	
4A			4B			4C	
5A			5B			5C	
6A			6B			6C	
7A			7B			7C	
Total			Total			Total	

D	Score		E	Score		F	Score
1D			1E			1F	
2D			2E			2F	
3D			3E			3F	
4D			4E			4F	
5D			5E			5F	
6D			6E			6F	
7D			7E			7F	
Total			Total			Total	

Below, you will find the designated letters that correspond to six different leadership archetypes.

Under each title, you will find an executive summary and more details on the skills and strengths of each leadership archetype.

Plotting your Score

If you purchased the Pro version of the PMAS, the results are automatically plotted for you on a Radar Pie Chart. On the other hand, if you administered the quiz via paper or webforms, you can use a spreadsheet tool to plot the results and acquire the relative score of each Archetype, as shown below.

The plots for this quiz are then overlaid on top of the plots from other quizzes to compare them in terms of target states and aspired scores. For more information on which comparisons are relevant and how to interpret the gaps for each comparison, please refer to the PMAS eBook.

Found below are examples of how graphical representation can

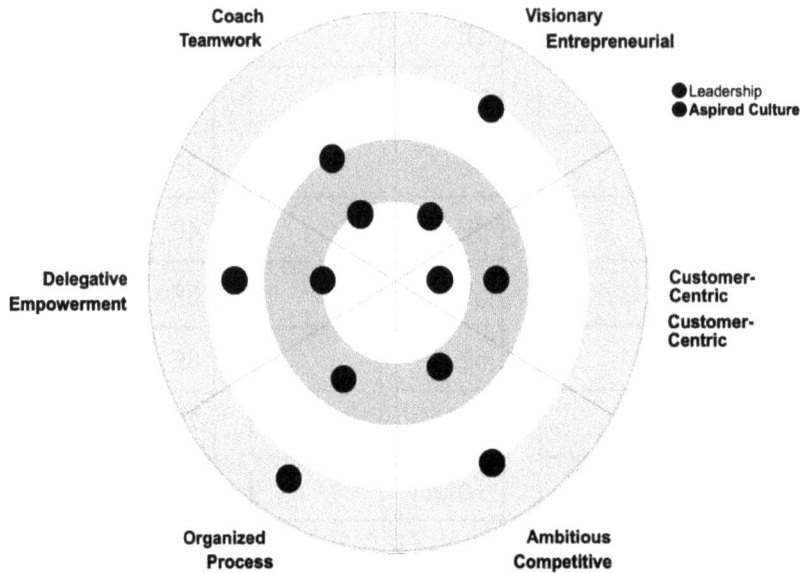

provide insight into assessments—in particular when performing

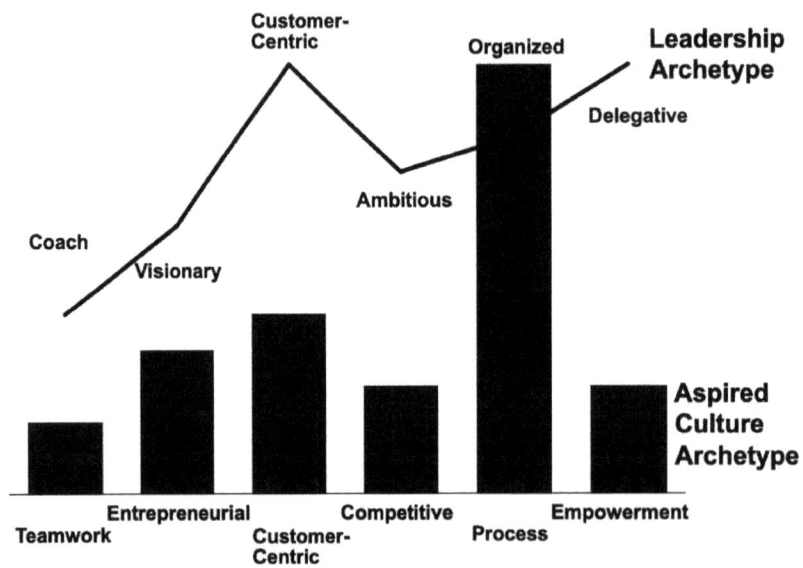

comparisons with other metrics.

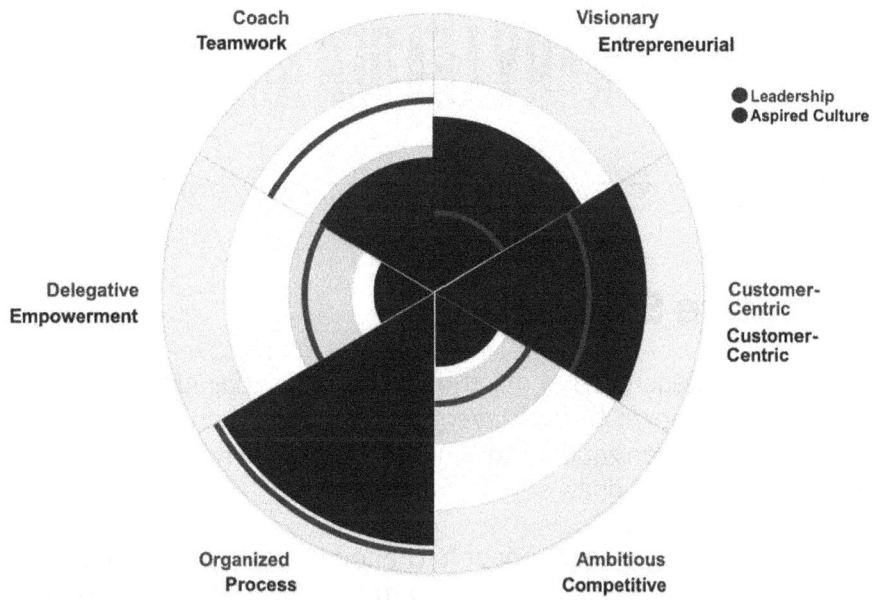

Coach
Teamwork

Visionary
Entrepreneurial

● Leadership
● Aspired Culture

Delegative
Empowerment

Customer-
Centric

Customer-
Centric

Organized
Process

Ambitious
Competitive

A. THE VISIONARY LEADER ARCHETYPE

"If things are not failing, you are not innovating enough." – Elon Musk

Executive Summary:

Visionary Leaders fall under the innovative leader Archetype, as they are known to be clever and creative when it comes to managing the organization. They invest their time and energy in the pursuit of achieving goals set out for the team.

Visionary Leaders easily adapt to changing circumstances and are more likely to display agility as a key attribute. Accordingly, they are able to recognize the upsides of unprecedented circumstances quite impressively.

They are forward-looking leaders who can easily envision change. They constantly remind themselves and those around them to focus on where the organization is and where it should be.

Exploring Skills and Strengths:

Innovative Visionary Leaders ("**Visionaries**") mainly focus on exploring and perfecting cutting-edge approaches towards objectives and performance goals. Their competitive side often emerges and their innovative side constantly shines through. Visionaries encourage others to join them across their journeys, and they constantly remind their teams that results can be achieved through improvement. They enjoy completing tasks through unconventional means, especially if it means a few heads will be turned.

Visionary leadership displays the following three attributes:

144

Innovative

Visionaries encourage individuals to be innovative and expand their alternatives. They push their colleagues and employees to be as creative as possible and to generate as many new ideas as they can.

Such leaders are crucial when it comes to solving problems in an out-of-the-box way. Visionaries are creative individuals that take pride in their originality, as they typically display a high degree of aesthetic sensitivity, and they work well with individuals who also have an eye for detail. Visionaries enjoy working in a team and strive to have coherent relationships with peers who communicate well and share the same passion for creativity and uniqueness. They want people to share their ideas and innovations, and they aim to adopt radical approaches within their organizations.

Visionary Leaders engage in experimentation, creativity, and non-normative thinking. Accordingly, they thrive amidst uncertainty and are comfortable even amidst ambiguous circumstances. They are likely to be impulsive, spontaneous, and quick to respond to information. Furthermore, these leaders often rely on their creative side to gather information and engage in brainstorming. They are inductive thinkers who usually have a wide array of interests.

Visionary Leaders usually achieve their goals using non-traditional means, as they rely on intuitive hunches more than any other means of processing and/or organization. They don't strive for perfection and even recognize the value of deviating from imposed rules and regulations. Instead, they prefer to excel creatively rather than to follow typical textbook methods. Visionaries stumble upon their best ideas when they least expect them, and they would sometimes rather be left alone than be part of a crowd. As such, these leaders usually use their private time to expand on their ideas and projects by means of both logic and intuition. Moreover, they are most at ease when employing specific techniques that engage their creative sides.

Entrepreneurial

Visionaries clearly identify their future goals and work towards them. Their vision is one of abundant growth, success, and positive future outcomes. The kind of vision these leaders set helps their team tap into its potential, because it satisfies a universal desire to make a sustainable difference. Visionaries, a.k.a entrepreneurs, help employees commit to that vision and adopt it as their own by encouraging colleagues to work toward its accomplishment. They are able to harness their team's potential to implement their creative strategies.

Visionaries have a vivid imagination that allows them to generate new ideas and adopt radical approaches to problem-solving. They are experimental and speculative, as they develop unique visions with endless possibilities. When faced with difficult problems, Visionaries try to tackle the issues at hand by coming up with revolutionary possibilities and distinctive solutions.

Like entrepreneurs, Visionaries are more willing to engage in risky projects and they are less alienated from their work environments. These individuals are also more satisfied with their work, and they experience less job strain and more position mobility.

Entrepreneurs and Visionaries alike expect to gain respect within their positions, so they tend to avoid situations that make them feel inferior to others. They have a distinct way of leading others, as they focus on reinforcing their team's strengths rather than on overcoming weaknesses. When discussing ideas and/or resolutions, these leaders engage their teams both mentally and emotionally. Furthermore, Visionaries place high importance on having their teams commit to a shared organizational vision. They believe a positive workplace is necessary to generate ideas, so they express gratitude and commend their team when needed.

Agile

Visionary Leaders are experts when it comes to adaptability and agility. This makes room for unique visions and complex approaches.

They handle uncertainty with much ease and encourage flexibility and productive change among individuals in their spaces.

Given the turbulent nature of the business world, most employees look up to someone who can easily guide them towards a more agile work approach. Visionaries encourage those around them to take initiatives that lead to cutting-edge approaches. Such leaders consider the workplace to be a 'tent' rather than a 'palace', meaning everything is temporary and subject to change when necessary. In a space where overload and uncertainty are on the rise, Visionaries show leadership skills that help bring flexibility and adaptability to the center, making those around them feel comfortable and confident in their day-to-day work. Team formation and functioning under Visionary leadership do not foster centralized power and authoritative relationships. Instead, power goes to whomever holds the best skills—i.e. to those who are able to adapt to changes and confront issues directly. Visionaries are trendsetters who enjoy pushing their team to take risks and enter new market spaces.

Summary

Overall, Visionaries possess leadership skills that are admired by those around them. They are considered to be dependable managers and leaders. Their skills are useful in times of sheer uncertainty and their thirst for innovation and creativity is contagious. Moreover, they help others feel confident in their abilities to progress and improve, and they ensure a calm and collected work environment during times of stress by adapting well to ambiguous situations. They are the leaders to be and the leaders to beat, as they inspire, attract, and motivate those around them.

B. THE CUSTOMER-CENTRIC LEADER ARCHETYPE

"We see our customers as invited guests to the party, and we are the hosts. It's our job every day to make every important aspect of the customer experience a little bit better." – Jeff Bezos

Executive Summary:

Customer-Centric Leaders ("**CC-Leaders**") are considered creative and imaginative individuals that always put their best foot forward when tackling customer-related problems.

Such customer-oriented leaders value the feedback received from their best clients and make sure to consider customers' needs when implementing organizational decisions.

These leaders have extremely high expectations for both themselves and their organization, as they strive to provide five-star customer service and excellent satisfaction ratings.

Exploring Skills and Strengths:

Customer-Centric Leaders prefer to tackle customer-related problems with utmost creativity. To ensure customer satisfaction is always high, these leaders encourage their team to prioritize customer feedback at all times. CC-Leaders aim to satisfy customers' wants, wishes, and desires.

Customer-Centric Leaders display the following three key attributes:

Creative Problem Solvers

Customer-Centric Leaders are experts at dealing with problems head-on while keeping the customer in mind at all times. They prefer to do so in a manner that ensures customer satisfaction, all while displaying high degrees of creativity and spontaneity. They recognize the importance of continuous improvement when keeping up with the dynamic customer market. Rather than focusing on what competitors are doing or what the company has been doing in the past, such leaders prioritize customers and their respective needs.

Customer-Centric Leaders aim to satisfy customer needs creatively, in unexpected and unique ways. To do so, CC-leaders utilize four methods, the first of which includes generating new ideas. This is because having an expansive imagination is a key trait of customer-centric leaders, and it often helps them tackle and understand their customers' needs. These leaders also focus on incremental improvement and constantly work hard to build upon what already exists, as this allows organizations to readily anticipate and keep up with any changes in customer demand. Thirdly, CC-Leaders tackle their customers' problems as quickly and as efficiently as possible by being first in line to handle any issue customers may have. Finally, these leaders focus on harnessing and sustaining creativity within the organization, as they consider ingenuity to be a key factor in organizational functioning and customer satisfaction.

Customer-Driven

CC-Leaders guide employees and colleagues towards customer-centric thinking by emphasizing the importance of customers' wants and needs. Such leaders consistently satisfy and even surpass customer expectations.

As previously mentioned, when it comes to both individual and collective improvement, CC-Leaders emphasize building on what already exists rather than starting from scratch. They voice their opinions openly, even though it may lead to disagreements. As such, CC-Leaders try following what is right rather than pleasing others.

In terms of priorities, CC-Leaders are externally-focused. They enjoy fulfilling customers' demands and thrive when exceeding expectations. CC-Leaders recognize the value of impeccable customer service and are known for treating customers with the utmost respect. CC-Leaders enjoy being "go-to" people for anyone looking to receive top-notch services. They're always fully ready to constantly deliver high-quality products and services.

Strategic

CC-Leaders remain up-to-date with the ever-changing technological landscape that shapes increasingly demanding customer wants and needs. CC-Leaders recognize the importance of placing customers at the center of all important and strategic business decisions. They deliver products and services while seeking ongoing feedback from existing and potential customers to accurately anticipate their needs.

CC-Leaders can adapt to change and adjust their vision, strategies, goals, products and services accordingly. CC leaders work on motivating both their team and those of other departments—marketing, product design, customer service, etc.—to meet and exceed customers' expectations. Their main focus is to rally the organization as a whole towards prioritizing customer feedback and incorporating it into their plans and strategies.

Summary

CC-Leaders are valued and appreciated by customers and vice versa. CC-Leaders measure success by surpassing goals whose aims are increasing customer loyalty, enhancing customer experience and maintaining high-levels of customer satisfaction. CC-Leaders pride themselves on being able to accurately anticipate customers' needs and on adopting creative means of solving customer-related problems.

C. THE AMBITIOUS LEADER ARCHETYPE

"If you don't have a competitive advantage, don't compete." –
Jack Welch

Executive Summary:

Ambitious Leaders are known for being competitive and motivating, all while being assertive. They are quite demanding, as they have a very specific way of getting things done. Also, they actively pursue goals and targets and are driven by competition and benchmarks.

Winning is a dominant objective for Ambitious Leaders. They are predominantly externally focused and are driven by their performance against competitors.

One key personality trait of Ambitious Leaders is their dedication to their work. They believe that hard work and perseverance, by means of setting and achieving targets and goals, lead to excellence.

Exploring Skills and Strengths:

Ambitious Leaders are driven by healthy competition. They pride themselves on being dependable managers who set themselves apart from their competitors by studying, analyzing and outperforming their business opponents. Ambitious Leaders are known to be high-energy individuals who push their organizations towards pursuing and accomplishing highly ambitious goals.

Ambitious Leaders display the three following attributes that set them apart from other leaders:

151

Competitiveness

Ambitious Leaders place their work ahead of anything else and constantly strive for excellence. Their ambitious personality makes it difficult for them not to reach the goals they set out to achieve for themselves and others. Their daily goal is heightened productivity, and they build upon this desire with their teammates on an everyday basis. Their competitive nature drives them to invest serious time and effort into making sure they are up to date with the latest research on market trends and developments.

Ambitious Leadership fosters a competitive work environment where outranking competitors is the goal. Ambitious Leaders motivate their teams by promoting internal competition between employees, teams, and departments and by keeping track of individual contributions.

Performance and Achievement

The fast-paced work-life leaves no room for error, so Ambitious Leaders set goals to ensure that any strategy redundancy is eliminated.

Ambitious Leaders recognize the importance of high workplace morale and strive to be role models that subordinates look up to for inspiration and advice. These leaders want to be accessible to everyone. They lead others towards success with a great deal of enthusiasm and support, as they readily recognize employee accomplishments. They enjoy challenging themselves and those around them by setting specific tasks and goals. Also, when problems arise, these leaders take on a guiding role and wholeheartedly express their confidence in their employees' abilities.

Ambitious Leaders readily set challenging targets that can be achieved through hard work. Under this type of leadership, the "work hard, play hard" ethic is applied. Ambitious Leaders recognize and celebrate individual and collective efforts and achievements.

If anything goes wrong, they need those responsible to be held accountable for their actions and to understand why errors have occurred, rather than lazily pass the blame on to others. If a mistake is made, the right solution needs to be found and implemented by wrongdoers to avoid future problems. Ambitious Leaders encourage their employees to accept responsibility, to learn the appropriate lessons, and to adopt a solution-driven attitude.

Motivation

When it comes to working as a team, Ambitious Leaders make it clear what the vision moving forward should be and what they, as leaders, want everyone to accomplish. They work with strict deadlines, and they motivate employees by adopting a carrot-and-stick approach, that may combine meritocracy with an "Up or Out" policy, to keep people alert, focused, and motivated.

Ambitious Leaders make sure they have a fair system in place by setting measurable goals and objectives ahead of time and by frequently updating these targets. They expect everyone around them to excel and improve over time, and they may adopt a forced ranking approach that uses bell-curve rating, when setting targets and evaluating employees. They treat their team equitably by making sure every employee is held accountable for his/her actions and results. For example, these leaders assign mutually exclusive and collectively exhaustive individual key performance indicators to ensure that employees sign off on targets ahead of time.

Ambitious leaders readily reward success and give credit where it is due. They utilize this strategy when energizing employees and when getting difficult tasks done. Moreover, under Ambitious Leadership, challenging targets are broken down into smaller tasks with strict deadlines, in order to make frequent celebration of small wins a key driver of motivation.

Summary

Overall, Ambitious Leaders are strategic, externally-focused, and driven by competition. Despite having a reputation of being stern, they are still able to motivate employees to give their full potential. They are natural leaders who unite people around common goals and try to gain knowledge of their own strengths and weaknesses; as well as those of their teams, in order to progress. They despise mediocrity and do not accept excuses for failure. They value dedication, commitment, high achievement, meritocracy, ambition and winning above all else. They credit, recognize and reward successes, and they learn from failure to ensure it doesn't happen again. They thrive on internal and external competition and promote knowledge and continuous self and collective development.

D. THE ORGANIZED LEADER ARCHETYPE

"A leader is one who knows the way, goes the way and shows the way." – John C. Maxwell

Executive Summary:

Organized Leaders are typically known for being well-informed technical experts. They do things by textbook standards and feel at ease with systematic problem-solving. They adopt and follow clear processes and procedures, and they actively pursue consistency and uniformity.

Organized Leaders are praised for being dependable and reliable. They base their day-to-day work life on practicing situational engineering, managing schedules, giving assignments and ensuring order by maintaining structure in the workplace.

They challenge themselves to improve on what already exists through systematic and thorough planning and execution. They thrive on stability and control and tend to be the go-to leaders for analytical problem-solvers.

Exploring Skills and Strengths:

Organized Leaders exhibit notable self-awareness and self-knowledge. These two traits are considered to be key characteristics of organized leadership, as organized leaders are very punctual and prioritize time management when dealing with both workplace and non-workplace individuals.

Within the workplace, organized Leaders heavily rely on clear structure and thorough organization. Therefore, three main attributes are found:

155

Time Management

Organized Leaders help individuals understand organizational culture and its subsequent expectations, including structure. Organized Leaders ensure that their employees are well aware of workplace standards and principles, and this helps them better acclimate to the workplace and meet expectations their leaders have set for them. In terms of work ethic, Organized Leaders are known for being extremely punctual, as they take both their own time management and that of others very seriously. Accordingly, they adopt effective time-management methods such as keeping track of time, making to-do lists, and prioritizing necessary tasks over less immediate obligations. They find relief in breaking down large tasks into smaller ones, as this helps reduce anxiety and makes work feel less overwhelming.

Organized Leaders are typically well-prepared and can easily follow up with their teams when it comes to tasks and projects. Their daily agenda focuses on setting and meeting deadlines. Such leaders rarely procrastinate with their work and make sure not to waste time during the day. They plan their days in advance and they fill up any free time they may have with smaller assignments to make sure they're always on track and continue progressing smoothly.

Process and Structure

Organized Leaders don't work well with ambiguity, so they require all tasks, goals, and actions to be clearly identified ahead of time. They work in a very structured way to ensure that processes, measurements, and monitoring systems are implemented as they should be.

They would rather tackle tasks and challenges that leverage their current capabilities, as they believe this is the best means of achieving continuous progress. That being said, Organized Leaders do not let feelings get the better of them, as they can separate themselves from any workplace negativity by remaining calm and collected when emotions and stress are running high. They're highly organized and prefer to do things logically, in a manner that conforms to conventional procedures and maintains a stable routine. One area of strength is information-processing, as Organized Leaders are able to condense large amounts of data into concise, cohesive, and logical forms. When faced with unpleasant situations in the workplace, Organized Leaders are known to maintain self-control and clear-headed thinking.

These leaders maintain control by ensuring compliance and managing information and documentation. They try to abide by a set of rules that allows them to optimize monitoring, reporting, and control systems. Accordingly, these administrators are praised for their organizational skills, as they provide their employees and colleagues with clear expectations, policies, values, objectives, job descriptions, and performance targets. In turn, Organized Leaders are able to measure and monitor employee performance and take the necessary corrective actions that ensure consistency, quality and predictability.

Authority and Control

Organized Leaders cannot imagine a workplace without authority or control, as they like to be in control of any and all situations. They ensure that standardized measures, monitoring systems, and reporting mechanisms are in place to maintain control. They consistently emphasize an adherence to organizational policy, processes, and procedures.

They drive compliance and control through standard business and best practice tools, an example of which is ensuring their organization has updated and clearly-defined reporting and hierarchical structures. Furthermore, Organized Leaders always provide details about job descriptions for every position, and they expand upon fixed roles and responsibilities for units, groups, and individuals within the organization. These are combined with an up-to-date authority matrix that defines how the decision-making process is divided across different levels of the organization (down to the position). This includes definitions such as accountability, responsibility, recommendation, consultation and the sharing of information.

Efficiency, Consistency and Stability

Organized Leaders are efficient and consistent at what they do. They like predictability and plan as far ahead as possible by preparing for their coming days, weeks, and months. They constantly anticipate risks and build contingency plans and preventative measures to avoid disruptions and interruptions. They have a systematic methodology for gathering and responding to information, as well as clear agendas, well-developed outlines, and clear processes to aid them as they seek, interpret, and deal with information.

They focus on ensuring consistent quality when delivering a product or a service (e.g., six sigma), and they cultivate a quality-driven culture around them. Consistency drives everything they do, from quality assurance to quality of business processes and procedures they put in place. This ultimately maintains stability and smooth-running, efficient, and undisrupted operations.

Summary

Overall, Organized Leaders emphasize the need to have structure, rules and routine in the workplace. Their way of work is very systematic and often includes the use of daily to-do tasks backed up with processes and procedures on how to follow through with them and what standards need to be maintained. They are often sought out when structure is needed and chaos is on the rise. Their impeccable self-understanding and self-control help keep everyone at work in check and in turn, Organized Leaders are better able to understand themselves and those they work with. They are less inclined to acquire information by interacting with others but rather sway towards thinking things through more logically and rationally. They excel at inductive reasoning and organizing material into a consistent whole. They bring a sense of calm to the workplace by ensuring order and structure always exist within the organization. This allows them to be successful and competent Organized Leaders.

E. THE DELEGATIVE LEADER ARCHETYPE

"Leadership is about empowering others to achieve things they did not think possible." - Simon Sinek

Executive Summary:

Delegative Leaders ("**Delegators**") adopt a hands-off approach to management by empowering those around them and by delegating authority to individuals, teams, units and/or organizations they manage.

Delegators foster an inclusive culture and encourage personal growth that allows employees to gain autonomy and freedom within the decision-making process.

They promote the free flow of information and enhance interdepartmental communication and cooperation by assisting in analytics and providing the support needed to address capability gaps across the organization.

Exploring Skills and Strengths:

Delegative Leaders are skilled at passing on and allocating responsibilities across individuals and departments. This empowers team members to bring out the best of their abilities. They enhance interdepartmental communication and information-sharing while ensuring the utmost inclusivity within their daily practices.

Some common traits of Delegators include:

Empowerment

Delegators tend to manage their organization by trusting those around them and by delegating tasks and major and minor responsibilities. This helps create a culture centered around

159

employee empowerment and inclusivity. They believe that autonomy, self-awareness, and self-confidence are the way forward when it comes to building a strong and capable organization. These leaders are able to instill confidence within their employees, and they help team members feel more included in the organization as a whole.

Delegators foster high-level coordination and cooperation within and across departments, all while making it a priority that the organization function as a consistent unit. They facilitate this by promoting data free flow and effective communication, and by ensuring collective alignment with the organization's visions, goals, objectives, projects, and day-to-day tasks.

When it comes to teamwork and problem-solving, they delegate tasks to well-performing, highly competent employees, and they emphasize collective involvement in problem-solving. They make sure to provide their staff with the necessary assignments, opportunities, and training needed for ongoing personal growth and development, all while helping them move up within the organization.

Inclusivity

Delegators tend to steer clear of authoritative leadership, and they do not recognize any added value in micromanaging and pressuring employees. Instead, they emphasize freedom and collective involvement within the workspace, as they encourage multiple people to join forces and pitch ideas, recommendations, and solutions to higher-ups and fellow team members. They provide their staff with proper guidance, constructive criticism, adequate resources, and the necessary support to enable them to reach their full potential.

Delegators help team members discover hidden strengths and weaknesses to ensure that delegated tasks are given to the right employees. Delegators would rather employees overcome their weaknesses on their own than be actively involved as leaders. As previously mentioned, this reinforces empowerment-led culture under Delegative leadership.

Analytics

Delegators are analytical decision-makers and problem-solvers. They rely heavily on numbers and data in their work and steer clear of cognitive biases that may affect their decision-making. When crunching numbers and/or research data—whether personally or through delegation—Delegative Leaders make sure to apply and incorporate thorough analysis into their leadership strategy. These leaders enforce the use of reporting systems in order to remain up-to-date on unit performance. They do not prioritize data extraction mechanisms. Instead, they focus on obtaining the actual data at hand and on assisting their teams in making this happen. Having a systematic methodology for gathering and responding to information is important to these types of leaders, as they engage in a meticulous follow-up process in order to produce clear and concise outlines.

Tending to problems analytically means that Delegators look for rationality, validity and proof of data when attempting to complete tasks and goals. They guide their team towards an accurate and credible presentation of information.

Summary

Overall, Delegative Leaders are admired and appreciated by their team. Employees feel that such leaders help bring out their best qualities and they feel comfortable seeking their leaders' guidance when it comes to ideas and recommendations. Delegators create a positive culture at work all while maintaining a stern attitude that produces impressive results. Logic and reasoning are at an all-time high when having a conversation with Delegators. Every step taken is meticulously-planned and researched to ensure that results meet necessary expectations. As such, these leaders take their time when making decisions. They are more focused on the problem itself rather than on the people/person behind the issue, hence why problem-solving for Delegators tends to be more straightforward and less interpersonal.

F. THE COACH LEADER ARCHETYPE

"Great things in business are never done by one person. They're done by a team of people" - Steve Jobs

Executive Summary:

Coaches fall under the Leader Archetype. Typically, individuals within this category find ease in building and strengthening positive relationships, and they are able to communicate with people in a way that enhances feelings of trust, openness, and support.

Coaches are considered to be people-oriented facilitators. They manage conflict, seek consensus and positively influence others by involving every member of the workplace in decision-making and problem-solving. They actively encourage participation and openness and boost morale and commitment.

Coaches are looked at as caring and empathetic mentors. They are aware of and care for the needs of those around them. Their influence is based on mutual respect and trust.

A Coach Leader Archetype ("Coach") is considered to be natural when it comes to supportive communication and managing interpersonal relationships with colleagues, subordinates and peers. A Coach first listens, then provides feedback when needed, and is the go-to person when resolving any interpersonal problems between team members.

Exploring Skills and Strengths:

We define "**Coaches**" as Leaders who tend to focus on both their own wellbeing and that of others when it comes to workplace interactions. Coaches easily establish mentor-mentee relationships and prioritize providing their team with necessary feedback for improvement. These types of Leaders encourage and uplift others

162

and they place the utmost importance on highlighting their colleagues' and employees' skills and strengths.

Interpersonal Relationships

Coaches build positive interpersonal relationships with those around them by emphasizing supportive feedback, active listening, and efficient resolution of interpersonal problems. Such healthy interactions create positive group environments, as employees tend to feel more calm and optimistic when around Coaches. On the other hand, interactions with negative leaders can be difficult and depleting, both mentally and emotionally, and this creates a toxic workspace.

Employees and team members are more inclined to seek information and resources from individuals, like Coaches, who motivate them and make them feel secure. Accordingly, research has shown that productivity increases when a workplace is filled with positive-minded individuals— Coaches.

Coaches allow for positive interpersonal change to take place not only within the confines of the workplace but also within employees' personal lives. As previously mentioned, team members feel safe and encouraged when working and interacting with Coaches. Such healthy relationships generate long-term physiological, emotional, intellectual, and social development.

Being around Coaches can help employees better deal with stress, and it can reduce distractions caused by feelings of anxiety, frustration, or uncertainty from negative relationships.

Communication and Openness

One of the most important skills in building positive interpersonal relationships is the ability to communicate with people in a way that enhances feelings of trust, openness, and support. Coaches are effective communicators, as they excel in transmitting and receiving clear and precise messages with transparency and honesty, especially during difficult circumstances. Coaches attempt to do so without jeopardizing personal relationships with colleagues.

Coaches help others work harder and smarter by providing specific feedback and not making haphazard assumptions. They enjoy emphasizing corrective behavior in a positive and respectful manner, and they would rather have their encounters with others end on an encouraging note. Their exceptional interpersonal communication skills help them maneuver their teams around difficult circumstances in a manner that encourages honesty and efficiency. Coaches find it easy to communicate supportively, even when it comes to sensitive matters such as correcting negative behavior, highlighting shortcomings, or delivering negative feedback.

Managing Conflicts and Collaboration

Coaches manage conflict, seek consensus, and actively encourage their teams to get involved with decision-making and problem-solving. As previously mentioned, Coaches thrive in open work environments, and they support employees by communicating productively and encouragingly, without lashing out. This unique set of skills shines through during difficult situations.

In cases of conflict, Coaches focus on reliable facts and consider multiple perspectives in order to effectively engage in debate and reach fair, objective solutions. When trying to resolve issues, Coaches share commonly agreed-upon goals with their employees, and they incorporate humor into the decision-making process, all while maintaining a power balance with others. Moreover, these Leaders establish superordinate goals and focus on commonalities, by distinguishing people from the issues they are involved in and by clarifying the mutual benefits to be gained from problem-resolution.

When moving towards a vision, Coaches utilize the knowledge they have gained about their team's core competencies and unique strengths in order to evaluate the best means of moving forward. Even if other team members don't necessarily agree with the leader's perspective, common ground is still reached to ensure that all perspectives are taken into consideration.

Mentoring

Coaches foster mentoring relationships and teamwork, as mentoring is known to enhance interpersonal resilience between team members. Research shows that career success, work satisfaction, and resilience against stress improve under a well-established mentor-mentee relationship, as this type of dynamic is characterized by commitment, trust, and cooperation. Employees consider Coaches to be role models who provide them with personal attention and validation, especially throughout uncertain, crucial, and/or stressful situations. Accordingly, Coaches actively seek and foster a mentoring relationship that is mutually satisfying and mutually beneficial for both parties.

Team Development and Team Building

Coaches consider coordination and team development to be very important. They attempt to generate and facilitate effective, cohesive, and high-performance teamwork. They do so by being aware of others and caring deeply for their needs. They actively influence others to practice mutual trust and respect within the workspace. Consequently, commitment and positive morale are some of their key attributes.

The organization's overall performance depends on the types of relationships it fosters. Coaches can act as catalysts for enhancing cooperation between team members, as they help reduce—and maybe even eliminate—conflicts and disagreements that hinder performance. Loyalty and commitment have been shown to increase when TEDIs are in charge of organizations.

Coaches demonstrate leadership integrity and behave in alignment with their values—fairness and justice". Furthermore, coaches are clear, consistent, and certain about what they want and where they are going, without being dogmatic or stubborn. This allows team members to trust their leaders, as these individuals have no hidden agendas or motives.

Coaches create positive energy and stay optimistic, and they manage agreements/ disagreements remarkably well, all while using commonality and reciprocity in a complimentary manner. By providing team members with useful information and advice and assisting them with task requirements.

Coaches are knowledgeable about their teams' preferences, talents, and daily tasks. By frequently checking in with team members about levels of agreement, obstacles, dissatisfactions, needs and interpersonal or team-related issues, coaches are able to understand a multitude of perspectives and gain others' credibility and trust. As such, Coaches are highly effective team leaders who continually expand their knowledge about the team and its environment.

Coaches enjoy helping employees improve their performance, expand their competencies and obtain personal development opportunities. This allows for higher job performance, as tasks are completed more readily and effectively. Moreover, Coaches boost collective morale by recognizing and celebrating the team's small successes. Also, Coaches aid others in developing personal mastery of their work by motivating mentees to take on more complex and demanding tasks.

Summary

Overall, Coaches are leaders that teams can look up to and be inspired by. They are managers that individuals love to work with. Their caring nature makes it easy to reach them, and their need to support others shines through with their positive feedback. By having a positive attitude, they empower their colleagues and employees and make their teams feel at ease. They rarely make enemies in the workplace and constantly strive for fairness and honesty which is what keeps the organization running smoothly and efficiently.

ORGANIZATION CULTURE ARCHETYPE ASSESSMENT WORKBOOK

INTRODUCTION

We define organizational culture as the beliefs, values, mindsets and practices of a group of people (whether an entire organization or a subset thereof) within an organization. Decades of wide-reaching empirical evidence have proven undisputedly that organizational cultures have a major impact on company performance. If you have ever led a team, department, business unit, or company, you may have reflected upon the role that organizational culture plays when it comes to overall performance. As such, it is important to mention that the relationship between an organization's culture and its performance has been the leading cause of industry and corporation fallouts, no matter the prestige of the conglomerates at hand.

For example, if we look at the organizational cultures within the steel industry and their subsequent resistance to change, we would see that they have prevented American steel companies from innovating and modernizing. This has led to their subsequent domination by Korean, Japanese, and European producers. More recent examples include the fallout of the newspaper industry and the retail apocalypse. Because organizational culture has been influenced by industry functioning, organizations have failed to find a balance between traditional and new activities. The reason behind this is that leaders have not adequately responded to the uncertainty brought about by changes within the external environment. An example of such changes is the tension between the old organizational culture—that of monopoly newspapers and 20% profit margins—and the new organizational culture which emerged from disruptive changes in the industry. The same can be said about retail giants such as *Sears, Radioshack, Toys R Us* and *Blockbuster.*

Organizational culture creates friction and tension between groups, as whenever ten or more people share a space that allows them to engage in a multitude of dynamics, an entire collective culture emerges within a very short period of time. Furthermore, more recent evidence has come to light regarding organizational culture requirements and the subsequent work environments they generate. These studies were conducted across all industry sectors, within many international settings, and for every organization type. Accordingly, research shows that different organizations need to adopt their own specific cultures—there isn't one that works for all. In parallel, various factors need to be taken into consideration such as the growth stage, the market and competitive dynamics of the industry, and the organization's vision, mission, and strategy.

For example, a startup organization with a small team of founders and new-hires is likely to be entrepreneurial in its culture, and it would function with much agility and flexibility. As the organization grows in size, its original entrepreneurial culture would not be sustained in the long-term, as more measures and processes would be taken to ensure long-lasting growth. Also, as new hires import cultures from former to current places of employment, a new dominant culture emerges and becomes the norm.

The purpose of this workbook is to provide all members of an organization with information regarding what it means to be part of specific work culture. It should be noted that this workbook is intended for leaders, managers, employees and anyone actively involved in running organizations, as each of these parties contributes towards creating and maintaining organizational cultures. We hope that, by the end of this workbook, readers would have gained vital information that allows organizations to better understand what way of work suits them, what form of authority they prefer and what truly drives them towards working well together and reaching their desired goals.

LIMITATIONS OF NON-PRO VERSION

The paper version of the quiz, despite containing the same questions as those of the "Pro" version, is more limited in its capacities. This is because the Pro quiz is designed in a manner that utilizes nested processing, as questions are continuously generated according to previous results. As such, unlike its pencil-paper counterpart, the Pro version contains built-in intelligence that allows for more thorough, complex analysis.

Within today's market, traditional employee surveys rarely have the built-in capacities that allow for complex business and managerial investigations to occur. This is why many of these surveys produce results that do not accurately reflect the reality of the situation. Consequently, these questionnaires seldom provide their users with a precise understanding of organizational gaps and challenges and, subsequently, hinder processes such as transformation and change management. Another drawback of conventional surveys is the number of complications that occur when administering and collecting information. These obstacles challenge surveys' ability to measure progress over a short period of time and to produce an accurate portrayal of the organization's reality.

Despite the aforementioned limitations of the non-Pro version, it still generates more information than most surveys out there do and can, subsequently, identify the primary, secondary, and tertiary dominant culture Archetypes. As discussed later and in the PMAS book, the quiz is structured in a manner that allows for any potential bias to be limited via the types of answer options in the multiple-choice section.

The Pro version, on the other hand, can reveal all primary, secondary and tertiary archetypes with more precision and can be easily administered with the click of a button. Furthermore, the Pro's results can be measured accurately and rapidly on a monthly basis. If you have not signed up for the Pro version, you can do so by following up with Business Model Hackers through the account generated alongside this book's purchase.

INTERPRETING RESULTS

The answer choices provided in the quiz are structured in such a way as to capture various cultural attributes. This was done in accordance with the concept of paradoxicality, as discussed in the PMAS book, in order to effectively reduce human bias. For more details and background information on how the quiz was structured, please refer to the main PMAS book.

The assessment for each Archetype (whether primary, secondary, or tertiary) is provided separately and divided into two sections: The Executive Summary and the Detailed Assessment.

The Culture Archetypes

A paradox mindset highlights the extent to which individuals embrace tensions. This is because the adoption of a paradox mindset can help people leverage tensions and produce creative outputs. However, most people tend to have a preference for one direction over the other, which is why they experience cognitive dissonance when they are pulled towards opposing extremes. Yet, research suggests that these conflicts can often work in a person's favor. Several studies conducted by psychologists and organizational researchers have found that people who learn to embrace, rather than reject, opposing sides of a paradox display more creativity, flexibility and productivity, as duality can lead to enhanced overall performance.

The Culture Archetype Assessment design follows a structure that presents values in opposing axes across two key dimensions, Agility and Orientation, which are further broken down into six subcategories. These subcategories are grouped into three paradoxical pairs along the two main axes as shown below. Accordingly, the six Culture Archetypes are as follows:

- **Entrepreneurial:** The Entrepreneurial Culture Archetype is characterized by innovation and trendsetting activities. The

171

work environment is dynamic and agile, and creativity, risk-taking, and innovation are encouraged and rewarded. Employees take pride in their unique work execution, and they are typically driven by ulterior motives, such as a desire to positively change the world and/or disrupt the markets that they serve.

- **Customer-Centric:** The Customer-Centric Culture Archetype is characterized by its focus on customers, as they weigh in heavily on organizational decisions and influence the organization's strategic direction. The work environment encourages incremental innovation and creative problem-solving, and employees are typically driven by the desire to please customers and provide products/services that exceed customers' expectations.

- **Competitive:** The Competitive Culture Archetype is one that is driven by marketplace competitors. Its work environment practices meritocracy, encourages high achievements, and rewards performance. Competition, benchmarks, and market trends drive the organization's strategic direction. Employees continuously monitor their markets and are motivated by the desire to achieve excellence and to consistently beat their competitors.

- **Process:** The Process Culture Archetype is one that is driven by clearly-defined processes and procedures, in an environment that is organized, hierarchical and structured. Stability, consistency, and quality drive the organization's day-to-day operations. Employees know exactly what's expected of them, and they are motivated by job security and by their ability to perform and deliver exactly what's expected of them.

- **Empowerment:** The Empowerment Culture Archetype is one that is driven by empowerment and accountability, in a work environment that emphasizes inclusivity and accountability. A "laissez-faire" approach characterized by the delegation of authority is what drives the organization's management. Employees have a sense of purpose and always feel included in key decisions. Two factors motivate the employees of such a culture: an acceptance of responsibility and an autonomous management of their work.

- **Teamwork:** The Teamwork Culture Archetype is one that is based on active participation and openness. Two factors drive the organization forward: a teamwork-based approach, and individual team members' collective involvement in the workplace. Such an environment is very people-friendly, and its members feel like an extended family. Employees know that they are able to achieve greatness by means of having their individual capabilities leveraged equally with those of everyone else, so they are motivated when working as a unit.

Each Culture Archetype is detailed in the next section.

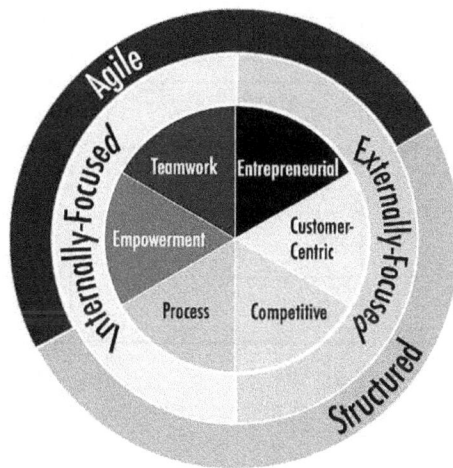

Scoring

Scoring the quiz is simple and requires you to add up the points from the six different sections and the total in each category (ranging from A-F). Accordingly, whichever category ranks the highest indicates the most dominant culture archetype. Below, you'll find tables that you can use to help with the scoring process; you will also find 6 tables representing the 6 different categories (A-F).

Answers for questions 1-6 are each worth 14 points. Please note that question 7 is worth 16 points.

For example, if 'A' were chosen for questions 3, 5, and 7, 14 points would be placed in rows 3 and 5 in the first table, and 16 points would be placed in row 7 for that same table. Follow through with the tables according to the quiz answers. Any number-letter combination that does not have an answer is worth 0 points and, subsequently, has a score of "0."

Eventually, you will be able to add up the scores in each table, and the table containing the highest total indicates the primary culture archetype.

A	Score
1A	
2A	
3A	
4A	
5A	
6A	
7A	
Total	

B	Score
1B	
2B	
3B	
4B	
5B	
6B	
7B	
Total	

C	Score
1C	
2C	
3C	
4C	
5C	
6C	
7C	
Total	

D	Score
1D	
2D	
3D	

E	Score
1E	
2E	
3E	

F	Score
1F	
2F	
3F	

4D		4E		4F	
5D		5E		5F	
6D		6E		6F	
7D		7E		7F	
Total		Total		Total	

Below, you will find the designated letters that correspond to six different culture archetypes.

Under each title, you will find an executive summary and more details on the attributes of each culture archetype.

Plotting your Score

If you purchased the Pro version of the PMAS, the results are automatically plotted for you on a Radar Pie Chart. On the other hand, if you administered the quiz via paper or webforms, you can use a spreadsheet tool to plot the results and acquire the relative score of each Archetype, as shown below.

The plots for this quiz are then overlaid on top of the plots from other quizzes to compare them in terms of target states and aspired scores. For more information on which comparisons are relevant and how to interpret the gaps for each comparison, please refer to the PMAS eBook.

Found below are examples of how graphical representation can provide insight into assessments—in particular when performing comparisons with other metrics.

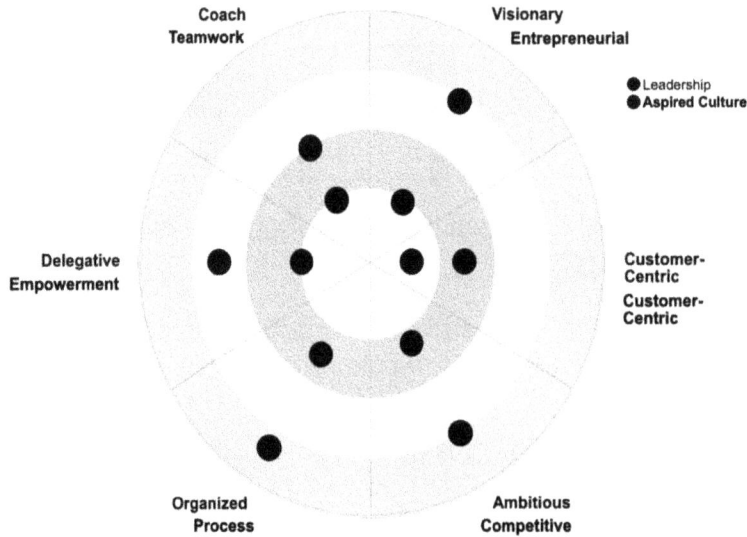

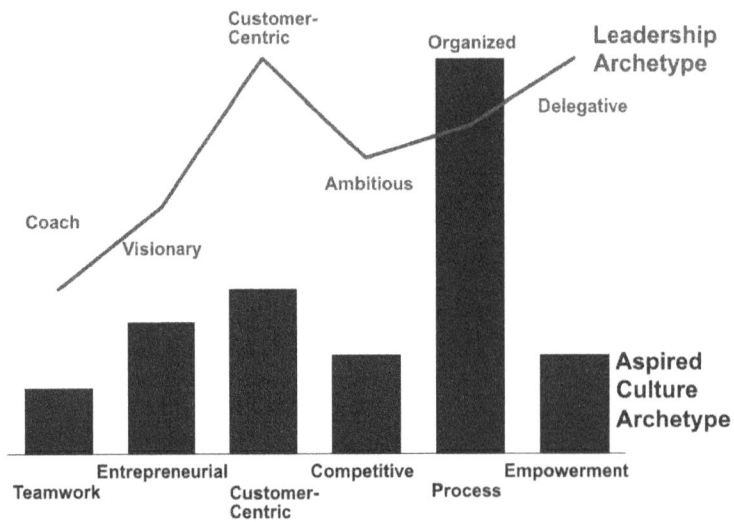

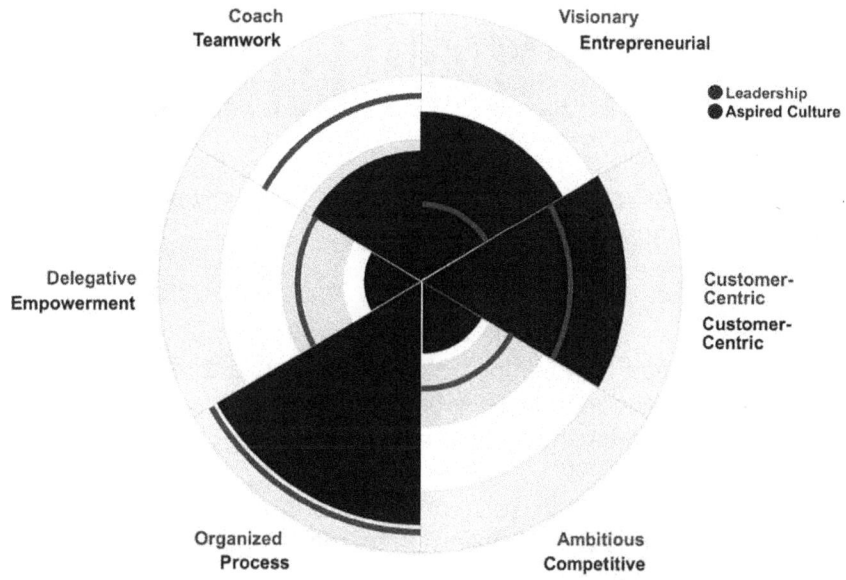

Coach
Teamwork

Visionary
Entrepreneurial

● Leadership
● Aspired Culture

Delegative
Empowerment

Customer-
Centric

Customer-
Centric

Organized
Process

Ambitious
Competitive

A. ENTREPRENEURIAL CULTURE

"Creative thinking inspires ideas. Ideas inspire change." – Barbara Januszkiewicz

Executive Summary:

Continuous innovation and creativity are at the heart of Entrepreneurial organizational cultures. Organizational goals are usually met in inventive, uncharacteristic ways.

Employees within such organizations are consistently bending and breaking the rules in order to reach unprecedented results in unconventional ways.

Change (internal and external) is easy for such organizations, as colleagues continuously find themselves in a multitude of situations that allow them to be adaptable.

Deep Dive:

Entrepreneurial Culture emphasizes exploring and perfecting cutting-edge approaches that allow companies to reach their goals. Colleagues are constantly reminded how satisfying it is to see results through exciting new methods; consequently, creative culture is created that allows everyone to exceed their limits and let their creativity run loose. If tasks aren't completed in an unconventional way, they simply haven't met the mark.

In Entrepreneurial Culture, three characteristics shine through:

Innovation

Team members are commended for being outside-the-box thinkers, innovative hard workers, and creative problem-solvers. Entrepreneurial workplace culture leaves no room for routine, and

178

the team prides itself on having a high degree of aesthetic sensitivity. They work well with each other and feed off of their shared passion for creativity and uniqueness when completing tasks. In Entrepreneurial Cultures, people openly share their ideas and innovations with others and adopt radical approaches when tackling problems.

The path to an end goal is anything but traditional within this culture, as team members are encouraged to rely on intuition above all and subsequently take pleasure in breaking rules. Team meetings usually allow people to stumble upon their best ideas when they least expect them.

Entrepreneurship

Fostering an entrepreneurial mindset among team members is important for such cultures. Leaders often encourage their team members to bring forth their own ideas and to pursue their own goals. Furthermore, Entrepreneurial culture encourages employees to "put it all on the table" in order to commit to visions and follow through with what they think works for the organization.

Team meetings have employees bouncing ideas off each other, as individuals readily speak up about the path they wish to take and how they aim to develop their own ideas. In such an entrepreneurial environment, It's very rare for individual and collective creativity/ideas to be rejected, thus creating an endless flow of ideas, projects, creativity, and risk-taking.

This culture encourages managers and employees to utilize their vivid imaginations to create new ideas. As such, problem-solving takes place via breakthroughs and the adoption of radical approaches. In such a culture, it is essential to engage both experimentation and speculation, as this provides the organization with endless possibilities. Moreover, those who propose risky yet exciting ideas are applauded for their creative efforts. This influences other team members to also engage in risk-taking, which allows creative culture to flourish. When faced with difficult problems, the organization often adopts an approach that is more focused on revolutionary possibilities and unique solutions.

Agility

Ambiguity is a common feature of everyday life in an Entrepreneurial Culture. Team members can effectively deal with workplace uncertainty, and this makes for great entrepreneurs with unique visions and complex approaches. Entrepreneurial teams pride themselves on using less structured tasks to make room for more creative and non-conventional approaches.

Any risky and/or high-effort task is right down the team's alley, as employees are willing to dedicate time and effort to make sure all tasks are carried out impeccably. When addressing projects and conflicts, teams always have alternative solutions to any problems they may face, allowing everyone to quickly get back on track.

Given the turbulent nature of today's businesses, entrepreneurial culture adapts fairly quickly to turbulent times through creativity and innovation. Meetings are often an opportunity to discuss the importance of having multiple solutions to a problem. Different approaches are used to address change, whether it be in the market or in the organization, and this promotes fast adaptability. As such, the workplace is looked at as a 'tent' rather than as a 'palace', meaning everything is temporary and subject to change when necessary. Finally, Entrepreneurial culture does not encourage centralized power or authoritative relationships. Instead, power goes to whoever can best adapt to situations and deal with them head-on.

Summary

Overall, entrepreneurial culture promotes creativity and fearless innovation, and this allows teams to pull through in times of uncertainty. Moreover, team members help each other feel confident in their ability to progress and improve. Everyone on the team adapts well to uncertain situations, as stressful situations are dealt with calmly and readily. This culture is admirable in that it encourages employees to reach new limits and discover their potential.

B. CUSTOMER-CENTRIC CULTURE

"We see our customers as invited guests to the party, and we are the hosts. It's our job everyday to make every important aspect of the customer experience a little bit better." – Jeff Bezos

Executive Summary:

Customer-Centric ("CC") organizations place customers at the center of key decisions. Customer feedback and customer's needs/wants are at the heart of everything they do.Employees put their best foot forward when tackling any customer-related problems, and they strive to exceed customer expectations.

This culture focuses on customer service, customer satisfaction, and customer expectations, and the organization strives to always exceed customer-centric targets.

Deep Dive:

A Customer-Centric organization focuses on its customers, and its main attributes include creative problem solving, ongoing improvement, and effective communication.

The team works towards prioritizing customers and their subsequent needs, desires, and wishes at all times. As a collective, the team continuously strives to exceed customer expectations.

Three main attributes characterize the CC culture:

Creative Problem Solving and Incremental Wins

CC Teams master the ability to handle any problem head-on while always keeping customers in mind. Most team members do so in a way that's creative and unexpected, making sure customer satisfaction is always high. Moreover, incremental and continuous improvement are key when keeping pace with the market trends. Rather than focusing on what competitors are doing or what the company has done in the past, the team navigates itself towards customers and the fulfillment of their needs.

Customer demands are always a priority, and a CC Culture thrives when customers' expectations are exceeded. Moreover, CC organizations aim to solve customer problems by way of thorough understanding that generates creative solutions. As such, teams start and end their days by focusing on customer feedback. When producing and evaluating products and services, it is not the CEO or production manager who calls the shots, but rather customer feedback. This ensures that customer requests and complaints are taken into account, and customers are involved in every step of the process, with loyal customers even considered to be part of the organization. Factors of success within this organizational culture include a consideration of customer feedback and an incremental improvement of customer satisfaction.

Customer-Driven Adaptability

CC organizations are willing to adapt to change since nothing can be set-in-stone when it comes to customer demand. Customer demands and customer feedback are used as key inputs when improving or developing new products and services that compete well in the market space. Moreover, a main goal for the organization is to always have high-level performance and impeccable internal communication, both within the organization and externally, with clients.

The team recognizes the importance of having loyal customers who can be counted on and who can count on the organization in return. Within this culture, customer service is impeccable, and organizations are well-known for treating customers with respect and giving them the importance they deserve. As such, the success of the company depends on the feedback received from external parties. When dealing with complaints, designated departments take them in, process them, and amend anything that needs to be changed in order to meet customer needs. The number of complaints, recalls, refunds, replacements, etc. are key performance indicators that are targeted for eradication. Teams will get to the bottom of all possible hiccups and work on their resolution.

Strategic

Technological advances are the leading cause of a constantly changing market customer needs. In order to remain up-to-date with these changes, in CC cultures, the customer is at the forefront and is the key determining factor in the overall organization's forward-looking strategic direction, vision, mission, goals, and products/services. Accordingly, the customers' continuous feedback and input are what drive key decisions, such as evaluating and selecting features when designing new products/services. Whether introducing new products/services or improving existing ones, the feedback received from customers is vital and a key determinant before such products/services are offered to the public for CC organizations.

Customer-facing departments (e.g., customer service, marketing, sales) work with internal functions and departments (e.g., manufacturing, engineering, design, production) harmoniously, in order to ensure that anything targeted towards customers actually fulfills their needs and that any customer feedback, whether positive or negative, is always prioritized in a feedback loop.

Summary

As a whole, the organization creates a culture that prioritizes customers' wants and expectations. Customers appreciate how much the team values them and know they can always count on the organization to take their feedback into consideration and truly give them what they need. Long-time customers stay loyal to the organization because they know it's very unlikely for them to be disappointed with what they receive, whether it be flawless customer service, a product/service they truly need, or a place in the organization where they feel important and valued. Ultimately, teams prefer to work on filling in gaps when it comes to customer needs, as opposed to generating products and services that merely meet organizational goals.

C. COMPETITIVE CULTURE

"If you don't have a competitive advantage, don't compete." – Jack Welch

Executive Summary:

In Competitive Culture, the organization prides itself on being competitive and aggressive in its approach towards success. Teams present themselves as tough and intimidating. They have demanding ways of getting things done.

Stretch goals are actively set and high targets are actively pursued, allowing the team to thrive under competitive circumstances.

Winning is a dominant objective, and the focus of the organization is on external competitors and marketplace positions.

Team members are considered to be workaholics. Peers are commended for being task-oriented and work-focused, as the only way to get things done is hard work.

Deep Dive:

Competitive organizations aim to aggressively and vigorously outrank the competition. Everyone within such a culture is energetic with a thirst for achievement which makes such teams tough contenders in competitive markets.

The characteristics of a Competitive Culture are:

Competitiveness

A Competitive culture is driven by staying ahead of the competition and by continuously benchmarking and tracking

competitors' performance. Extensive time and effort are put into making sure everyone is up to date with the latest research on market trends and developments. Accordingly, competitive organizations quickly look into new products and services that hit the market.

Teams and employees are enthusiastic about beating their competition. In some organizations, daily meetings consist of setting aggressively high targets or checking them off as 'complete'. Within this culture, it's very unlikely to encounter team members or team leaders who are intimidated by competitors, as they are typically driven by competition and a winning attitude. Moreover, teams don't shy away from exploring new niches if they know it's something that can beat their competitors.

Performance and Achievement

Work always comes first for Competitive Culture, and teams are able to reach their goals as dedicated team members who are constantly working towards excellence. High ambitions reign dominant within such an environment where a strategy focused on dominating the market is a top priority. Team meetings and projects often revolve around finding and monetizing off of as many marketplace sub-niches as possible. This occurs via the production of high-quality products and services, as competitive organizations consider anything below the team's best efforts to be unacceptable.

Employees are expected to have a natural ability to work well under pressure and adhere to strict deadlines. If anything goes wrong, those responsible should be ready to accept the blame and take charge in order to provide proper solutions and make sure that mistakes are not repeated.

Motivation

Leaders in Competitive Culture organizations are concerned with pushing everyone towards achieving world-class competitive performance. On that basis, clear visions, goals, and objectives drive the key performance indicators of teams, units and individual

employees. Targets are set by monitoring competitors closely and performance is measured according to how well the organization does against the competition. Team members know what's expected of them, and they know they will be recognized when targets are reached.

Tackling challenges is a daily practice within a competitive culture, as it promotes high-reaching tasks and goals. There's a strong emphasis on competitiveness throughout the organization with a drive to consistently outperform competitors. Everyone involved is tested when it comes to their skills, responsibilities and autonomy. This leaves no room for anything except improvement.

The leadership of such organizations bolsters a highly competitive environment that energizes and keeps employees on their toes. Team members are often rewarded and commended for their hard work, to keep work functioning rigorously in a fast-paced and intense work culture where high achievers always shine.

Summary

Overall, Competitive Culture gives way to a stringent and driven work ethic, leaving no room for failure. Emphasis is placed on high-performance in the workplace where the bar is set high and overachievers shine. Team members are more than willing to be daring when setting and achieving those high targets. Within this culture, rewards outweigh hard work, and that is what keeps organization members going.

D. PROCESS CULTURE

"A leader is one who knows the way, goes the way and shows the way." – John C. Maxwell

Executive Summary:

Consistency and uniformity are well-entrenched in Process Culture organizations, through the adoption of systematic and structured approaches. Employees work with textbook processes and feel confident knowing that desired results can be achieved when following procedures.

Continuous improvement is often prioritized through systematic, careful, and thorough steps forward. Everyone on the team works well by following specific processes and procedures, in order to attain precise and predictable results.

Process Culture teams are known for being dependable and reliable. Day-to-day tasks focus on situational engineering, monitoring and evaluation and ensuring that order and structure are always maintained.

Maintaining high productivity, efficiency, consistency, and quality are considered key factors to success, thus are continuously monitored and reported on. When problems occur or targets are missed, they are tackled by adopting conventional and best practice methods with zero tolerance for risk-taking in the process.

Deep Dive:

Teams exhibit exemplary levels of self-awareness and, in turn, copious degrees of self-knowledge. These two traits are intertwined and are considered key when adopting and maintaining Process Culture. Furthermore, other key attributes are punctuality and time management.

The characteristics of a Process Culture are:

Control and Structure

Process Cultures are bounded by clearly defined organization structures, reporting relationships, chain of commands, job descriptions, processes, procedures, and well-articulated visions/missions and values. Control measures are typically in place to continuously ensure stability, productivity, quality, and consistency as well as monitor and maintain accountability.

Everyone knows who and what they are responsible for and who they should be reporting to, all while adhering to the values and direction of the organization, as these two factors are at the center of any steps taken forward. Emphasis is placed on ensuring a predictable and secure work environment, and where activities are continuously monitored and measured against performance criteria that are designed to maintain efficiency and smooth-running operations.

Processes and Procedures

Employees in Process Culture organizations work according to a well-developed set of standards and principles that help guide their behavior and communication. Everything is highly organized and systematic with clearly defined processes and procedures governing everything employees do.

The team fits and works well together and team members have no trouble integrating themselves into the work setting when they adopt and follow the rules, regulations, processes and procedures. Accordingly, teams work well when adequate monitoring systems and measurement procedures are in place.

Employees within such organizations are highly dependable, well-coordinated, and extremely organized. In the unlikely event that projects or tasks go astray, Process Culture teams would not fall victim to anxiety and stress, as they are able to develop solutions that minimize-risk and guarantee outcomes. This level of collective emotional intelligence is what allows Process Culture organizations to consistently improve.

Time Management, Consistency, and Quality

Time management and effective scheduling of tasks are important factors for Process Culture organizations, and time spent wastefully is not tolerated. Effective time-management and productivity tools/methods such as keeping track of time, making to-do lists, and prioritizing tasks, are often adopted to help organization members structure and complete their tasks on time. Being punctual and having impeccable time management skills are important parts of this culture.

Productivity, efficiency, consistency, and quality are typically the benchmarks of success in such organizations. Procrastination is frowned upon, and encouragement is ever-present, as colleagues push each other to complete tasks efficiently and productively. For example, priorities may be constantly discussed to determine what is truly important and immediate. Moreover, consistency is key, particularly when it comes to quality. A key success factor of Process Cultures is having reliable systems in place that continuously monitor, measure, report, and ensure the consistent delivery of high-quality products and service excellence.

Summary

Overall, this is a culture centered around processes and control, and its participants strive to enforce structure even amidst chaotic circumstances. Employees understand what is expected of them, what organizational culture and standards look like, and what best fits team members within their respective work settings. People are comfortable with routine tasks and feel safe and secure knowing exactly what to do when they come to work in the morning. Moreover, Process Culture teams handle difficult situations with ease, as they enforce structure over challenging issues. The organization has a clear hierarchy and a clearly-defined chain of command that follows clear-cut standards and utilizes comprehensive means of performance measurement and evaluation, and all this leaves little room for failure.

E. EMPOWERMENT CULTURE

"Leadership is about empowering others to achieve things they did not think possible." - Simon Sinek

Executive Summary:

Empowerment Culture emphasizes cooperation and inclusion across functional and organizational boundaries, with a focus on empowering employees and making sure they accept their responsibilities and manage their work with full autonomy.

In this culture, high levels of 'delegation of authority' are compensated by means of emphasizing sound data analysis and analytics when seeking authorization of key and major decisions. This is achieved by ensuring that adequate data is made available through the continuous and constant flow of accurate information and frequent (dynamic) reporting.

Employees take on an all-hands-on-deck approach when accomplishing tasks, and this makes everyone feel valued and needed.

Interpersonal and cross-functional coordination are key factors in keeping things running smoothly and efficiently.

Deep Dive:

Autonomy is considered to be the best means of improvement when building a strong, empowerment-centered organization. When team members feel confident and believe in their potential, their sense of inclusion within the organization is heightened, and they feel more qualified to occupy their respective positions. Moreover, communication runs effectively throughout the Empowerment Culture organizations. Proven results, accurate reporting, coordination, and transparency are key when it comes to keeping underlying collective values and behaviors aligned.

A more laissez-faire approach consisting of the following key attributes is adopted in such a culture:

Empowerment

There is a high level of autonomy present within Empowerment Culture organizations, so team members tend to diagnose their own strengths and weaknesses and take on tasks that they know will play to their advantage. Moreover, team members usually overcome their weaknesses on their own, and this further reinforces empowerment culture. An effort is made to ensure that tasks assigned to subordinates match their capabilities and capacity. This allows work to be balanced at all times, as members are very rarely overworked or unsure of what is expected of them. The fact that everyone is actively involved in their respective departments fosters a lot of self-confidence and allows people to discover hidden talents and new potential. Within Empowerment Culture, people are just as responsible for their successes as they are for their failures.

As teams take on decisions and key tasks that are vital to the organization, this delegation of authority that comes with Empowerment Culture shifts the responsibility to individual units/teams and team members, and they are then expected to commit to key performance indicators targets and continuously report their performance to higher-ups and stakeholders (e.g., owners, shareholders, executives, etc.). As such, delegation is typically sustained and goes hand-in-hand with high levels of coordination among units and functions, requiring the entire organization to work more coherently as a unit. This is only achievable when organization members are in alignment when it comes to tasks and projects, daily communication, and goals to be attained.

Analytics

In an Empowerment Culture, the increased level of autonomy and the emphasis 'delegation of authority' are both typically sustained when strategies are backed by analytical decision-making based on sound analysis. This is especially the case when it comes to high-stakes decision-making by higher-level stakeholders (e.g., owners, shareholders, executives, headquarters). Teams and individual team members are required to do their homework when it comes to seeking approval on key decisions such as acquiring key resources and/or seeking major investments.

Therefore, with empowerment comes a necessary fact-checking of information, as to accuracy and meticulousness that help sustain such cultures. For example, when employees come together to pitch ideas, recommendations, or solutions, control measures and constraints are eliminated when the analysis is solid, the information is well backed and the content is presented in a clear and concise manner. This helps put people at ease and keeps team members motivated, stimulated, and oriented towards specific goals.

Inclusivity

In Empowerment Cultures, employees of all departments and levels are actively involved in decision-making and participate in deciding the strategic direction of the organization as a whole. Both teams and individuals are aware of and accountable for their actions. As a result, people feel valued and appreciated, and if there ever comes a time when control needs to be handed over, it is usually done so without a fault due to the inclusivity and coordination present within this culture.

Team members and units consistently share their ideas and thoughts with others. Collaboration with other departments, teams and units is highly encouraged. Mechanisms are usually in place to allow everyone's thoughts and ideas to be heard, collected, and taken seriously through active participation in decision-making. This is made possible by empowering everyone in the organization across functions (horizontal lines) and levels (vertical lines) to speak up,

and by facilitating the flow of information throughout the organization.

Summary

Overall, team members accept their responsibilities and take them seriously. Within empowerment culture, organization members are comfortable sharing their ideas and recommendations and, subsequently, their best qualities are brought forward. When tasks are handed down, so are their associated responsibilities. This allows members to grow and discover their potential as leaders, managers, and heads of departments. Communication is the most successful attribute, and employees don't shy away from sharing ideas, notes, or remarks in order to ensure multilevel efficiency. This culture thrives on delegation, and the ability of power to flow easily throughout the organization reinforces inclusivity.

F. TEAMWORK CULTURE

"Leadership is a way of thinking, a way of acting, and most importantly, a way of communicating." - Simon Sinek

Executive Summary:

Teamwork organizations are focused on setting comfortable and inclusive spaces to help transform and aid their members.

Teamwork-driven organizations emphasize collective involvement in decision-making and problem-solving. As such, participation, openness, morale, and commitment are consistently pursued within teamwork cultures. The environment is people-oriented and people-friendly, so managing conflict and seeking consensus is of the utmost importance.

The culture is one of care and empathy. Team members are aware of others and their needs, and they exhibit mutual respect and trust towards each other.

Supportive communication and the management of interpersonal relationships come naturally to teamwork-driven organizations, and they are able to do so while understanding problems and responding to them with the needed support and mentorship. This allows the organization to feel a lot like an extended family.

Deep Dive:

Teamwork Culture focuses on the well-being of others when it comes to workspace interactions. Mentor-mentee relationships are easily established, and it is considered important to always provide others with the necessary feedback for improvement. Some common actions that take place include praising, encouraging, and uplifting

194

others, as it is necessary to highlight the skills and strengths of peers.

Some common behaviors found within Teamwork Culture include:

Interpersonal Relationships

There is usually a build-up of interpersonal relationships in the workplace. Positive relationships have shown to create positive energy, as one feels safe and secure within their workspace. These healthy relationships offer a multitude of physiological, emotional, intellectual, and social benefits, and team members are less likely to experience feelings of anxiety, frustration, or uncertainty. Furthermore, within a positive workplace, employees are more likely to turn to each other and consequently, work more productively. Employees feel competent in their work, as their successes are recognized and celebrated.

Studies have shown that when employees have a more positive outlook on their jobs, their attention spans increase, their memories improve and their decision-making skills are heightened. Furthermore, employees functioning within a positive workspace learn more efficiently and make fewer mental errors. As a result, interactions between team members are more productive, as they are more likely to exchange knowledge and advice with one another.

Communication and Openness

This collaborative workplace culture encourages everyone to work harder and smarter, as specific feedback is regularly provided. It is well-known that in order to help the organization reach its true potential, corrective behavior is necessary. This is done in a positive/respectful manner, and it ends on an encouraging note.

Peers within Teamwork Culture often practice supportive communication, as they interact with confidence, trust, and openness with one another when the organization is functioning well. This is even the case when it comes to correcting negative behavior, pointing out shortcomings, and delivering negative feedback, as these challenging situations are addressed with ease.

Managing Conflicts and Collaboration

Teamwork creates an environment whereby employees recognize the importance of dealing with conflict head-on to ensure openness and honesty and so that relationships remain intact. When problems arise, teams are encouraged to communicate respectfully without lashing out.

When conflict arises, teamwork culture emphasizes the use of multiple solutions and the sharing of common goals to maintain the power balance and ensure that all agreements are reached unanimously. Teamwork differentiates people from their problems by clarifying mutual benefits to be gained when addressing potential conflicts. As such, teamwork employees and managers use objective criteria when evaluating alternatives and determining what is fair.

Mentoring

When teamwork culture is achieved and maintained, it enables and encourages the development of mentoring among coworkers. Within such a culture, employees address stressful situations with confidence and high esteem. Having a mentor-mentee relationship is important, as it's proven to be mutually beneficial for both parties. Employees gain a wide range of information and skills from their mentors, while managers benefit from reduced stress. Subsequently, mentor-mentee trust improves, cooperation increases, and teamwork becomes smoother. A mentor's guidance can help employees avoid stressful situations and cope when necessary.

Team Development and Team Building

Working as a team helps everyone in the organization better understand their own strengths and those of their peers. Performance runs more smoothly and efficiently, and project tasks become individualized. Also, teamwork keeps the main goals in focus while employees exhibit trust and integrity throughout their projects. As such, taking on tasks as a team aids in the personal development of all team members and allows employees to further explore their competencies and skills in order to improve within their teams.

The team focuses on building strengths rather than overcoming weaknesses. A Teamwork Culture prioritizes commitment to a vision and the recognition of hard work. As such, gratitude is readily shown, and this contributes towards the creation of a positive work environment where ideas flow abundantly.

Summary

Overall, within Teamwork Culture, organizations are considered to be nurturing and comfortable spaces where colleagues are eager to work every day and are able to reach their full potential. Teamwork fosters a strong sense of team spirit and a positive attitude. The relationship between any two team members can feel like the relationship among family members. The workplace is seen as an environment not only for working but also for forging friendships and connections. When adopting a teamwork culture, organizations emphasize fairness and honesty across all their practices. This is what keeps everything running smoothly and efficiently, making Teamwork culture the one to beat!

ASPIRED ORGANIZATION CULTURE ASSESSMENT WORKBOOK

INTRODUCTION

There are two versions of the aspired culture assessment. One version is meant to be taken by the leader and another should be utilized by the team or unit being assessed. This version is designed to assess the individual responses, i.e. those taken from the perspective of the team or employees being assessed. The aspired culture quiz aims to evaluate the unit's aspirational state considering six of your organization's elements, as described below.

By answering quiz questions, your employees provided responses that reflected their aspirations for their organization—unless their status quo already reflected their aspirations, in which case their aspirations reflected their current state.

That said, both the Aspired Culture's assessment method and its attributes are the same as those of the Culture Archetype Assessment. Nevertheless, they've been added here to save you the trouble of referring to another document when reviewing your quiz assessment results.

In the context of organizational culture, we define organizational culture as the beliefs, values, mindsets and practices of a group of people (whether an entire organization or a subset thereof) within an organization. Decades of wide-reaching empirical evidence have proven undisputedly, that organizational cultures have a major impact on company performance. If you have ever led a team, department, business unit, or company, you may have reflected upon the role that organizational culture plays when it comes to overall performance. As such, it is important to mention that the relationship between an organization's culture and its performance has been the leading cause of industry and corporation fallouts, no matter the prestige of the conglomerates at hand.

For example, if we look at the organizational cultures within the steel industry and their subsequent resistance to change, we would see that they have prevented American steel companies from innovating

199

and modernizing. This has led to their subsequent domination by Korean, Japanese, and European producers. More recent examples include the fallout of the newspaper industry and the retail apocalypse. Because organizational culture has been influenced by industry functioning, organizations have failed to find a balance between traditional and new activities. The reason behind this is that leaders have not adequately responded to the uncertainty brought about by changes within the external environment. An example of such changes is the tension between the old organizational culture—that of monopoly newspapers and 20% profit margins—and the new organizational culture which emerged from disruptive changes in the industry. The same can be said about retail giants such as *Sears, Radioshack, Toys R Us* and *Blockbuster.*

Organizational culture creates friction and tension between groups, as whenever ten or more people share a space that allows them to engage in a multitude of dynamics, an entire collective culture emerges within a very short period of time. Furthermore, more recent evidence has come to light regarding organizational culture requirements and the subsequent work environments they generate. These studies were conducted across all industry sectors, within many international settings, and for every organization type. Accordingly, research shows that different organizations need to adopt their own specific cultures—there isn't one that works for all. In parallel, various factors need to be taken into consideration such as the growth stage, the market and competitive dynamics of the industry, and the organization's vision, mission, and strategy.

For example, a startup organization with a small team of founders and new-hires is likely to be entrepreneurial in its culture and functions with much agility and flexibility. As the organization grows in size, its original entrepreneurial culture would not be sustained in the long-term, as more measures and processes would be taken to ensure long-lasting growth. Also, as new hires import cultures from former to current places of employment, a new dominant culture emerges and becomes the norm.

The purpose of this workbook is to provide all members of an organization with information regarding what it means to be part of a specific work culture. It should be noted that this workbook is intended for leaders, managers, employees and anyone actively involved in running organizations, as each of these parties contributes towards creating and maintaining organizational cultures. We hope that, by the end of this workbook, readers would have gained vital information that allows organizations to better understand what way of work suits them, what form of authority they prefer and what truly drives them towards working well together and reaching their desired goals.

LIMITATIONS OF NON-PRO VERSION

The paper version of the quiz, despite containing the same questions as those of the "Pro" version, is more limited in its capacities. This is because the Pro quiz is designed in a manner that utilizes nested processing, as questions are continuously generated according to previous results. As such, unlike its pencil-paper counterpart, the Pro version contains built-in intelligence that allows for more thorough, complex analysis.

Within today's market, traditional employee surveys rarely have the built-in capacities that allow for complex business and managerial investigations to occur. This is why many of these surveys produce results that do not accurately reflect the reality of the situation. Consequently, these questionnaires seldom provide their users with a precise understanding of organizational gaps and challenges and, subsequently, hinder processes such as transformation and change management. Another drawback of conventional surveys is the number of complications that occur when administering and collecting information. These obstacles challenge surveys' ability to measure progress over a short period of time and to produce an accurate portrayal of the organization's reality.

Despite the aforementioned limitations of the non-Pro version, it still generates more information than most surveys out there do and can, subsequently, identify the primary, secondary, and tertiary dominant aspired culture Archetypes. As discussed later and in the PMAS book, the quiz is structured in a manner that allows for any potential bias to be limited via the types of answer options in the multiple-choice section.

The Pro version, on the other hand, can reveal all primary, secondary and tertiary archetypes with more precision and can be easily administered with the click of a button. Furthermore, the Pro's results can be measured accurately and rapidly, on a monthly basis. If you have not signed up for the Pro version, you can do so by following up with Business Model Hackers through the account generated alongside this book's purchase.

INTERPRETING RESULTS

The answer choices provided in the quiz are structured in such a way as to capture various aspired cultural attributes. This was done in accordance with the concept of paradoxicality, as discussed in the PMAS book, in order to effectively reduce human bias. For more details and background information on how the quiz was structured, please refer to the main PMAS book.

The assessment for each Archetype (whether primary, secondary, or tertiary) is provided separately and divided into two sections: The Executive Summary and the Detailed Assessment.

The (Aspired) Culture Archetypes

A paradox mindset highlights the extent to which individuals embrace tensions. This is because the adoption of a paradox mindset can help people leverage tensions and produce creative outputs. However, most people tend to have a preference for one direction over the other, which is why they experience cognitive dissonance when they are pulled towards opposing extremes. Yet, research suggests that these conflicts can often work in a person's favor. Several studies conducted by psychologists and organizational researchers have found that people who learn to embrace, rather than reject, opposing sides of a paradox display more creativity, flexibility and productivity, as duality can lead to enhanced overall performance.

The (aspired) Culture Archetype Assessment design follows a structure that presents values in opposing axes across two key dimensions, Agility and Orientation, which are further broken down into six subcategories. These subcategories are grouped into three paradoxical pairs along the two main axes as shown below. Accordingly, the six Culture Archetypes are as follows:

A. Entrepreneurial: The Entrepreneurial Culture Archetype is characterized by innovation and trendsetting activities. The

work environment is dynamic and agile, and creativity, risk-taking, and innovation are encouraged and rewarded. Employees take pride in their unique work execution, and they are typically driven by ulterior motives, such as a desire to positively change the world and/or disrupt the markets that they serve.

B. **Customer-Centric**: The Customer-Centric Culture Archetype is characterized by its focus on customers, as they weigh in heavily on organizational decisions and influence the organization's strategic direction. The work environment encourages incremental innovation and creative problem-solving, and employees are typically driven by the desire to please customers and provide products/services that exceed customers' expectations.

C. **Competitive**: The Competitive Culture Archetype is one that is driven by marketplace competitors. Its work environment practices meritocracy, encourages high achievements, and rewards performance. Competition, benchmarks, and market trends drive the organization's strategic direction. Employees continuously monitor their markets and are motivated by the desire to achieve excellence and to consistently beat their competitors.

D. **Process**: The Process Culture Archetype is one that is driven by clearly defined processes and procedures, in an environment that is organized, hierarchical and structured. Stability, consistency, and quality drive the organization's day-to-day operations. Employees know exactly what's expected of them, and they are motivated by job security and by their ability to perform and deliver exactly what's expected of them.

E. **Empowerment**: The Empowerment Culture Archetype is one that is driven by empowerment and accountability, in a work environment that emphasizes inclusivity and accountability. A "laissez-faire" approach characterized by the delegation of authority is what drives the organization's management. Employees have a sense of purpose and always feel included in key decisions. Two factors motivate the employees of such a culture: an acceptance of responsibility and an autonomous management of their work.

F. Teamwork: The Teamwork Culture Archetype is one that is based on active participation and openness. Two factors drive the organization forward: a teamwork-based approach, and individual team members' collective involvement in the workplace. Such an environment is very people-friendly, and its members feel like an extended family. Employees know that they are able to achieve greatness by means of having their individual capabilities leveraged equally with those of everyone else, so they are motivated when working as a unit.

Each Culture Archetype is detailed in the next section.

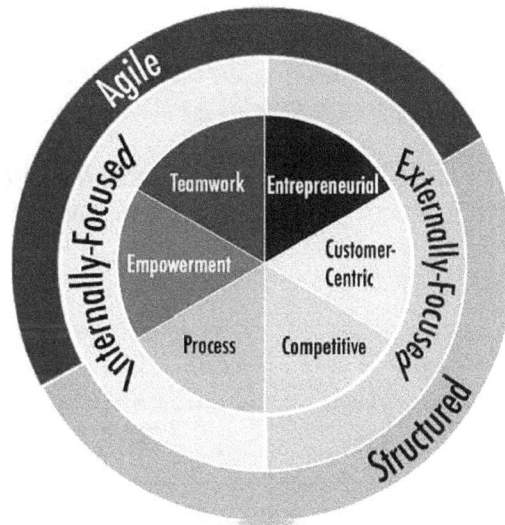

Scoring

Scoring the quiz is simple and requires you to add up the points from the six different sections and the total in each category (ranging from A-F). Accordingly, whichever category ranks the highest indicates the most dominant aspired culture archetype. Below, you'll find tables that you can use to help with the scoring process; you will also find 6 tables representing the 6 different categories (A-F).

Answers for questions 1-6 are each worth 14 points. Please note that question 7 is worth 16 points.

For example, if 'A' were chosen for questions 3, 5, and 7, 14 points would be placed in rows 3 and 5 in the first table, and 16 points would be placed in row 7 for that same table. Follow through with the tables according to the quiz answers. Any number-letter combination that does not have an answer is worth 0 points and, subsequently, has a score of "0."

Eventually, you will be able to add up the scores in each table, and the table containing the highest total indicates the primary aspired culture archetype.

Below, you will find the designated letters that correspond to six different aspired culture archetypes.

Under each title, you will find an executive summary and more details on the attributes of each aspired culture archetype.

A	Score
1A	
2A	
3A	
4A	
5A	
6A	
7A	

B	Score
1B	
2B	
3B	
4B	
5B	
6B	
7B	

C	Score
1C	
2C	
3C	
4C	
5C	
6C	
7C	

Total	
Total	

Total	

Total	

D	Score
1D	
2D	
3D	
4D	
5D	
6D	
7D	
Total	

E	Score
1E	
2E	
3E	
4E	
5E	
6E	
7E	
Total	

F	Score
1F	
2F	
3F	
4F	
5F	
6F	
7F	
Total	

Plotting your Score

If you purchased the Pro version of the PMAS, the results are automatically plotted for you on a Radar Pie Chart. On the other hand, if you administered the quiz via paper or webforms, you can use a spreadsheet tool to plot the results and acquire the relative score of each Archetype, as shown below.

The plots for this quiz are then overlaid on top of the plots from other quizzes to compare them in terms of target states and aspired scores. For more information on which comparisons are relevant and how to interpret the gaps for each comparison, please refer to the PMAS eBook.

Found below are examples of how graphical representation can provide insight into assessments—in particular when performing comparisons with other metrics.

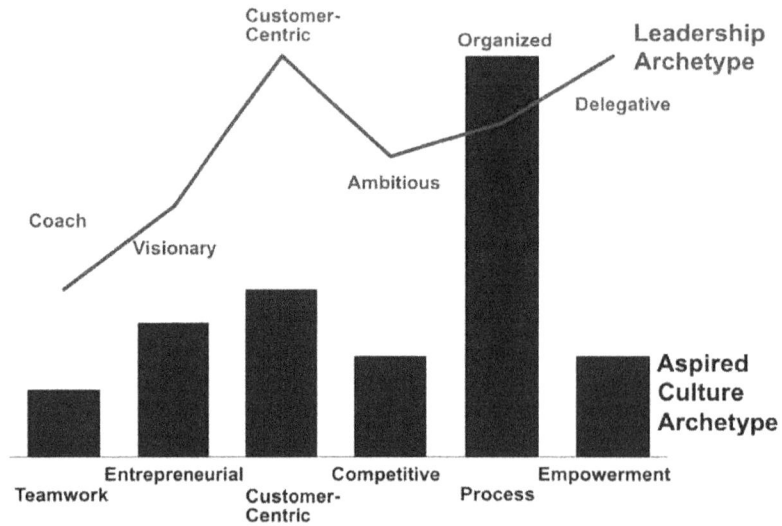

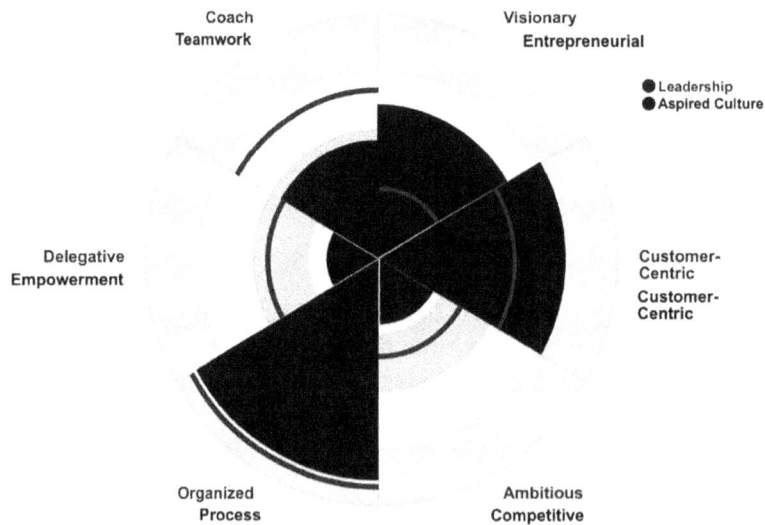

A. ENTREPRENEURIAL CULTURE

"Creative thinking inspires ideas. Ideas inspire change." – Barbara Januszkiewicz

Executive Summary:

Continuous innovation and creativity are at the heart of Entrepreneurial organizational cultures. Organizational goals are usually met in inventive, uncharacteristic ways.

Employees within such organizations are consistently bending and breaking the rules in order to reach unprecedented results in unconventional ways.

Change (internal and external) is easy for such organizations, as colleagues continuously find themselves in a multitude of situations that allow them to be adaptable.

Deep Dive:

Entrepreneurial Culture emphasizes exploring and perfecting cutting-edge approaches that allow companies to reach their goals. Colleagues are constantly reminded how satisfying it is to see results through exciting new methods; consequently, creative culture is created that allows everyone to exceed their limits and let their creativity run loose. If tasks aren't completed in an unconventional way, they simply haven't met the mark.

In Entrepreneurial Culture, three characteristics shine through:

Innovation

Team members are commended for being outside-the-box thinkers, innovative hard workers, and creative problem-solvers. Entrepreneurial workplace culture leaves no room for routine, and the team prides itself on having a high degree of aesthetic

209

sensitivity. They work well with each other and feed off of their shared passion for creativity and uniqueness when completing tasks. In Entrepreneurial Cultures, people openly share their ideas and innovations with others and adopt radical approaches when tackling problems.

The path to an end goal is anything but traditional within this culture, as team members are encouraged to rely on intuition above all and subsequently take pleasure in breaking rules. Team meetings usually allow people to stumble upon their best ideas when they least expect them.

Entrepreneurship

Fostering an entrepreneurial mindset among team members is important for such cultures. Leaders often encourage their team members to bring forth their own ideas and to pursue their own goals. Furthermore, Entrepreneurial culture encourages employees to "put it all on the table" in order to commit to visions and follow through with what they think works for the organization.

Team meetings have employees bouncing ideas off each other, as individuals readily speak up about the path they wish to take and how they aim to develop their own ideas. In such an entrepreneurial environment, It's very rare for individual and collective creativity/ideas to be rejected, thus creating an endless flow of ideas, projects, creativity, and risk-taking.

This culture encourages managers and employees to utilize their vivid imaginations to create new ideas. As such, problem-solving takes place via breakthroughs and the adoption of radical approaches. In such a culture, it is essential to engage both experimentation and speculation, as this provides the organization with endless possibilities. Moreover, those who propose risky yet exciting ideas are applauded for their creative efforts. This influences other team members to also engage in risk-taking, which allows creative culture to flourish. When faced with difficult problems, the organization often adopts an approach that is more focused on revolutionary possibilities and unique solutions.

Agility

Ambiguity is a common feature of everyday life in an Entrepreneurial Culture. Team members can effectively deal with workplace uncertainty, and this makes for great entrepreneurs with unique visions and complex approaches. Entrepreneurial teams pride themselves on using less structured tasks to make room for more creative and non-conventional approaches.

Any risky and/or high-effort task is right down the team's alley, as employees are willing to dedicate time and effort to make sure all tasks are carried out impeccably. When addressing projects and conflicts, teams always have alternative solutions to any problems they may face, allowing everyone to quickly get back on track.

Given the turbulent nature of today's businesses, entrepreneurial culture adapts fairly quickly to turbulent times through creativity and innovation. Meetings are often an opportunity to discuss the importance of having multiple solutions to a problem. Different approaches are used to address change, whether it be in the market or in the organization, and this promotes fast adaptability. As such, the workplace is looked at as a 'tent' rather than as a 'palace', meaning everything is temporary and subject to change when necessary. Finally, Entrepreneurial culture does not encourage centralized power or authoritative relationships. Instead, power goes to whoever can best adapt to situations and deal with them head-on.

Summary

Overall, entrepreneurial culture promotes creativity and fearless innovation, and this allows teams to pull through in times of uncertainty. Moreover, team members help each other feel confident in their ability to progress and improve. Everyone on the team adapts well to uncertain situations, as stressful situations are dealt with calmly and readily. This culture is admirable in that it encourages employees to reach new limits and discover their potential.

B. CUSTOMER-CENTRIC CULTURE

"We see our customers as invited guests to the party, and we are the hosts. It's our job everyday to make every important aspect of the customer experience a little bit better." – Jeff Bezos

Executive Summary:

Customer-Centric ("CC") organizations place customers at the center of key decisions. Customer feedback and customer's needs/wants are at the heart of everything they do.

Employees put their best foot forward when tackling any customer-related problems, and they strive to exceed customer expectations.

This culture focuses on customer service, customer satisfaction, and customer expectations, and the organization strives to always exceed customer-centric targets.

Deep Dive:

A Customer-Centric organization focuses on its customers, and its main attributes include creative problem solving, ongoing improvement, and effective communication.

The team works towards prioritizing customers and their subsequent needs, desires, and wishes at all times. As a collective, the team continuously strives to exceed customer expectations.

Three main attributes characterize the CC culture:

Creative Problem Solving and Incremental Wins

CC Teams master the ability to handle any problem head-on while always keeping customers in mind. Most team members do so in a way that's creative and unexpected, making sure customer satisfaction is always high. Moreover, incremental and continuous improvement are key when keeping pace with the market trends. Rather than focusing on what competitors are doing or what the company has done in the past, the team navigates itself towards customers and the fulfillment of their needs.

Customer demands are always a priority, and a CC Culture thrives when customers' expectations are exceeded. Moreover, CC organizations aim to solve customer problems by way of thorough understanding that generates creative solutions. As such, teams start and end their days by focusing on customer feedback. When producing and evaluating products and services, it is not the CEO or production manager who calls the shots, but rather customer feedback. This ensures that customer requests and complaints are taken into account, and customers are involved in every step of the process, with loyal customers even considered to be part of the organization. Factors of success within this organizational culture include a consideration of customer feedback and incremental improvement of customer satisfaction.

Customer-Driven Adaptability

CC organizations are willing to adapt to change since nothing can be set-in-stone when it comes to customer demand. Customer demands and customer feedback are used as key inputs when improving or developing new products and services that compete well in the market space. Moreover, a main goal for the organization is to always have high-level performance and impeccable internal communication, both within the organization and externally, with clients.

The team recognizes the importance of having loyal customers who can be counted on and who can count on the organization in return. Within this culture, customer service is impeccable, and organizations are well-known for treating customers with respect and giving them the importance they deserve. As such, the success of the company depends on the feedback received from external parties. When dealing with complaints, designated departments take them in, process them and amend anything that needs to be changed in order to meet customer needs. The number of complaints, recalls, refunds, replacements, etc. are key performance indicators that are targeted for eradication. Teams will get to the bottom of all possible hiccups and work on their resolution.

Strategic

Technological advances are the leading cause of a constantly changing market customer needs. In order to remain up-to-date with these changes, in CC cultures, the customer is at the forefront and is the key determining factor in the overall organization's forward-looking strategic direction, vision, mission, goals, and products/services. Accordingly, the customers' continuous feedback and input are what drive key decisions such as evaluating and selecting features when designing new products/services. Whether introducing new products/services or improving existing ones, the feedback received from customers is vital and a key determinant before such products/services are offered to the public for CC organizations.

Customer-facing departments (e.g., customer service, marketing, sales) work with internal functions and departments (e.g., manufacturing, engineering, design, production) harmoniously in order to ensure that anything targeted towards customers actually fulfills their needs and that any customer feedback, whether positive or negative, is always prioritized in a feedback loop.

Summary

As a whole, the organization creates a culture that prioritizes customers' wants and expectations. Customers appreciate how much the team values them and know they can always count on the organization to take their feedback into consideration and truly give them what they need. Long-time customers stay loyal to the organization because they know it's very unlikely for them to be disappointed with what they receive, whether it be flawless customer service, a product/service they truly need, or a place in the organization where they feel important and valued. Ultimately, teams prefer to work on filling in gaps when it comes to customer needs, as opposed to generating products and services that merely meet organizational goals.

C. COMPETITIVE CULTURE

"If you don't have a competitive advantage, don't compete." –
Jack Welch

Executive Summary:

In Competitive Culture, the organization prides itself on being competitive and aggressive in its approach towards success. Teams present themselves as tough and intimidating. They have demanding ways of getting things done.

Stretch goals are actively set and high targets are actively pursued, allowing the team to thrive under competitive circumstances.

Winning is a dominant objective, and the focus of the organization is on external competitors and marketplace positions.

Team members are considered to be workaholics. Peers are commended for being task-oriented and work-focused, as the only way to get things done is hard work.

Deep Dive:

Competitive organizations aim to aggressively and vigorously outrank the competition. Everyone within such a culture is energetic with a thirst for achievement which makes such teams tough contenders in competitive markets.

The characteristics of a Competitive Culture are:

Competitiveness

A Competitive culture is driven by staying ahead of the competition and by continuously benchmarking and tracking

215

competitors' performance. Extensive time and effort are put into making sure everyone is up to date with the latest research on market trends and developments. Accordingly, competitive organizations quickly look into new products and services that hit the market.

Teams and employees are enthusiastic about beating their competition. In some organizations, daily meetings consist of setting aggressively high targets or checking them off as 'complete'. Within this culture, it's very unlikely to encounter team members or team leaders who are intimidated by competitors, as they are typically driven by competition and a winning attitude. Moreover, teams don't shy away from exploring new niches if they know it's something that can beat their competitors.

Performance and Achievement

Work always comes first for Competitive Culture, and teams are able to reach their goals as dedicated team members who are constantly working towards excellence. High ambitions reign dominant within such an environment where a strategy focused on dominating the market is a top priority. Team meetings and projects often revolve around finding and monetizing off of as many marketplace sub-niches as possible. This occurs via the production of high-quality products and services, as competitive organizations consider anything below the team's best efforts to be unacceptable.

Employees are expected to have a natural ability to work well under pressure and adhere to strict deadlines. If anything goes wrong, those responsible should be ready to accept the blame and take charge in order to provide proper solutions and make sure that mistakes are not repeated.

Motivation

Leaders in Competitive Culture organizations are concerned with pushing everyone towards achieving world-class competitive performance. On that basis, clear visions, goals, and objectives drive the key performance indicators of teams, units and individual

employees. Targets are set by monitoring competitors closely and performance is measured according to how well the organization does against the competition. Team members know what's expected of them, and they know they will be recognized when targets are reached.

Tackling challenges is a daily practice within a competitive culture, as it promotes high-reaching tasks and goals. There's a strong emphasis on competitiveness throughout the organization with a drive to consistently outperform competitors. Everyone involved is tested when it comes to their skills, responsibilities and autonomy. This leaves no room for anything except improvement.

The leadership of such organizations bolsters a highly competitive environment that energizes and keeps employees on their toes. Team members are often rewarded and commended for their hard work, to keep work functioning rigorously in a fast-paced and intense work culture where high achievers always shine.

Summary

Overall, Competitive Culture gives way to a stringent and driven work ethic, leaving no room for failure. Emphasis is placed on high-performance in the workplace where the bar is set high and overachievers shine. Team members are more than willing to be daring when setting and achieving those high targets. Within this culture, rewards outweigh hard work, and that is what keeps organization members going.

D. PROCESS CULTURE

"A leader is one who knows the way, goes the way and shows the way." – John C. Maxwell

Executive Summary:

Consistency and uniformity are well-entrenched in Process Culture organizations, through the adoption of systematic and structured approaches. Employees work with textbook processes and feel confident knowing that desired results can be achieved when following procedures.

Continuous improvement is often prioritized through systematic, careful, and thorough steps forward. Everyone on the team works well by following specific processes and procedures, in order to attain precise and predictable results.

Process Culture teams are known for being dependable and reliable. Day-to-day tasks focus on situational engineering, monitoring and evaluation and ensuring that order and structure are always maintained.

Maintaining high productivity, efficiency, consistency, and quality are considered key factors to success, thus are continuously monitored and reported on. When problems occur or targets are missed, they are tackled by adopting conventional and best practice methods with zero tolerance for risk-taking in the process.

Deep Dive:

Teams exhibit exemplary levels of self-awareness and, in turn, copious degrees of self-knowledge. These two traits are intertwined and are considered key when adopting and maintaining Process Culture. Furthermore, other key attributes are punctuality and time management.

218

The characteristics of a Process Culture are:

Control and Structure

Process Cultures are bounded by clearly defined organization structures, reporting relationships, chain of commands, job descriptions, processes, procedures, and well-articulated visions/missions and values. Control measures are typically in place to continuously ensure stability, productivity, quality, and consistency as well as monitor and maintain accountability.

Everyone knows who and what they are responsible for and who they should be reporting to, all while adhering to the values and direction of the organization, as these two factors are at the center of any steps taken forward. Emphasis is placed on ensuring a predictable and secure work environment, and where activities are continuously monitored and measured against performance criteria that are designed to maintain efficiency and smooth-running operations.

Processes and Procedures

Employees in Process Culture organizations work according to a well-developed set of standards and principles that help guide their behavior and communication. Everything is highly organized and systematic with clearly defined processes and procedures governing everything employees do.

The team fits and works well together and team members have no trouble integrating themselves into the work setting when they adopt and follow the rules, regulations, processes and procedures. Accordingly, teams work well when adequate monitoring systems and measurement procedures are in place.

Employees within such organizations are highly dependable, well-coordinated, and extremely organized. In the unlikely event that projects or tasks go astray, Process Culture teams would not fall victim to anxiety and stress, as they are able to develop solutions that minimize-risk and guarantee outcomes. This level of collective emotional intelligence is what allows Process Culture organizations to consistently improve.

Time Management, Consistency, and Quality

Time management and effective scheduling of tasks are important factors for Process Culture organizations, and time spent wastefully is not tolerated. Effective time-management and productivity tools/methods such as keeping track of time, making to-do lists, and prioritizing tasks, are often adopted to help organization members structure and complete their tasks on time. Being punctual and having impeccable time management skills are important parts of this culture.

Productivity, efficiency, consistency, and quality are typically the benchmarks of success in such organizations. Procrastination is frowned upon, and encouragement is ever-present, as colleagues push each other to complete tasks efficiently and productively. For example, priorities may be constantly discussed to determine what is truly important and immediate. Moreover, consistency is key, particularly when it comes to quality. A key success factor of Process Cultures is having reliable systems in place that continuously monitor, measure, report, and ensure the consistent delivery of high-quality products and service excellence.

Summary

Overall, this is a culture centered around processes and control, and its participants strive to enforce structure even amidst chaotic circumstances. Employees understand what is expected of them, what organizational culture and standards look like, and what best fits team members within their respective work settings. People are comfortable with routine tasks and feel safe and secure knowing exactly what to do when they come to work in the morning. Moreover, Process Culture teams handle difficult situations with ease, as they enforce structure over challenging issues. The organization has a clear hierarchy and a clearly defined chain of command that follows clear-cut standards and utilizes comprehensive means of performance measurement and evaluation, and all this leaves little room for failure.

E. EMPOWERMENT CULTURE

"Leadership is about empowering others to achieve things they did not think possible." - Simon Sinek

Executive Summary:

Empowerment Culture emphasizes cooperation and inclusion across functional and organizational boundaries with a focus on empowering employees and making sure they accept their responsibilities and manage their work with full autonomy.

In this culture, high-level authority delegation is compensated by means of emphasizing sound data analysis and analytics when seeking authorization of key and major decisions. This is achieved by ensuring that adequate data is made available through the continuous and constant flow of accurate information and frequent (dynamic) reporting.

Employees take on an all-hands-on-deck approach when accomplishing tasks, and this makes everyone feel valued and needed.

Interpersonal and cross-functional coordination are key factors in keeping things running smoothly and efficiently.

Deep Dive:

Autonomy is considered to be the best means of improvement when building a strong, empowerment-centered organization. When team members feel confident and believe in their potential, their sense of inclusion within the organization is heightened, and they feel more qualified to occupy their respective positions. Moreover, communication runs effectively throughout the Empowerment Culture organizations. Proven results, accurate reporting,

221

coordination, and transparency are key when it comes to keeping the underlying collective values and behaviors aligned.

A more laissez-faire approach consisting of the following key attributes is adopted in such a culture:

Empowerment

There is a high level of autonomy present within Empowerment Culture organizations, so team members tend to diagnose their own strengths and weaknesses and take on tasks that they know will play to their advantage. Moreover, team members usually overcome their weaknesses on their own, and this further reinforces empowerment culture. An effort is made to ensure that tasks assigned to subordinates match their capabilities and capacity. This allows work to be balanced at all times, as members are very rarely overworked or unsure of what is expected of them. The fact that everyone is actively involved in their respective departments fosters a lot of self-confidence and allows people to discover hidden talents and new potential. Within Empowerment Culture, people are just as responsible for their successes as they are for their failures.

As teams take on decisions and key tasks that are vital to the organization, this delegation of authority that comes with Empowerment Culture shifts the responsibility to individual units/teams and team members, and they are then expected to commit to key performance indicators targets and continuously report their performance to higher-ups and stakeholders (e.g., owners, shareholders, executives, etc.). As such, delegation is typically sustained and goes hand-in-hand with high levels of coordination among units and functions, requiring the entire organization to work more coherently as a unit. This is only achievable when organization members are in alignment when it comes to tasks and projects, daily communication and goals to be attained.

Analytics

In an Empowerment Culture, the increased level of autonomy and the emphasis on authority delegation are both typically sustained when strategies are backed by analytical decision-making based on sound analysis. This is especially the case when it comes to high-stakes decision-making by higher-level stakeholders (e.g., owners, shareholders, executives, headquarters). Teams and individual team members are required to do their homework when it comes to seeking approvals on key decisions such as acquiring key resources and/or seeking major investments.

Therefore, with empowerment comes a necessary fact-checking of information, as to accuracy and meticulousness that help sustain such cultures. For example, when employees come together to pitch ideas, recommendations, or solutions, control measures and constraints are eliminated when the analysis is solid, the information is well backed and the content is presented in a clear and concise manner. This helps put people at ease and keeps team members motivated, stimulated, and oriented towards specific goals.

Inclusivity

In Empowerment Cultures, employees of all departments and levels are actively involved in decision-making and participate in deciding the strategic direction of the organization as a whole. Both teams and individuals are aware of and accountable for their actions. As a result, people feel valued and appreciated, and if there ever comes a time when control needs to be handed over, it is usually done so without a fault due to the inclusivity and coordination present within this culture.

Team members and units consistently share their ideas and thoughts with others. Collaboration with other departments, teams and units is highly encouraged. Mechanisms are usually in place to allow everyone's thoughts and ideas to be heard, collected, and taken seriously through active participation in decision-making. This is made possible by empowering everyone in the organization across functions (horizontal lines) and levels (vertical lines) to speak up,

and by facilitating the flow of information throughout the organization.

Summary

Overall, team members accept their responsibilities and take them seriously. Within empowerment culture, organization members are comfortable sharing their ideas and recommendations and, subsequently, their best qualities are brought forward. When tasks are handed down, so are their associated responsibilities. This allows members to grow and discover their potential as leaders, managers, and heads of departments. Communication is the most successful attribute, and employees don't shy away from sharing ideas, notes, or remarks in order to ensure multilevel efficiency. This culture thrives on delegation, and the ability of power to flow easily throughout the organization reinforces inclusivity.

F. TEAMWORK CULTURE

"Leadership is a way of thinking, a way of acting, and most importantly, a way of communicating." - Simon Sinek

Executive Summary:

Teamwork organizations are focused on setting comfortable and inclusive spaces to help transform and aid their members.

Teamwork-driven organizations emphasize collective involvement in decision-making and problem-solving. As such, participation, openness, morale, and commitment are consistently pursued within teamwork cultures. The environment is people-oriented and people-friendly, so managing conflict and seeking consensus is of the utmost importance.

The culture is one of care and empathy. Team members are aware of others and their needs, and they exhibit mutual respect and trust towards each other.

Supportive communication and the management of interpersonal relationships come naturally to teamwork-driven organizations, and they are able to do so while understanding problems and responding to them with the needed support and mentorship. This allows the organization to feel a lot like an extended family.

Deep Dive:

Teamwork Culture focuses on the well-being of others when it comes to workspace interactions. Mentor-mentee relationships are easily established, and it is considered important to always provide others with the necessary feedback for improvement. Some common actions that take place include praising, encouraging, and uplifting others, as it is necessary to highlight the skills and strengths of peers.

Some common behaviors found within Teamwork Culture include:

Interpersonal Relationships

There is usually a build-up of interpersonal relationships in the workplace. Positive relationships have shown to create positive energy, as one feels safe and secure within their workspace. These healthy relationships offer a multitude of physiological, emotional, intellectual, and social benefits, and team members are less likely to experience feelings of anxiety, frustration, or uncertainty. Furthermore, within a positive workplace, employees are more likely to turn to each other and consequently, work more productively. Employees feel competent in their work, as their successes are recognized and celebrated.

Studies have shown that when employees have a more positive outlook on their jobs, their attention spans increase, their memories improve and their decision-making skills are heightened. Furthermore, employees functioning within a positive workspace learn more efficiently and make fewer mental errors. As a result, interactions between team members are more productive, as they are more likely to exchange knowledge and advice with one another.

Communication and Openness

This collaborative workplace culture encourages everyone to work harder and smarter, as specific feedback is regularly provided. It is well-known that in order to help the organization reach its true potential, corrective behavior is necessary. This is done in a positive/respectful manner, and it ends on an encouraging note.

Peers within Teamwork Culture often practice supportive communication, as they interact with confidence, trust, and openness with one another when the organization is functioning well. This is even the case when it comes to correcting negative behavior, pointing out shortcomings, and delivering negative feedback, as these challenging situations are addressed with ease.

Managing Conflicts and Collaboration

Teamwork creates an environment whereby employees recognize the importance of dealing with conflict head-on to ensure openness and honesty and so that relationships remain intact. When problems arise, teams are encouraged to communicate respectfully without lashing out.

When conflict arises, teamwork culture emphasizes the use of multiple solutions and the sharing of common goals to maintain the power balance and ensure that all agreements are reached unanimously. Teamwork differentiates people from their problems by clarifying mutual benefits to be gained when addressing potential conflicts. As such, teamwork employees and managers use objective criteria when evaluating alternatives and determining what is fair.

Mentoring

When teamwork culture is achieved and maintained, it enables and encourages the development of mentoring among coworkers. Within such a culture, employees address stressful situations with confidence and high esteem. Having a mentor-mentee relationship is important, as it's proven to be mutually beneficial for both parties. Employees gain a wide range of information and skills from their mentors, while managers benefit from reduced stress. Subsequently, mentor-mentee trust improves, cooperation increases, and teamwork becomes smoother. A mentor's guidance can help employees avoid stressful situations and cope when necessary.

Team Development and Team Building

Working as a team helps everyone in the organization better understand their own strengths and those of their peers. Performance runs more smoothly and efficiently, and project tasks become individualized. Also, teamwork keeps the main goals in focus while employees exhibit trust and integrity throughout their projects. As such, taking on tasks as a team aids in the personal development of all team members and allows employees to further explore their competencies and skills in order to improve within their teams.

The team focuses on building strengths rather than overcoming weaknesses. A Teamwork Culture prioritizes commitment to a vision and the recognition of hard work. As such, gratitude is readily shown, and this contributes towards the creation of a positive work environment where ideas flow abundantly.

Summary

Overall, within Teamwork Culture, organizations are considered to be nurturing and comfortable spaces where colleagues are eager to work every day and are able to reach their full potential. Teamwork fosters a strong sense of team spirit and a positive attitude. The relationship between any two team members can feel like the relationship among family members. The workplace is seen as an environment not only for working but also for forging friendships and connections. When adopting a teamwork culture, organizations emphasize fairness and honesty across all their practices. This is what keeps everything running smoothly and efficiently, making Teamwork culture the one to beat!

ASPIRED ORGANIZATION CULTURE ASSESSMENT WORKBOOK—LEADER VERSION

INTRODUCTION

There are two versions of the aspired culture assessment. One is meant to be taken by the leader, and the second is for the team/unit under assessment. This specific version is designed to assess leader responses, i.e, those that consider the leader's perspective. The aspired culture quiz aims to evaluate the leader's aspirational state considering six of your organization's elements, as described below.

By answering quiz questions, the leaders provided responses that reflect their aspirations for their organization—unless their status quo already reflected their aspirations, in which case their aspirations reflected their current state.

That said, both the Aspired Culture Assessment—Leader Version's method and its attributes are the same as those of the Culture Archetype Assessment. Regardless, they have been added here to save you the trouble of referring to another document when reviewing your quiz assessment results.

In the context of organizational culture, we define organizational culture as the beliefs, values, mindsets and practices of a group of people (whether an entire organization or a subset thereof) within an organization. Decades of wide-reaching empirical evidence have proven, undisputedly, that organizational cultures have a major impact on company performance. If you have ever led a team, department, business unit, or company, you may have reflected upon the role that organizational culture plays when it comes to overall performance. As such, it is important to mention that the relationship between an organization's culture and its performance has been the leading cause of industry and corporation fallouts, no matter the prestige of the conglomerates at hand.

For example, if we look at the organizational cultures within the steel industry and their subsequent resistance to change, we would see that they have prevented American steel companies from innovating and modernizing. This has led to their subsequent domination by Korean, Japanese and European producers. More recent examples include the fallout of the newspaper industry and the retail apocalypse. Because organizational culture has been influenced by industry functioning, organizations have failed to find a balance between traditional and new activities. The reason behind this is that leaders have not adequately responded to the uncertainty brought about by changes within the external environment. An example of such changes is the tension between the old organizational culture—that of monopoly newspapers and 20% profit margins—and the new organizational culture which emerged from disruptive changes in the industry. The same can be said about retail giants such as *Sears, Radioshack, Toys R Us* and *Blockbuster*.

Organizational culture creates friction and tension between groups, as whenever ten or more people share a space that allows them to engage in a multitude of dynamics, an entire collective culture emerges within a very short period of time. Furthermore, more recent evidence has come to light regarding organizational culture requirements and the subsequent work environments they generate. These studies were conducted across all industry sectors, within many international settings, and for every organization type. Accordingly, research shows that different organizations need to adopt their own specific cultures—there isn't one that works for all. In parallel, various factors need to be taken into consideration such as the growth stage, the market and competitive dynamics of the industry, and the organization's vision, mission, and strategy.

For example, a startup organization with a small team of founders and new-hires is likely to be entrepreneurial in its culture and functions with much agility and flexibility. As the organization grows in size, its original entrepreneurial culture would not be sustained in the long-term, as more measures and processes would be taken to ensure long-lasting growth. Also, as new hires import cultures from former to current places of employment, a new dominant culture emerges and becomes the norm.

The purpose of this workbook is to provide all members of an organization with information regarding what it means to be part of a specific work culture. It should be noted that this workbook is intended for leaders, managers, employees, and anyone actively involved in running organizations, as each of these parties contributes towards creating and maintaining organizational cultures. We hope that, by the end of this workbook, readers would have gained vital information that allows organizations to better understand what way of work suits them, what form of authority they prefer, and what truly drives them towards working well together and reaching their desired goals.

LIMITATIONS OF NON-PRO VERSION

The paper version of the quiz, despite containing the same questions as those of the "Pro" version, is more limited in its capacities. This is because the Pro quiz is designed in a manner that utilizes nested processing, as questions are continuously generated according to previous results. As such, unlike its pencil-paper counterpart, the Pro version contains built-in intelligence that allows for more thorough, complex analysis.

Within today's market, traditional employee surveys rarely have the built-in capacities that allow for complex business and managerial investigations to occur. This is why many of these surveys produce results that do not accurately reflect the reality of the situation. Consequently, these questionnaires seldom provide their users with a precise understanding of organizational gaps and challenges and, subsequently, hinder processes such as transformation and change management. Another drawback of conventional surveys is the number of complications that occur when administering and collecting information. These obstacles challenge surveys' ability to measure progress over a short period of time and to produce an accurate portrayal of the organization's reality.

Despite the aforementioned limitations of the non-Pro version, it still generates more information than most surveys out there do and can, subsequently, identify the primary, secondary, and tertiary dominant aspired culture Archetypes. As discussed later and in the PMAS book, the quiz is structured in a manner that allows for any potential bias to be limited via the types of answer options in the multiple-choice section.

The Pro version, on the other hand, can reveal all primary, secondary, and tertiary archetypes with more precision and can be easily administered with the click of a button. Furthermore, the Pro's results can be measured accurately and rapidly, on a monthly basis. If you have not signed up for the Pro version, you can do so by following up with Business Model Hackers through the account generated alongside this book's purchase.

233

INTERPRETING RESULTS

The answer choices provided in the quiz are structured in such a way as to capture various aspired cultural attributes. This was done in accordance with the concept of paradoxicality, as discussed in the PMAS book, in order to effectively reduce human bias. For more details and background information on how the quiz was structured, please refer to the main PMAS book.

The assessment for each Archetype (whether primary, secondary, or tertiary) is provided separately and divided into two sections: The Executive Summary and the Detailed Assessment.

The (Aspired) Culture Archetypes

A paradox mindset highlights the extent to which individuals embrace tensions. This is because the adoption of a paradox mindset can help people leverage tensions and produce creative outputs. However, most people tend to have a preference for one direction over the other, which is why they experience cognitive dissonance when they are pulled towards opposing extremes. Yet, research suggests that these conflicts can often work in a person's favor. Several studies conducted by psychologists and organizational researchers have found that people who learn to embrace, rather than reject, opposing sides of a paradox display more creativity, flexibility and productivity, as duality can lead to enhanced overall performance.

The (aspired) Culture Archetype Assessment design follows a structure that presents values in opposing axes across two key dimensions, Agility and Orientation, which are further broken down into six subcategories. These subcategories are grouped into three paradoxical pairs along the two main axes as shown below. Accordingly, the six Culture Archetypes are as follows:

A. **Entrepreneurial**: The Entrepreneurial Culture Archetype is characterized by innovation and trendsetting activities. The

work environment is dynamic and agile, and creativity, risk-taking, and innovation are encouraged and rewarded. Employees take pride in their unique work execution, and they are typically driven by ulterior motives, such as a desire to positively change the world and/or disrupt the markets that they serve.

B. **Customer-Centric**: The Customer-Centric Culture Archetype is characterized by its focus on customers, as they weigh in heavily on organizational decisions and influence the organization's strategic direction. The work environment encourages incremental innovation and creative problem-solving, and employees are typically driven by the desire to please customers and provide products/services that exceed customers' expectations.

C. **Competitive**: The Competitive Culture Archetype is one that is driven by marketplace competitors. Its work environment practices meritocracy, encourages high achievements, and rewards performance. Competition, benchmarks, and market trends drive the organization's strategic direction. Employees continuously monitor their markets and are motivated by the desire to achieve excellence and to consistently beat their competitors.

D. **Process**: The Process Culture Archetype is one that is driven by clearly-defined processes and procedures, in an environment that is organized, hierarchical and structured. Stability, consistency, and quality drive the organization's day-to-day operations. Employees know exactly what's expected of them, and they are motivated by job security and by their ability to perform and deliver exactly what's expected of them.

E. **Empowerment**: The Empowerment Culture Archetype is one that is driven by empowerment and accountability, in a work environment that emphasizes inclusivity and accountability. A "laissez-faire" approach characterized by the delegation of authority is what drives the organization's management. Employees have a sense of purpose and always feel included in key decisions. Two factors motivate the employees of such a culture: an acceptance of responsibility and an autonomous management of their work.

F. Teamwork: The Teamwork Culture Archetype is one that is based on active participation and openness. Two factors drive the organization forward: a teamwork-based approach, and individual team members' collective involvement in the workplace. Such an environment is very people-friendly, and its members feel like an extended family. Employees know that they are able to achieve greatness by means of having their individual capabilities leveraged equally with those of everyone else, so they are motivated when working as a unit.

Each Culture Archetype is detailed in the next section.

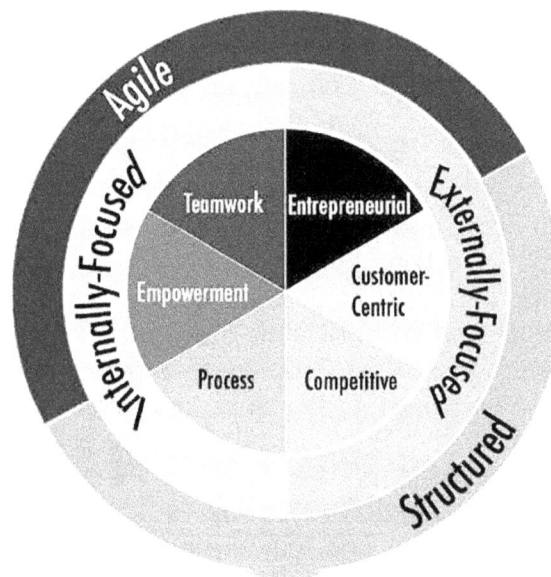

Scoring

Scoring the quiz is simple and requires you to add up the points from the six different sections and the total in each category (ranging from A-F). Accordingly, whichever category ranks the highest indicates the most dominant aspired culture archetype. Below, you'll find tables that you can use to help with the scoring process; you will also find 6 tables representing the 6 different categories (A-F).

Answers for questions 1-6 are each worth 14 points. Please note that question 7 is worth 16 points.

For example, if 'A' were chosen for questions 3, 5, and 7, 14 points would be placed in rows 3 and 5 in the first table, and 16 points would be placed in row 7 for that same table. Follow through with the tables according to the quiz answers. Any number-letter combination that does not have an answer is worth 0 points and, subsequently, has a score of "0."

Eventually, you will be able to add up the scores in each table, and the table containing the highest total indicates the primary aspired culture archetype.

Below, you will find the designated letters that correspond to six different aspired culture archetypes.

Under each title, you will find an executive summary and more details on the attributes of each aspired culture archetype.

A	Score		B	Score		C	Score
1A			1B			1C	
2A			2B			2C	
3A			3B			3C	
4A			4B			4C	
5A			5B			5C	
6A			6B			6C	
7A			7B			7C	

Total	

Total	

Total	

D	Score
1D	
2D	
3D	
4D	
5D	
6D	
7D	
Total	

E	Score
1E	
2E	
3E	
4E	
5E	
6E	
7E	
Total	

F	Score
1F	
2F	
3F	
4F	
5F	
6F	
7F	
Total	

Plotting your Score

If you purchased the Pro version of the PMAS, the results are automatically plotted for you on a Radar Pie Chart. On the other hand, if you administered the quiz via paper or webforms, you can use a spreadsheet tool to plot the results and acquire the relative score of each Archetype, as shown below.

The plots for this quiz are then overlaid on top of the plots from other quizzes to compare them in terms of target states and aspired scores. For more information on which comparisons are relevant and how to interpret the gaps for each comparison, please refer to the PMAS eBook.

Found below are examples of how graphical representation can provide insight into assessments—in particular when performing comparisons with other metrics.

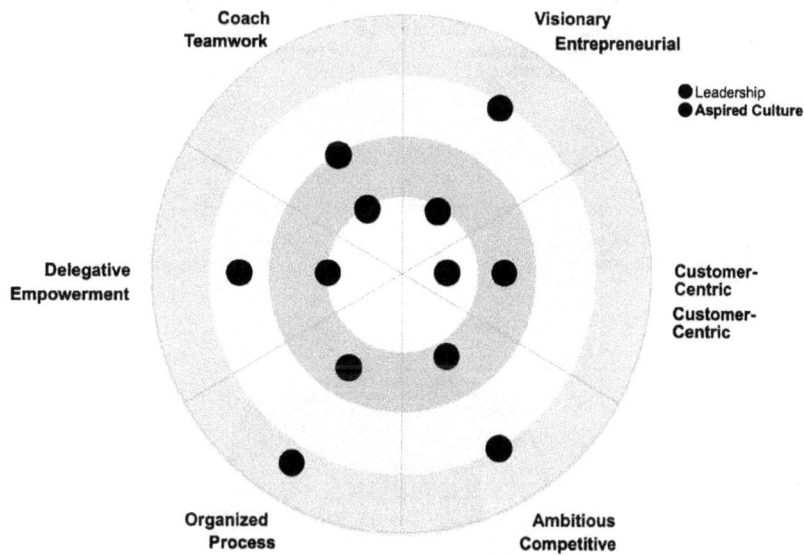

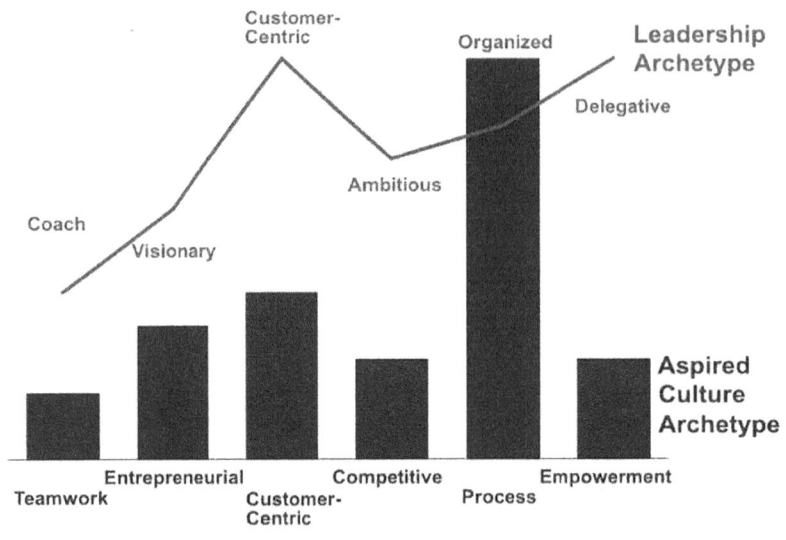

Customer-
Centric

Organized

Leadership
Archetype

Delegative

Ambitious

Coach

Visionary

Aspired
Culture
Archetype

Teamwork

Entrepreneurial

Customer-
Centric

Competitive

Process

Empowerment

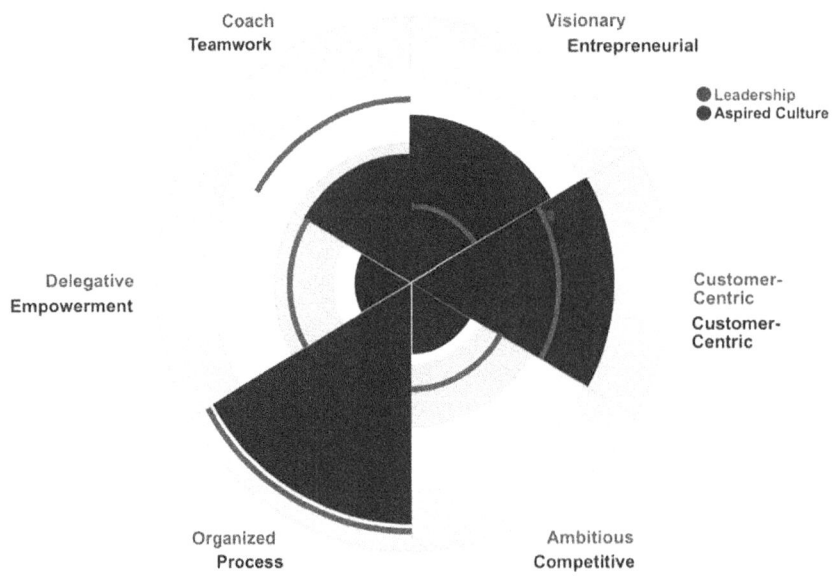

Coach
Teamwork

Visionary
Entrepreneurial

● Leadership
● Aspired Culture

Delegative
Empowerment

Customer-
Centric

Customer-
Centric

Organized
Process

Ambitious
Competitive

240

A. ENTREPRENEURIAL CULTURE

"Creative thinking inspires ideas. Ideas inspire change." –
Barbara Januszkiewicz

Executive Summary:

Continuous innovation and creativity are at the heart of Entrepreneurial organizational cultures. Organizational goals are usually met in inventive, uncharacteristic ways.

Employees within such organizations are consistently bending and breaking the rules in order to reach unprecedented results in unconventional ways.

Change (internal and external) is easy for such organizations, as colleagues continuously find themselves in a multitude of situations that allow them to be adaptable.

Deep Dive:

Entrepreneurial Culture emphasizes exploring and perfecting cutting-edge approaches that allow companies to reach their goals. Colleagues are constantly reminded how satisfying it is to see results through exciting new methods; consequently, creative culture is created that allows everyone to exceed their limits and let their creativity run loose. If tasks aren't completed in an unconventional way, they simply haven't met the mark.

In Entrepreneurial Culture, three characteristics shine through:

Innovation

Team members are commended for being outside-the-box thinkers, innovative hard workers, and creative problem-solvers. Entrepreneurial workplace culture leaves no room for routine, and

241

the team prides itself on having a high degree of aesthetic sensitivity. They work well with each other and feed off of their shared passion for creativity and uniqueness when completing tasks. In Entrepreneurial Cultures, people openly share their ideas and innovations with others and adopt radical approaches when tackling problems.

The path to an end goal is anything but traditional within this culture, as team members are encouraged to rely on intuition above all and subsequently take pleasure in breaking rules. Team meetings usually allow people to stumble upon their best ideas when they least expect them.

Entrepreneurship

Fostering an entrepreneurial mindset among team members is important for such cultures. Leaders often encourage their team members to bring forth their own ideas and to pursue their own goals. Furthermore, Entrepreneurial culture encourages employees to "put it all on the table" in order to commit to visions and follow through with what they think works for the organization.

Team meetings have employees bouncing ideas off each other, as individuals readily speak up about the path they wish to take and how they aim to develop their own ideas. In such an entrepreneurial environment, It's very rare for individual and collective creativity/ideas to be rejected, thus creating an endless flow of ideas, projects, creativity, and risk-taking.

This culture encourages managers and employees to utilize their vivid imaginations to create new ideas. As such, problem-solving takes place via breakthroughs and the adoption of radical approaches. In such a culture, it is essential to engage both experimentation and speculation, as this provides the organization with endless possibilities. Moreover, those who propose risky yet exciting ideas are applauded for their creative efforts. This influences other team members to also engage in risk-taking, which allows creative culture to flourish. When faced with difficult problems, the organization often adopts an approach that is more focused on revolutionary possibilities and unique solutions.

Agility

Ambiguity is a common feature of everyday life in an Entrepreneurial Culture. Team members can effectively deal with workplace uncertainty, and this makes for great entrepreneurs with unique visions and complex approaches. Entrepreneurial teams pride themselves on using less structured tasks to make room for more creative and non-conventional approaches.

Any risky and/or high-effort task is right down the team's alley, as employees are willing to dedicate time and effort to make sure all tasks are carried out impeccably. When addressing projects and conflicts, teams always have alternative solutions to any problems they may face, allowing everyone to quickly get back on track.

Given the turbulent nature of today's businesses, entrepreneurial culture adapts fairly quickly to turbulent times through creativity and innovation. Meetings are often an opportunity to discuss the importance of having multiple solutions to a problem. Different approaches are used to address change, whether it be in the market or in the organization, and this promotes fast adaptability. As such, the workplace is looked at as a 'tent' rather than as a 'palace', meaning everything is temporary and subject to change when necessary. Finally, Entrepreneurial culture does not encourage centralized power or authoritative relationships. Instead, power goes to whoever can best adapt to situations and deal with them head-on.

Summary

Overall, entrepreneurial culture promotes creativity and fearless innovation, and this allows teams to pull through in times of uncertainty. Moreover, team members help each other feel confident in their ability to progress and improve. Everyone on the team adapts well to uncertain situations, as stressful situations are dealt with calmly and readily. This culture is admirable in that it encourages employees to reach new limits and discover their potential.

B. CUSTOMER-CENTRIC CULTURE

"We see our customers as invited guests to the party, and we are the hosts. It's our job everyday to make every important aspect of the customer experience a little bit better." – Jeff Bezos

Executive Summary:

Customer-Centric **("CC")** organizations place customers at the center of key decisions. Customer feedback and customer's needs/wants are at the heart of everything they do.

Employees put their best foot forward when tackling any customer-related problems, and they strive to exceed customer expectations.

This culture focuses on customer service, customer satisfaction, and customer expectations, and the organization strives to always exceed customer-centric targets.

Deep Dive:

A Customer-Centric organization focuses on its customers, and its main attributes include creative problem solving, ongoing improvement, and effective communication.

The team works towards prioritizing customers and their subsequent needs, desires, and wishes at all times. As a collective, the team continuously strives to exceed customer expectations.

Three main attributes characterize the CC culture:

244

Creative Problem Solving and Incremental Wins

CC Teams master the ability to handle any problem head-on while always keeping customers in mind. Most team members do so in a way that's creative and unexpected, making sure customer satisfaction is always high. Moreover, incremental and continuous improvement are key when keeping pace with the market trends. Rather than focusing on what competitors are doing or what the company has done in the past, the team navigates itself towards customers and the fulfillment of their needs.

Customer demands are always a priority, and a CC Culture thrives when customers' expectations are exceeded. Moreover, CC organizations aim to solve customer problems by way of thorough understanding that generates creative solutions. As such, teams start and end their days by focusing on customer feedback. When producing and evaluating products and services, it is not the CEO or production manager who calls the shots, but rather customer feedback. This ensures that customer requests and complaints are taken into account, and customers are involved in every step of the process, with loyal customers even considered to be part of the organization. Factors of success within this organizational culture include a consideration of customer feedback and incremental improvement of customer satisfaction.

Customer-Driven Adaptability

CC organizations are willing to adapt to change since nothing can be set-in-stone when it comes to customer demand. Customer demands and customer feedback are used as key inputs when improving or developing new products and services that compete well in the market space. Moreover, a main goal for the organization is to always have high-level performance and impeccable internal communication, both within the organization and externally, with clients.

The team recognizes the importance of having loyal customers who can be counted on and who can count on the organization in return. Within this culture, customer service is impeccable, and organizations are well-known for treating customers with respect and giving them the importance they deserve. As such, the success of the company depends on the feedback received from external parties. When dealing with complaints, designated departments take them in, process them and amend anything that needs to be changed in order to meet customer needs. The number of complaints, recalls, refunds, replacements, etc. are key performance indicators that are targeted for eradication. Teams will get to the bottom of all possible hiccups and work on their resolution.

Strategic

Technological advances are the leading cause of a constantly changing market customer needs. In order to remain up-to-date with these changes, in CC cultures, the customer is at the forefront and is the key determining factor in the overall organization's forward-looking strategic direction, vision, mission, goals, and products/services. Accordingly, the customers' continuous feedback and input are what drive key decisions such as evaluating and selecting features when designing new products/services. Whether introducing new products/services or improving existing ones, the feedback received from customers is vital and a key determinant before such products/services are offered to the public for CC organizations.

Customer-facing departments (e.g., customer service, marketing, sales) work with internal functions and departments (e.g., manufacturing, engineering, design, production) harmoniously in order to ensure that anything targeted towards customers actually fulfills their needs and that any customer feedback, whether positive or negative, is always prioritized in a feedback loop.

Summary

As a whole, the organization creates a culture that prioritizes customers' wants and expectations. Customers appreciate how much the team values them and know they can always count on the organization to take their feedback into consideration and truly give them what they need. Long-time customers stay loyal to the organization because they know it's very unlikely for them to be disappointed with what they receive, whether it be flawless customer service, a product/service they truly need, or a place in the organization where they feel important and valued. Ultimately, teams prefer to work on filling in gaps when it comes to customer needs, as opposed to generating products and services that merely meet organizational goals.

C. COMPETITIVE CULTURE

"If you don't have a competitive advantage, don't compete." – Jack Welch

Executive Summary:

In Competitive Culture, the organization prides itself on being competitive and aggressive in its approach towards success. Teams present themselves as tough and intimidating. They have demanding ways of getting things done.

Stretch goals are actively set and high targets are actively pursued, allowing the team to thrive under competitive circumstances.

Winning is a dominant objective, and the focus of the organization is on external competitors and marketplace positions.

Team members are considered to be workaholics. Peers are commended for being task-oriented and work-focused, as the only way to get things done is hard work.

Deep Dive:

Competitive organizations aim to aggressively and vigorously outrank the competition. Everyone within such a culture is energetic with a thirst for achievement which makes such teams tough contenders in competitive markets.

The characteristics of a Competitive Culture are:

Competitiveness

A Competitive culture is driven by staying ahead of the competition and by continuously benchmarking and tracking

competitors' performance. Extensive time and effort are put into making sure everyone is up to date with the latest research on market trends and developments. Accordingly, competitive organizations quickly look into new products and services that hit the market.

Teams and employees are enthusiastic about beating their competition. In some organizations, daily meetings consist of setting aggressively high targets or checking them off as 'complete'. Within this culture, it's very unlikely to encounter team members or team leaders who are intimidated by competitors, as they are typically driven by competition and a winning attitude. Moreover, teams don't shy away from exploring new niches if they know it's something that can beat their competitors.

Performance and Achievement

Work always comes first for Competitive Culture, and teams are able to reach their goals as dedicated team members who are constantly working towards excellence. High ambitions reign dominant within such an environment where a strategy focused on dominating the market is a top priority. Team meetings and projects often revolve around finding and monetizing off of as many marketplace sub-niches as possible. This occurs via the production of high-quality products and services, as competitive organizations consider anything below the team's best efforts to be unacceptable.

Employees are expected to have a natural ability to work well under pressure and adhere to strict deadlines. If anything goes wrong, those responsible should be ready to accept the blame and take charge in order to provide proper solutions and make sure that mistakes are not repeated.

Motivation

Leaders in Competitive Culture organizations are concerned with pushing everyone towards achieving world-class competitive performance. On that basis, clear visions, goals, and objectives drive the key performance indicators of teams, units and individual

employees. Targets are set by monitoring competitors closely and performance is measured according to how well the organization does against the competition. Team members know what's expected of them, and they know they will be recognized when targets are reached.

Tackling challenges is a daily practice within a competitive culture, as it promotes high-reaching tasks and goals. There's a strong emphasis on competitiveness throughout the organization with a drive to consistently outperform competitors. Everyone involved is tested when it comes to their skills, responsibilities and autonomy. This leaves no room for anything except improvement.

The leadership of such organizations bolsters a highly competitive environment that energizes and keeps employees on their toes. Team members are often rewarded and commended for their hard work, to keep work functioning rigorously in a fast-paced and intense work culture where high achievers always shine.

Summary

Overall, Competitive Culture gives way to a stringent and driven work ethic, leaving no room for failure. Emphasis is placed on high-performance in the workplace where the bar is set high and overachievers shine. Team members are more than willing to be daring when setting and achieving those high targets. Within this culture, rewards outweigh hard work, and that is what keeps organization members going.

D. PROCESS CULTURE

"A leader is one who knows the way, goes the way and shows the way." – John C. Maxwell

Executive Summary:

Consistency and uniformity are well-entrenched in Process Culture organizations, through the adoption of systematic and structured approaches. Employees work with textbook processes and feel confident knowing that desired results can be achieved when following procedures.

Continuous improvement is often prioritized through systematic, careful, and thorough steps forward. Everyone on the team works well by following specific processes and procedures, in order to attain precise and predictable results.

Process Culture teams are known for being dependable and reliable. Day-to-day tasks focus on situational engineering, monitoring and evaluation and ensuring that order and structure are always maintained. Maintaining high productivity, efficiency, consistency, and quality are considered key factors to success, thus are continuously monitored and reported on. When problems occur or targets are missed, they are tackled by adopting conventional and best practice methods with zero tolerance for risk-taking in the process.

Deep Dive:

Teams exhibit exemplary levels of self-awareness and, in turn, copious degrees of self-knowledge. These two traits are intertwined and are considered key when adopting and maintaining Process Culture. Furthermore, other key attributes are punctuality and time management.

The characteristics of a Process Culture are:

251

Control and Structure

Process Cultures are bounded by clearly defined organization structures, reporting relationships, chain of commands, job descriptions, processes, procedures, and well-articulated visions/missions and values. Control measures are typically in place to continuously ensure stability, productivity, quality, and consistency as well as monitor and maintain accountability.

Everyone knows who and what they are responsible for and who they should be reporting to, all while adhering to the values and direction of the organization, as these two factors are at the center of any steps taken forward.

Emphasis is placed on ensuring a predictable and secure work environment, and where activities are continuously monitored and measured against performance criteria that are designed to maintain efficiency and smooth-running operations.

Processes and Procedures

Employees in Process Culture organizations work according to a well-developed set of standards and principles that help guide their behavior and communication. Everything is highly organized and systematic with clearly defined processes and procedures governing everything employees do.

The team fits and works well together and team members have no trouble integrating themselves into the work setting when they adopt and follow the rules, regulations, processes and procedures. Accordingly, teams work well when adequate monitoring systems and measurement procedures are in place.

Employees within such organizations are highly dependable, well-coordinated, and extremely organized. In the unlikely event that projects or tasks go astray, Process Culture teams would not fall victim to anxiety and stress, as they are able to develop solutions that minimize-risk and guarantee outcomes. This level of collective emotional intelligence is what allows Process Culture organizations to consistently improve.

Time Management, Consistency, and Quality

Time management and effective scheduling of tasks are important factors for Process Culture organizations, and time spent wastefully is not tolerated. Effective time-management and productivity tools/methods such as keeping track of time, making to-do lists, and prioritizing tasks, are often adopted to help organization members structure and complete their tasks on time. Being punctual and having impeccable time management skills are important parts of this culture.

Productivity, efficiency, consistency, and quality are typically the benchmarks of success in such organizations. Procrastination is frowned upon, and encouragement is ever-present, as colleagues push each other to complete tasks efficiently and productively. For example, priorities may be constantly discussed to determine what is truly important and immediate. Moreover, consistency is key, particularly when it comes to quality. A key success factor of Process Cultures is having reliable systems in place that continuously monitor, measure, report, and ensure the consistent delivery of high-quality products and service excellence.

Summary

Overall, this is a culture centered around processes and control, and its participants strive to enforce structure even amidst chaotic circumstances. Employees understand what is expected of them, what organizational culture and standards look like, and what best fits team members within their respective work settings. People are comfortable with routine tasks and feel safe and secure knowing exactly what to do when they come to work in the morning. Moreover, Process Culture teams handle difficult situations with ease, as they enforce structure over challenging issues. The organization has a clear hierarchy and a clearly-defined chain of command that follows clear-cut standards and utilizes comprehensive means of performance measurement and evaluation, and all this leaves little room for failure.

E. EMPOWERMENT CULTURE

"Leadership is about empowering others to achieve things they did not think possible." - Simon Sinek

---

Executive Summary:

Empowerment Culture emphasizes cooperation and inclusion across functional and organizational boundaries, with a focus on empowering employees and making sure they accept their responsibilities and manage their work with full autonomy.

In this culture, high-level authority delegation is compensated by means of emphasizing sound data analysis and analytics when seeking authorization of key and major decisions. This is achieved by ensuring that adequate data is made available through the continuous and constant flow of accurate information and frequent (dynamic) reporting.

Employees take on an all-hands-on-deck approach when accomplishing tasks, and this makes everyone feel valued and needed.

Interpersonal and cross-functional coordination are key factors in keeping things running smoothly and efficiently.

Deep Dive:

Autonomy is considered to be the best means of improvement when building a strong, empowerment-centered organization. When team members feel confident and believe in their potential, their sense of inclusion within the organization is heightened, and they feel more qualified to occupy their respective positions. Moreover, communication runs effectively throughout the Empowerment

254

Culture organizations. Proven results, accurate reporting, coordination, and transparency are key when it comes to keeping the underlying collective values and behaviors aligned.

A more laissez-faire approach consisting of the following key attributes is adopted in such a culture:

Empowerment

There is a high level of autonomy present within Empowerment Culture organizations, so team members tend to diagnose their own strengths and weaknesses and take on tasks that they know will play to their advantage. Moreover, team members usually overcome their weaknesses on their own, and this further reinforces empowerment culture. An effort is made to ensure that tasks assigned to subordinates match their capabilities and capacity. This allows work to be balanced at all times, as members are very rarely overworked or unsure of what is expected of them. The fact that everyone is actively involved in their respective departments fosters a lot of self-confidence and allows people to discover hidden talents and new potential. Within Empowerment Culture, people are just as responsible for their successes as they are for their failures.

As teams take on decisions and key tasks that are vital to the organization, this delegation of authority that comes with Empowerment Culture shifts the responsibility to individual units/teams and team members, and they are then expected to commit to key performance indicators targets and continuously report their performance to higher-ups and stakeholders (e.g., owners, shareholders, executives, etc.). As such, delegation is typically sustained and goes hand-in-hand with high levels of coordination among units and functions, requiring the entire organization to work more coherently as a unit. This is only achievable when organization members are in alignment when it comes to tasks and projects, daily communication and goals to be attained.

Analytics

In an Empowerment Culture, the increased level of autonomy and the emphasis on authority delegation are both typically sustained when strategies are backed by analytical decision-making based on sound analysis. This is especially the case when it comes to high-stakes decision-making by higher-level stakeholders (e.g., owners, shareholders, executives, headquarters). Teams and individual team members are required to do their homework when it comes to seeking approval on key decisions such as acquiring key resources and/or seeking major investments.

Therefore, with empowerment comes a necessary fact-checking of information, as to accuracy and meticulousness that help sustain such cultures. For example, when employees come together to pitch ideas, recommendations, or solutions, control measures and constraints are eliminated when the analysis is solid, the information is well backed and the content is presented in a clear and concise manner. This helps put people at ease and keeps team members motivated, stimulated, and oriented towards specific goals.

Inclusivity

In Empowerment Cultures, employees of all departments and levels are actively involved in decision-making and participate in deciding the strategic direction of the organization as a whole. Both teams and individuals are aware of and accountable for their actions. As a result, people feel valued and appreciated, and if there ever comes a time where control needs to be handed over, it is usually done so without a fault due to the inclusivity and coordination present within this culture.

Team members and units consistently share their ideas and thoughts with others. Collaboration with other departments, teams and units is highly encouraged. Mechanisms are usually in place to allow everyone's thoughts and ideas to be heard, collected, and taken seriously through active participation in decision-making. This is made possible by empowering everyone in the organization across functions (horizontal lines) and levels (vertical lines) to speak up,

and by facilitating the flow of information throughout the organization.

Summary

Overall, team members accept their responsibilities and take them seriously. Within empowerment culture, organization members are comfortable sharing their ideas and recommendations and, subsequently, their best qualities are brought forward. When tasks are handed down, so are their associated responsibilities. This allows members to grow and discover their potential as leaders, managers, and heads of departments. Communication is the most successful attribute, and employees don't shy away from sharing ideas, notes, or remarks in order to ensure multilevel efficiency. This culture thrives on delegation, and the ability of power to flow easily throughout the organization reinforces inclusivity.

F. TEAMWORK CULTURE

"Leadership is a way of thinking, a way of acting, and most importantly, a way of communicating." - Simon Sinek

---

Executive Summary:

Teamwork organizations are focused on setting comfortable and inclusive spaces to help transform and aid their members.

Teamwork-driven organizations emphasize collective involvement in decision-making and problem-solving. As such, participation, openness, morale, and commitment are consistently pursued within teamwork cultures. The environment is people-oriented and people-friendly, so managing conflict and seeking consensus is of the utmost importance.

The culture is one of care and empathy. Team members are aware of others and their needs, and they exhibit mutual respect and trust towards each other.

Supportive communication and the management of interpersonal relationships come naturally to teamwork-driven organizations, and they are able to do so while understanding problems and responding to them with the needed support and mentorship. This allows the organization to feel a lot like an extended family.

Deep Dive:

Teamwork Culture focuses on the well-being of others when it comes to workspace interactions. Mentor-mentee relationships are easily established, and it is considered important to always provide others with the necessary feedback for improvement. Some common actions that take place include praising, encouraging, and uplifting

258

others, as it is necessary to highlight the skills and strengths of peers.

Some common behaviors found within Teamwork Culture include:

Interpersonal Relationships

There is usually a build-up of interpersonal relationships in the workplace. Positive relationships have shown to create positive energy, as one feels safe and secure within their workspace. These healthy relationships offer a multitude of physiological, emotional, intellectual, and social benefits, and team members are less likely to experience feelings of anxiety, frustration, or uncertainty. Furthermore, within a positive workplace, employees are more likely to turn to each other and consequently, work more productively. Employees feel competent in their work, as their successes are recognized and celebrated.

Studies have shown that when employees have a more positive outlook on their jobs, their attention spans increase, their memories improve and their decision-making skills are heightened. Furthermore, employees functioning within a positive workspace learn more efficiently and make fewer mental errors. As a result, interactions between team members are more productive, as they are more likely to exchange knowledge and advice with one another.

Communication and Openness

This collaborative workplace culture encourages everyone to work harder and smarter, as specific feedback is regularly provided. It is well-known that in order to help the organization reach its true potential, corrective behavior is necessary. This is done in a positive/respectful manner, and it ends on an encouraging note.

Peers within Teamwork Culture often practice supportive communication, as they interact with confidence, trust, and openness with one another when the organization is functioning well. This is even the case when it comes to correcting negative behavior, pointing out shortcomings, and delivering negative feedback, as these challenging situations are addressed with ease.

Managing Conflicts and Collaboration

Teamwork creates an environment whereby employees recognize the importance of dealing with conflict head-on to ensure openness and honesty and so that relationships remain intact. When problems arise, teams are encouraged to communicate respectfully without lashing out.

When conflict arises, teamwork culture emphasizes the use of multiple solutions and the sharing of common goals to maintain the power balance and ensure that all agreements are reached unanimously. Teamwork differentiates people from their problems by clarifying mutual benefits to be gained when addressing potential conflicts. As such, teamwork employees and managers use objective criteria when evaluating alternatives and determining what is fair.

Mentoring

When teamwork culture is achieved and maintained, it enables and encourages the development of mentoring among coworkers. Within such a culture, employees address stressful situations with confidence and high esteem. Having a mentor-mentee relationship is important, as it's proven to be mutually beneficial for both parties. Employees gain a wide range of information and skills from their mentors, while managers benefit from reduced stress. Subsequently, mentor-mentee trust improves, cooperation increases, and teamwork becomes smoother. A mentor's guidance can help employees avoid stressful situations and cope when necessary.

Team Development and Team Building

Working as a team helps everyone in the organization better understand their own strengths and those of their peers. Performance runs more smoothly and efficiently, and project tasks become individualized. Also, teamwork keeps the main goals in focus while employees exhibit trust and integrity throughout their projects. As such, taking on tasks as a team aids in the personal development of all team members and allows employees to further explore their competencies and skills in order to improve within their teams.

The team focuses on building strengths rather than overcoming weaknesses. A Teamwork Culture prioritizes commitment to a vision and the recognition of hard work. As such, gratitude is readily shown, and this contributes towards the creation of a positive work environment where ideas flow abundantly.

Summary

Overall, within Teamwork Culture, organizations are considered to be nurturing and comfortable spaces where colleagues are eager to work every day and are able to reach their full potential. Teamwork fosters a strong sense of team spirit and a positive attitude. The relationship between any two team members can feel like the relationship among family members. The workplace is seen as an environment not only for working but also for forging friendships and connections. When adopting a teamwork culture, organizations emphasize fairness and honesty across all their practices. This is what keeps everything running smoothly and efficiently, making Teamwork culture the one to beat!

LEADERSHIP ARCHETYPE NUDGING HANDBOOK

INTRODUCTION

This book is intended as a companion to the Paradoxical Management Assessment System book as well as to The Leadership Archetype Nudging handbook. For this guide to help nudge you to work and ultimately achieve its objectives, it needs to start at the organizational level, and it needs to consider the organization's leadership.

Leadership styles are driven by the behaviors and communication styles of leaders, as these heads of organizations differ according to the competencies, values, skills and strengths they possess, embrace, and continually practice over time. However, this **does not** point to permanency when it comes to leadership styles adopted by managers and leaders, as leadership can be changed. Research shows that management skills and organizational management require a cognitive skill set that can be easily taught. Management Skills have certain traits in common:

- They can be developed and improved upon with the right training and practice. Unlike analytical skills, IQ-related skills, or certain personality attributes that can only be developed over a very long period of time (or sometimes never), managerial skills can be improved upon through practice and feedback.
- They are behavioral attributes existing separately from personality traits. They consist of an identifiable set of actions that individuals perform leading to certain outcomes. These behaviors can be observed by others, unlike attributes that are purely mental or personality-embedded. Although managers may have different styles leading to diverse skill set applications, the core of these skills is common all across a variety of styles.
- They are controllable by managers and can be consciously demonstrated, practiced, improved upon, or restrained by leaders when others are engaged.

263

To recap, the Leadership Archetypes that are adopted in the PMAS toolset is based on the paradoxical mindset which indicates the extent to which individuals are willing to embrace and be energized by tensions. The adoption of a paradoxical mindset can help people leverage tensions and produce creative outputs. However, most people tend to have a preference for one direction over the other and end up being dragged in two different directions, simultaneously, resulting in cognitive tension and stress. Yet, counter-intuitive research suggests that these conflicts can often work in a person's favor. Several studies conducted by psychologists and organizational researchers on the topic of the paradoxical mindset found that people who learn to embrace, rather than reject, opposing sides of this paradox have proven to be more creative, more flexible, and more productive. This duality leads to an enhanced overall performance well above the one used by someone who picked one of the sides.

The Leadership Archetype assessment is, by design, structured in a framework that presents the values in opposing axes across two key dimensions: agility and orientation. These two dimensions lead to six value sub-dimensions that characterize management and leadership styles. These are then grouped into three pairs in a paradoxical representation along the two main axes, as shown below. This leads us to six Archetypes in total, as follows:

A. **Visionary**: Visionary Archetypes are entrepreneurial and innovative, and they manage their organizations with agility while fostering creativity, risk-taking, and innovation in the organization's strategic direction

B. **Customer-Centric**: Customer-Centric Archetypes put the customer first and manage their organizations by letting customers heavily weigh in on and influence the organization's strategic direction.

C. **Ambitious**: Ambitious Archetypes are performance-oriented leaders who manage their organizations by monitoring their markets and having competitor benchmarks influence the organization's strategic direction.

D. Organized: Organized Archetypes are process-oriented and manage their organizations with clearly-defined processes and procedures that are designed to maintain efficiency, quality, consistency, structure, hierarchy, and order.

E. Delegative: Delegative Archetypes are empowerment-focused and manage their organizations with a "laissez-faire" approach that's designed to leverage their organization's capabilities and drive high cross-functional coordination.

F. Coach: Coach Archetypes are team-oriented and manage their organizations by emphasizing teamwork and team effort as means of getting the job done.

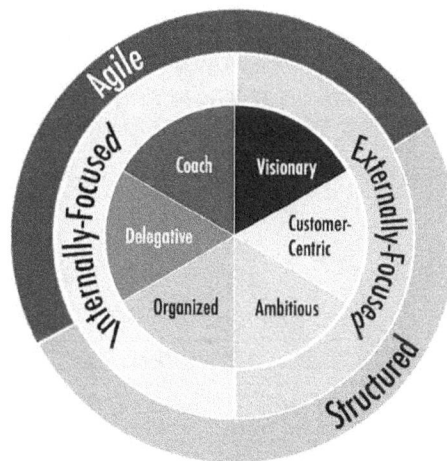

The main purpose of the book, based on the leadership archetype you wish to develop, is to help you select the most suitable list of initiatives and techniques highlighted for each leadership characteristic to drive rapid competency development and nudge leaders' values towards the targeted state, as identified earlier.

HOW TO USE THIS GUIDE

Each section below contains a brief description of each of the leadership archetypes. For a more detailed description, please refer to the 'Leadership Archetype Assessment Workbook'. The main purpose of each section is to provide leaders with the necessary tools and actions for developing the competencies required to achieve incremental nudges towards that section's particular archetype. As discussed in the PMAS toolset book and shown in the graph below, if you were to overlay the organizational culture and leadership archetype assessments on top of each other, you would recognize the gap between the leader and the organizational culture archetype.

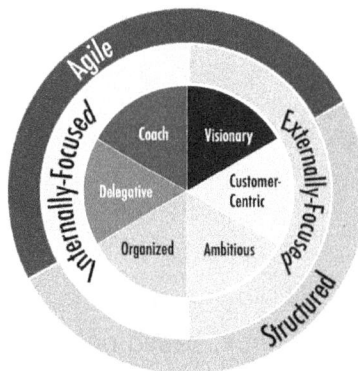

Ultimately, whether the gap you are trying to close relates to the company's organizational culture or to its leadership, you would require the nudging initiative for that particular archetype's leadership. So, whether you needed to bridge the gap between the status quo and the targeted state, or whether you needed to make sure that you maintained the status quo while working on nudging other archetypes, you would need to include the initiatives from the section of that particular archetype in your transformation program.

The culture-related initiatives would be added to the leadership initiative to form a comprehensive transformational program that achieves the desired nudges towards change.

266

The selection process would follow that of value-mapping, as discussed in the PMAS book. 'The Critical Gap Analysis Map' and 'The Transformation Program Plan' requirements are used together to select the initiative from each of the below leadership archetypes.

The initiatives would be combined with leaders' initiatives to develop a comprehensive nudge that would include one, more than one, or all the following types of initiatives:

1. Management tools
2. Leadership development initiatives
3. Cultural nudges
4. Incentive design

IMPORTANT: The leadership nudges and initiatives proposed herein are provided as a long list of suggestions designed to nudge your leadership style towards a particular archetype. The list is by no means exhaustive, or comprehensive, and will ultimately depend on your situation, your industry, and your specific context. We tried to make the list as general as possible, and we developed a number of key starters to help you develop initiatives and KPIs that apply to your situation.

On a final note, it's important to apply these initiatives to the formal and informal organization described in the PMAS.

In every section below, we will start with a brief recap and a description of the leadership style archetype, and we will describe the key values of each particular archetype. For a more detailed description of each archetype, you can refer to the Assessment Workbook.

To develop the skills required to achieve long-lasting managerial competencies for a particular archetype, a process of continuous improvement through continuous feedback should be developed. This can be achieved through 360 feedback and self-assessment. Assuming the objective is achieving alignment, progress can be measured by comparing the Leadership Archetype assessment with the Status Quo Culture Archetype assessment.

KEY CHARACTERISTICS OF LEADERSHIP AND MANAGEMENT SKILLS

Recapping from the material in the Leadership Archetype Assessment book, it is important to mention that Management skills have several defining attributes distinguishing them from other kinds of managerial characteristics and practices. Management skills are:

- **Contradictory or paradoxical**: The paradox mindset has been considered a key factor of a successful leader. Although paradoxes often throw us off guard, embracing contradictory ideas is the secret to creativity and leadership. For example, the core management skills are neither soft, nor hard-driven, and they are neither humanistic in orientation, nor directive in structure. They are oriented neither towards teamwork and interpersonal relations nor towards individualism and technical entrepreneurship. In fact, effective leaders possess a variety of skills that may be incompatible with one another.
- **Interrelated and overlapping**: It's hard to demonstrate just one skill in isolation from others. Skills are not simplistic, repetitive behaviors. Instead, they are integrated sets of complex responses. Successful leaders must rely on combinations of skills to achieve desired results. For example, to effectively motivate others, skills such as supportive communication, influence, empowerment, and self-awareness may be required. Effective leaders, in other words, develop a constellation of skills that overlap, support one another, and allow for flexibility in managing various situations.

- **Behavioral**: This consists of identifiable sets of actions that individuals perform in order to reach certain outcomes. Behavioral skills can be observed by others, whereas psychological or personality-driven attributes cannot. Therefore, people with different styles and personalities may apply their skills differently. There is a core set of observable attributes in effective skill performance that is common across a range of individuals.
- **Controllable**: Unlike organizational practices such as "selective hiring," or cognitive activities such as "transcending fear," skills can be consciously demonstrated, practiced, improved upon, or limited by individuals themselves. Skills may certainly engage other people and require cognitive work, but they are still behaviors that people can control and improve upon.
- **Developable**: Skills can be improved upon, whereas personality traits and temperament attributes remain relatively constant throughout life. Individuals can improve their skill performance competencies through practice and feedback, progressing from less competent to more competent.

Therefore, it is clear that developing paradoxical and overlapping leadership skills is essential to achieving both individual and organizational success.

Fortunately, research shows that leaders who have been exposed to the process of refining and enhancing their skills succeed in developing their managerial capacities. For example, studies performed over several decades have shown that managers who were given the knowledge and ability to develop their skills showed improvement by more than 300% in social skills.

A. THE VISIONARY LEADER ARCHETYPE

Visionary Leaders are innovative and entrepreneurial. They are known for fostering an environment of creativity and co-creation in the way they manage and run their organizations. They have a clear vision of their organization's future, and they excel at communicating with their teams and motivating them to make their vision a reality.

They are forward-looking leaders who can easily envision change. They constantly remind themselves and those around them to focus on where the organization is and where it should be.

By practicing organizational agility, Visionary Leaders are able to persevere during difficult situations and to easily adapt to changing circumstances.

They possess admirable leadership skills that are useful in times of sheer uncertainty. Moreover, these managers and leaders are considered to be highly dependable, and their thirst for innovation and creativity is contagious. They help others feel confident in their abilities to progress and improve, and they adapt well to uncertain circumstances, ensuring a calm and collected work environment during times of stress. They inspire, attract, and motivate those around them.

How to Be a Visionary Leader

A 'Visionary Leader' is someone who focuses on creating and enhancing an innovative culture within their workplace. These leaders are able to do the following: generate new means of task-completion, come up with revolutionary methods, and allow everyone's creative juices to run free. A carefree, innovative, and agile work environment needs its corresponding leader, i.e. someone who is willing and able to possess such traits.

It is important for such a leader to have the ability to be innovative and to want to see change. Visionary leaders should be able to nurture a high level of innovation and encourage those around them to do the same. Visionaries utilize experimental techniques and unprecedented methods, and they are not afraid to take risks in order for subordinates, and the organization as a whole, to practice innovation.

Visionaries are able to adapt to the ever-changing dynamics of the work environment and the marketplace. As pioneers of new technologies, strategies, and concepts, they're comfortable changing things up all the time, whether in terms of technology, organizational functioning, operations, or strategic vision.

Technology has been continuously evolving and integrating itself into our daily lives. As such, Visionaries are successful at incorporating new and emerging technologies into the workplace quickly and without hesitation. Being able to lead the team and make them more comfortable with different types of technology is also important to keep things running smoothly.

Visionaries learn how to face instability—in the form of shocks, events, and/or major changes in the marketplace and/or competition—with confidence and how to use this to their advantage. Factors nested in change demand that Visionary Leaders work, lead, and effectively manage diverse types of employees with vastly different technical skills and personalities.

As creative entrepreneurs, they are constantly coming up with new ideas for products, services, and innovative ways of reaching their goals. As such, stability and familiarity have a place in the innovative entrepreneur's dictionary. Visionary leaders are able to shine and lead positive change during unpredictable situations, as they believe that uncertainty allows for creativity to flourish and revolutionary ideas to arise. By leading the way towards constructive development, Visionaries are able to unlock the potential of those around them and reach new heights that are inaccessible to those who do not seek them out.

What Skills Should Visionaries Have?

Leaders looking to develop their Visionary archetype leadership skills should do as follows:

For Innovation

- Reward people for being innovative and make innovation a part of every team member's job description.
- Hold regular sprint workshops and/or hackathons that are designed to stimulate innovative problem-solving and/or innovative product/service development and improvement.
- Stay up-to-date with technology and innovation relevant to the organization's niche and continuously assess applicability to both the current situation and the organization's future.
- Leverage teams' existing collective knowledge and skills by staying up-to-date with different topics that one might not be knowledgeable about.
- Learn from others and allow different minds to join together to generate unique innovation.
- Allow for meetings to revolve around idea-sharing and idea-merging.
- Hold and encourage regular meetings for different teams to come together and share ideas.
- Appreciate and reward those who contribute to the innovation process, whether they initiate ideas or help others reach their innovative potential.
- Encourage team members to learn and gain inspiration from the innovation of others, both internally (within the organization) and externally (competition, parallels and analogs).
- Understand what methods have worked and what methods haven't and use this information to update and drive forward-looking strategy and future vision.
- Assess, review, and continuously reinforce an environment ideal for creative and innovative teamwork. Consider factors that inhibit innovation and work around them and celebrate small innovative wins.

272

For Agility

- o Establish an organization with teams that are dynamic when it comes to structure, processes, and people, yet stable in relation to primary or secondary axes.
- o Maintain flexibility and establish a mechanism to facilitate the quick assembly of multi-disciplinary teams with the right talent mix, and to assign resources and people that enable the organization to address new challenges and/or opportunities as they arise.
- o Allow the organization to continuously upgrade itself, adapt, change, and thrive in the rapidly changing, ambiguous, turbulent environment characterizing today's marketplace.
- o Minimize structural rigidity, eliminate stringent hierarchy, and provide employees, with human-centered experiences, with resources that enable creativity and co-creation.
- o Change goals and objectives according to how the organization is progressing and embrace and encourage adjustments as sources of positive change.
- o Hold workshops that allow attendees to learn the skills necessary for flexibility and adaptability in different work-related situations.

For Risk-Taking

- o Continuously try out new experiments, approaches and methods.
- o Encourage conversations where people do not hold back and are not afraid of pitching new ideas.
- o Allow teams to take risks and try out new techniques, regardless of possible successes or failures.
- o Create an environment that supports risk-taking, by not punishing employees who take smart, acceptable risks, yet end up failing. Instead, support these employees, help them learn from their mistakes, and encourage them to try again.
- o Praise those who have taken calculated risks, even if the risks didn't pay off in the end.
  - o Reward smart failures by setting up a mechanism that reviews failures and rewards best attempts.

273

B. THE CUSTOMER-CENTRIC LEADER ARCHETYPE

Customer-Centric Leaders ("**CC-Leaders**") are considered creative and imaginative individuals who always put their best foot forward when tackling customer-related problems.

Such customer-oriented leaders value the feedback received from their best clients and make sure to consider customers' needs when implementing organizational decisions.

These leaders have extremely high expectations for both themselves and their organizations, as they strive to provide five-star customer service and excellent satisfaction ratings.

A Customer-Centric Leader ("**CC-Leader**") leads and manages their organization by making sure every aspect of their day-to-day business revolves around the customer. In order to be customer-centric, it's important to combine various traits together: creative problem-solving, the ability to drive continuous and incremental improvement, and effective communication with external stakeholders (mainly customers).

How to Be a Customer-Centric Leader

As a CC-Leader, it's important to guide employees and colleagues towards prioritizing customers at all times by adhering to their needs, wants, and wishes. Successful leaders can consistently meet their customers' needs and exceed their customers' expectations.

Market expectations, needs, and technologies are constantly changing. Therefore, in order to be customer-oriented, one needs to remain up-to-date with these changes and to be willing and able to adapt and change visions, strategies, goals, and products accordingly. CC-Leaders accomplish this by placing customers at the center of any and all organizational decision-making. As such, customer feedback and input always dictate organizational strategy and the release of new or improved products or services to the market. CC-Leaders are able to withstand, absorb, and process criticism and complaints and amend whatever needs to be changed to meet customers' demands.

CC-leaders are able to solve their problems creatively. They consider that incremental and continuous improvement are key to keeping up with the dynamic customer market. Rather than focusing on what competitors are doing or on what the company has done in the past, CC-leaders navigate towards customers and see how their needs can be fulfilled.

As a CC-Leader, it's important to be willing to easily adapt to changes in customer needs, wants, and requirements, as nothing is set-in-stone when it comes to customer demand.

What Skills Should Customer-Centric Leaders Have?

Leaders looking to develop their CC Leadership archetype skills should do as follows:

For Customer-Centricity

o Monitor customer expectations, complaints, and preferences closely and regularly. Never underestimate what customers find to be wrong or below standard.
o Establish a mechanism that continuously collects customer feedback and responses.
o Make it easy for customers to voice their complaints or dissatisfaction and to suggest improvements according to their needs.
o Continuously measure customer satisfaction and determine why customers may be dissatisfied.
o Establish a post-delivery process to monitor and evaluate the products/services sold/provided to customers.

- Adopt a customer relationship management system that continuously maintains and updates customers' profiles, that ranks customers, and determines their lifetime value.
- Ensure that key customer-related performance indicators are clear and that targets are set for every level of the organization and for every employee in the organization.
- Establish a customer-specific reward mechanism for employee performance based on how well organization members serve their customers.
- Measure customer loyalty and set up a customer loyalty scheme that allows customers to be rewarded with exclusive perks and programs designed to increase customer loyalty.
- Surprise customers with a quality of service they would not have expected or requested.
- Praise and celebrate employees who exceed customer expectations and who provide high-level customer service.
- Collect data about negative performance indicators—complaints, recalls, refunds, warranty costs, replacements, repeat service, returns, grievances, worker complaints, and absenteeism—regularly. Work on consistently reducing these adverse indicators by including targets as key performance indicators.
- Follow through with an action, product, or service only if it is able to improve customer satisfaction.
- Set up a visible group dashboard that dynamically aggregates and reports the organization's customer-related key performance metrics. Ensure this dashboard is recognizable and is explained to every team member.

For Creative Problem-Solving

- Encourage creativity when it comes to solving customers' problems and complaints. Do not dismiss anything out-of-hand as outrageous or impossible. Use everyone's input and ideas (including those of customers) to stimulate different ways of approaching work.
- Consider a synectics technique when solving customer-related problems through a combination of different, unrelated elements.

- Modify current alternatives to problems and try to relate a problem's components together, specifically those relating to the actual state and the desired state.
- Encourage the establishment of joint team-customer boards that produce a consistent flow of new ideas.
- Allow employees to interact with customers and get better insights on how to creatively tackle their problems.
- Seek customer input and evaluation of new ideas before launching and/or implementing solutions to customers' problems.
- Consider running regular design sprints and/or sprint-style workshops to generate creative solutions for major problems.

For Forward-Looking Strategy

- Assign team members to continuously collect and process customer feedback, and ensure team members are aware that this process serves to influence the organization's future decisions.
- Encourage team members to remain up-to-date with market trends and to monitor them in order to gain knowledge about customers' future wants and needs. Combine this knowledge with that of customer feedback analysis.
- Engage team members for a collective analysis of customer feedback that allows information to be developed into useful and concise reports that can be shared with the wider organization.
- Hold regular team meetings and systematically conduct/facilitate/encourage regular workshops and sprints to the group. Also, prioritize customer feedback and market analysis as short-term and long-term initiatives for the organization.
- Incorporate (and/or advocate) long-term initiatives for developing products and services designed to exceed customer expectations into the organization's overall vision/mission and forward-looking strategy.
  - Assign short-term priority initiatives that maintain high-levels of customer satisfaction to team members and employees so that they can be incorporated into day-to-day operational plans.

C. THE AMBITIOUS LEADER ARCHETYPE

Ambitious Leaders are known for being competitive and motivational, all while being assertive. They are quite demanding, as they have a very specific way of getting things done. Also, they actively pursue goals and targets and are driven by competition and benchmarks.

Winning is a dominant objective for Ambitious Leaders. They are predominantly externally-focused and are driven by their performance against competitors.

One key personality trait of Ambitious Leaders is their dedication to their work. They believe that hard work and perseverance, by means of setting and achieving targets and goals, lead to excellence.

Despite having a reputation of being stern, Ambitious Leaders are still able to motivate employees to reach their full potential. They are natural leaders who unite people around common goals and try to gain knowledge of their own strengths and weaknesses as well as those of their teams, in order to progress. They despise mediocrity and do not accept excuses for failure. They value dedication, commitment, high achievement, meritocracy, ambition and winning above all else. They credit, recognize and reward successes, and they learn from failure to ensure it doesn't happen again. They thrive on internal and external competition and promote knowledge, continuous self-improvement, and collective development.

How to Be an Ambitious Leader

Ambitious leaders are reliable and legitimate, and they show a high level of expertise in their field. While a lack of expertise undermines authority, high-level expertise assures employees, team members, and colleagues that their leader is able to drive the organization very high up the marketplace ladder. Instead of worrying about pleasing those around them, Ambitious leaders need to be able to readily express their thoughts and opinions and prioritize reaching their end goals.

Ambitious leaders impose great mastery over their minds, emotions, and time in order to get the best out of themselves and their team members. They're very well aware of their team members' strengths and weaknesses, and they make sure to play to everyone's strengths. This ensures that the team is always working competitively to develop products, deliver services, or manage its day-to-day activities to the best of its abilities.

Ambitious leaders have a strong influence over the people they work with, which makes it easier for team members to follow in the footsteps of their leader. They use this influence to energize employees by driving internal competition and by providing team members with an environment that encourages them to thrive and overachieve in all aspects of their lives, not just job-related activities.

Ambitious leaders are able to energize their teams and push them towards working within a hyper turbulent work environment. When these leaders assign tasks, team members would be willing to put their best foot forward and to put their best efforts into every task and project assigned.

These leaders set ambitious goals that challenge their teams' status quo and standard benchmarks. They value hard work and dedication, and they foster a sense of competitiveness that drives team members to consistently work towards outperforming internal and external competitors.

What Skills Should Ambitious Leaders Have?

Leaders looking to develop their Ambitious archetype skills should do as follows:

For Market Leadership

- o Keep track of trends and predictions for the future of their industry or sector. Monitor competitors in order to gain knowledge to be applied in short-term and long-term strategic decision-making.

o Identify and select cutting-edge and trendsetting organizations/corporations for benchmarking. As such, study these companies' failures and successes in order to learn and progress.

o Maintain competitor data and information and adopt these as a "floor" benchmark to beat, and learn to improve and go beyond traditional best practices in these leaders' sectors/industries.

o Keep track of how competitors are performing and continuously monitor market trends and competition. Let market-driven feedback drive the organization's goals and objectives, by setting time-bound, "stretch" performance targets designed to dominate the marketplace and beat the competition.

o Set high-level performance goals and implement market-led differentiation to provide products/services that outperform those of competitors. May occasionally do business with competitors and identify their areas of superior functioning.

For Driving Competitiveness

o Identify personal strengths and weaknesses and develop self-awareness.

o Focus on overcoming weaknesses and on building strengths while continuously upgrading skills and knowledge to maintain top-notch expertise within the organization.

o Understand what others are doing differently and aim to do better by pushing team members towards achieving world-class success and by nurturing a high-performance organization whose environment is characterized by intense internal and external competitiveness.

o Drive team members and teams/units to consistently outperform competitors when it comes to generating products/services by doing the following: designing key performance indicators, setting reward mechanisms, and setting priority stretched goals and targets that aim for that objective.

- Promote internal competition through well-known tactics such as time-bound contests, leader boards, etc. Do this while ensuring that such tactics are mainly focused on the organization's goal and that they are equitably administered and not personalized.
- Find ways to learn from the successes and the failures of other units inside their organization.
- Identify and consistently evaluate the organization's core competencies and strategic advantages at the organizational, unit, and individual levels, highlighting strengths and weaknesses.
- Capitalize on strengths and establish ongoing initiatives and strategies to close weakness gaps and to maintain a personal dashboard that reports the status of internal gaps and challenges.
- Hold frequent discussion groups and take people out to a variety of events— work/business meals, business functions, and social events— designed as informal work meetings, and to internal networking events that extend beyond the workplace.

For Energizing Employees

- Establish a smart incentive system intrinsically designed to keep employees motivated and consistently eager to be challenged.
- Maintain (personal) individual and (visible) unit-level dashboards for key performance indicators with stretch targets that are driven by internal (departments/functions) and external (markets) competitor benchmarks. Combine this with a process that recognizes and rewards high-achievers, while keeping people on their toes.
- Recognize and celebrate small wins and reward big wins.
- Seek out challenging, high-intensity tasks and initiatives on a continual basis, as these are designed to nudge the organization towards achieving/maintaining market leadership.

D. THE ORGANIZED LEADER ARCHETYPE

Organized Leaders are typically known for being well-informed technical experts. They do things by textbook standards and feel at ease with systematic problem-solving. They adopt and follow clear processes and procedures, and actively pursue consistency and uniformity.

Organized Leaders are praised for being dependable and reliable. They base their day-to-day work life on practicing situational engineering, managing schedules, giving assignments, and ensuring order by maintaining structure in the workplace.

They challenge themselves to improve on what already exists through systematic, careful, and thorough planning and execution. They thrive on stability and control and tend to be the go-to leaders for analytical problem-solvers.

Organized Leaders emphasize the necessity for structure, rules, and routine in the workplace. Their way of work is very systematic and often includes the use of daily to-do tasks backed up with processes and procedures detailing the steps necessary for their follow-through, along with the appropriate standards to be maintained. They are often sought out when a structure is needed and when chaos is on the rise. Their impeccable self-understanding and self-control help keep everyone at work in check. In turn, Organized Leaders are better able to understand themselves and those they work with. They are less inclined to acquire information by interacting with others, instead opting for a logical and rational thinking process. They excel at inductive reasoning and at organizing material into a consistent whole. They bring a sense of calm into the workplace, as the presence of order and structure within their environments allows them to be successful and competent Organized Leaders.

How to Be an Organized Leader

Organized leaders are well-informed about operational details, standards, and protocols within their workplace. They're considered to be technical experts when it comes to organizational functioning and runs, and organizational goals and objectives.

As an Organized Leader, one should feel at ease with order and structure. Such a person is comfortable with systematic problem-solving and with having clear processes and procedures in place.

Under organized leadership, consistency and uniformity are key when dealing with employees or other external parties.

Organized leaders work well with stability and control, as they are comfortable exploring and improving their levels of self-awareness, which helps them readily display copious amounts of self-knowledge. These two traits are intertwined and are considered to be at the core of their behavior. They are admired by those who aim to maintain structure, order, organization, and consistency within the work.

When it comes to managing the organization, they focus on the quality of interconnectedness between colleagues and subordinates. For example, these leaders consider that every team member should be clear of what is expected of him/her and what his/her specific tasks are at all times. Employees working with Organized leaders are trained and selected to be comfortable with working in an environment where monitoring systems keep track of their individual and collective performance and aim for high standards that never drop but, rather, incrementally improve. This ensures targets are always met or exceeded, but never missed.

Organized Leaders train their teams on how to function within a controlled environment. They make it clear that all employees, and all those responsible for projects and tasks, are expected to follow procedure and to engage in standardized, routine, and structured behavior within stable and predictable work environments. They consider the organization's values, ethics, and code of conduct to be sacred, and they continuously monitor and report on compliance with such factors.

Organized leaders know their own strengths and weaknesses, as well as those of their colleagues. They have a high level of self-awareness that enables them to better manage and guide those they work with. Considering how dynamic and stressful the business world is, their ability to maintain self-control and a composed attitude during trying times is very helpful. In order to push through and succeed, Organized leaders distinguish between their anxieties and the tasks-at-hand.

They have little tolerance for ambiguity. In situations of uncertainty, Organized leaders compose themselves and pay attention to detail, in order to make sense out of seemingly nonsensical situations. They can break down large, overwhelming tasks into smaller ones without losing sight of the big picture.

Organized Leaders manage their time efficiently and have no tolerance for wasteful activities and tasks across the entire organization. They ensure that all their team members are trained on time-management and that productivity is in check at all times.

What Skills Should Organized Leaders Have?

Leaders looking to develop their Organized archetype leadership skills should do as follows:

For Process and Procedure

- o Develop a solid understanding of the organization's internal workings and operations by, for example, considering the organization to be a connected network of cause and effect relationships.
- o Maintain and update internal process maps and flowcharts, and develop documentation and procedures for every key process in the organization.

- Establish adequate hierarchy and maintain a standard set of processes, procedures, and policies. Draft a job description for every employee and aim to maintain a structured organization, clear roles, responsibilities, and reporting lines, and precise and efficient operations.
- Help employees apply/understand process maps, and roles and responsibilities. Ensure that they know how their role fits into the overall organization and its operations.
- Establish goals and objectives that are aligned with the organization's mission/vision and develop key performance indicators that align with the organization's goals.
- Ensure goals and objectives are cascaded top-down and aggregated bottom-up when developing performance metrics, to ensure a mutually exclusive and collectively exhaustive set of indicators.
- Collect, measure, and report accurate results when it comes to key performance indicators, levels of adherence to code of conduct, ethics and values, and the degree of compliance with key processes and procedures across the entire organization.
- Conduct regular personnel performance reviews and maintain time-phased progress data.
- Reduce any potential ambiguity and information complexity, and clarify or interpret confusing data.

For Efficiency, Consistency and Quality Assurance

- Set frequency of reporting metrics and performance evaluation metrics for each level of the organization.
- Maintain a database, and expertise industry, function benchmarks, and best practices for standardized and generally accepted principles relevant to the organization (e.g., Six Sigma, PMI, ISO, ASTM, IFRS, GAAP, etc.)
- Set key performance indicator targets based on the relevant industry benchmarks and on acceptable standards, where applicable.

- Set key performance indicator targets based on the company's strategic plans, goals, and objectives, where applicable.
- Emphasize consistency in the quality of (internal or external) products and services and incorporate related key performance indicators that measure quality in adherence with the overall organization metrics.
- Implement automated dashboards to visualize and report performance variance, and continuously monitor and optimize internal processes to meet/exceed targets and to trigger/initiate corrective action when targets are missed.
- Adopt a rational, stepwise system for defining, analyzing, and solving problems within their unit.
- Maintain process flowcharts and identify redundancies, irrelevancies, and work that add no value when targets, processes, and goals change.
- Assemble everyone involved in those processes to analyze overlaps, non-value-added work, obstacles to success, and necessary improvements.
- Establish a mechanism to assist employees in identifying and reporting blank spots and overlaps in their responsibilities.
- Ensure free flow of relevant information and establish communication channels that facilitate an efficient work environment free of hiccups and interruptions.
- Establish a budget for all critical resources and identify efficient ways in which each of these resources is allocated and expended.
- Analyze, with a critical eye, the key reports that are produced, to ensure their accuracy and usefulness. Discontinue the use of wasteful reports and the collection of non-essential data.
- Develop employees' time-management and productivity skills across the entire organization.
- Adopt time management and productivity tools and techniques designed to cut inefficient processes, prioritize activities, and eliminate time-wasting tasks. Adopt simple tools, such as "to-do lists", and keep track of time usage and productivity levels for everyone in the organization.

For Control, Stability and Job Security

o Establish initiation processes for new employees to provide them with on-the-job training and with formal training and orientation sessions tackling the organization's traditions, values, visions, and strategies.

o Maintain and update an authority matrix for the organization and communicate responsibilities and accountabilities to those involved in reviewing, reporting, informing, researching, recommending, and approving activities.

o Establish and maintain monitoring and reporting systems that allow teams and individuals to know how their units are performing against key performance indicators targets.

o Provide regular feedback to employees regarding their work performance, their strengths, their weaknesses, and their progress against their predefined, preset targets.

o Make sure that all employees know why they are doing what they're doing, and how that fits into the organization's broader picture.

o Institute regular internal and external audits of each unit in the organization to assess the robustness of reporting on key performance indicators, results, levels of adherence to code of conduct, ethics and values, and degree of compliance with key processes and procedures.

E. THE DELEGATIVE LEADER ARCHETYPE

Delegative Leaders ("**Delegators**") adopt a hands-off approach to management by empowering those around them and by delegating authority to the individuals, teams, units and/or organizations they manage.

Delegators foster a culture of inclusivity, and they encourage personal growth that allows employees to practice the decision-making process with autonomy and freedom.

They promote the free flow of information and enhance interdepartmental communication and cooperation by assisting in analytics and providing the support needed to address capability gaps across the organization.

Delegative leaders are admired and appreciated by their team. Employees feel that such leaders help bring out their best qualities, and they feel comfortable seeking their leaders' guidance when it comes to ideas and recommendations. Delegators create a positive culture at work, all while maintaining a stern attitude that produces impressive results. Logic and reasoning are at an all-time high when conversing with Delegators. Every step taken is meticulously-planned and researched to ensure that results meet necessary expectations. As such, these leaders take their time when making decisions. They are more focused on the problem itself rather than on the people/person behind the issue, hence why problem-solving for Delegators tends to be more straightforward and less interpersonal.

How to Be a Delegative Leader

A Delegative leader is comfortable delegating tasks to subordinates or teams he/she manages, as this leader has faith in them and trusts them to get the job done. This helps employees feel more included in the organization as a whole, which further empowers them. For delegation of authority to be successful, coordination among departments, functions, teams, and the company as a whole is essential. Delegative leaders achieve this by ensuring that expertise, best practices, capacity, and know-how are leveraged and optimized among the different teams by being aligned and by ensuring that all departments and functions can collaborate efficiently.

Delegative leaders empower their teams by making sure every task they set out to accomplish is within a team's or unit's capabilities, by letting employees overcome their obstacles on their own, and by matching the level of authority at hand with the level of responsibility given. That's how such leaders are willing to take risks when assigning a certain level of responsibility to employees. Key decisions, collaborations, and important projects are spread out across the entire organization to make sure everyone is actively involved. Rather than having employees be told what to do in an authoritative manner, team members are given the chance to exercise their skills and propose their own suggestions and ideas. This allows for diverse and joint efforts to be made. Consequently, company heads are able to face less pressure, and responsibility and creativity are evenly spread out across the organization.

It takes a great deal of vulnerability for employees to put their ideas and thoughts out in the open. If communication and coordination are not flowing consistently, empowerment and confidence within the organization are affected. In such cases, fear and conflict could arise, and this could affect the trust and morale present in the organization. So, effective communication is key.

Delegative Leaders must be well-aware of their teams' capabilities, gaps, constraints, and limitations. They set clear objectives, goals, performance indicators, and targets by matching teams' capabilities with the appropriate levels of delegated authority/ responsibility. In order to address and close their teams' capability gaps, these leaders provide the necessary guidance/support and allocate the appropriate resources. They clearly state what is expected of others and what results are required for end goals to be reached with maximal efficiency.

Their 'Laissez-Faire' leadership style enables employees to fend for themselves with very little guidance. Consequently, employees are given the chance to grow on their own, without being micromanaged the entire time. Rather than motivating, directing, or stimulating their teams, Delegative leaders provide their employees with freedom and do not control or constrain workflow.

Delegative leaders might find it easier to get things done when all hands are on deck. This provides employees with the necessary confidence and autonomy to further develop their skills and discover new capabilities within themselves. Finally, these leaders make sure that delegated actions are consistent, balanced, and not dependent on the leader's workload.

What Skills Should Delegative Leaders Have?

Leaders looking to develop their Delegative archetype leadership skills should do as follows:

For Delegation of Authority

- o Maintain a vision, a mission, values, goals, and objectives for the organization that is well-understood and properly transmitted to team/unit leaders/members. Ensure that the vision statement is consistent with the organization's basic principles and values.
- o Set clearly-defined key performance indicators based on the organization's vision and objectives. Set achievable and fair targets for delegated roles and responsibilities.
- o Assign accountabilities fairly, based on the organization's capabilities and available resources.
- o Maintain and update an authority matrix with high-level authority delegation and communicate responsibilities and accountabilities to those involved in key decision-making.
- o Establish a mechanism for measuring and reporting key performance indicators.

- Understand the strengths and weaknesses of the organization and assist in strengthening the organization's weaknesses and addressing its challenges and gaps.
- Provide opportunities for people/teams to learn new tasks. Continuously enrich and expand employees' job qualifications by adding responsibilities requiring them to learn new skills and abilities.
- Provide employees with a chance to learn on the job by having them take on responsibilities that are one level higher than those of their current organizational positions.
- Insist that subordinates not only highlight problems but also generate appropriate solutions. Discourage upward delegation accordingly.
- Empower everyone across functions, units and teams (horizontal lines), and levels (vertical lines) by embracing a "laissez-faire" and decentralized approach to decision-making with an increased level of downward autonomy.

For Inclusivity and Efficient Flow of Information

- Encourage team members to be actively involved in decision-making and involve everyone when formulating, or updating, the organizational vision and mission statements.
- Involve team members when devising strategies to accomplish the organization's vision. Build consensus through inclusion and through the flow of meaningful information.
- Establish cross-functional teams and task forces and leverage diversity and cooperation within such teams, in order to bring in fresh perspectives that contribute to new ideas. On an individual level, expose employees to a variety of organizational perspectives by involving them in cross-functional and cross-level teams.
- Maintain an internal system for gathering information—related to best practices, relevant benchmarks, new ideas, performance improvement suggestions, employee development, etc.—across the organization. Encourage everyone to contribute to progress. Encourage everyone to

291

take risks when contributing to the organization's development and competitiveness.

- o Assign projects and tasks that enable team members to do the following: explore and expand their skills, gain responsibilities, and increase their levels of autonomy. Establish a mechanism that ensures that employees are given the necessary feedback to improve.
- o Invest time in developing the right systems for analytical decision-making and information sharing, as well as for employee and human capital development. This leverages productivity and time-management benefits obtained as a result of increased empowerment and delegation of authority.

For Analytical Decision-Making

- o Identify important information that should be made available, in order to drive the organization's success. Pass this vital and strategic information along, even if not requested.
- o Bring what is hidden to the forefront and establish a mechanism that synthesizes, processes, and maintains relevant data relating to key performance indicators and market intelligence. This is crucial for stimulating high performance and competitiveness within the organization.
- o Set up a mechanism to analyze and disseminate data, and transfer the information to stakeholders in formats that can be easily understood and processed for better decision-making.

F. THE COACH ARCHETYPE

We define Coaches as individuals who find ease in building and strengthening positive relationships, as they are able to communicate with people in a way that enhances feelings of trust, openness, and support.

Coaches are considered to be people-oriented facilitators. They manage conflict, seek consensus, and positively influence others by involving every member of the workplace in decision-making and problem-solving. They actively encourage participation and openness and boost morale and commitment.

Coaches are looked at as caring and empathetic mentors. They are aware of and care for the needs of those around them. Their influence is based on mutual respect and trust.

A Coach Leader Archetype ("**Coach**") is considered to be natural when it comes to supportive communication and managing interpersonal relationships with colleagues, subordinates, and peers. A Coach first listens, then provides feedback when needed, and he/she is the go-to person when resolving any interpersonal problems between team members.

Coaches are leaders who teams can look up to and be inspired by. They are managers with who individuals love to work with. Their caring nature makes them emotionally accessible, and their need to support others shines through with their positive feedback. By having a positive attitude, they empower their colleagues and employees and make their teams feel at ease. They rarely make enemies in the workplace and constantly strive for fairness and honesty, and this keeps the organization running smoothly and efficiently.

How to Be a Coach

To be considered a "Coach Archetype Leader", one must actively embrace certain types of skills and pursue his/her strengths. Such leaders practice supportive communication, team building, team empowerment, active listening, and they have a genuine desire to help others in need. Coaches are able to nurture those involved in the organization, and they can deal with difficult situations in a compassionate and empathetic manner.

Supportive communication requires the development of positive interpersonal relationships. This helps create positive energy in the workplace, and it resonates well in the organization, allowing people to always feel comfortable and appreciated. Studies have shown that this positive energy is not only important for the sake of a healthy workplace, but also for better and more productive employee performance. Furthermore, as a Coach leader, it's important to foster, encourage, and make room for effective communication, whether this be between leaders and their subordinates or amongst employees. Effective communication occurs when messages are relayed honestly and accurately, keeping in mind the importance of maintaining interpersonal relationships. This can mean anything from having a face-to-face conversation with colleagues to relaying messages to subordinates, or to delegating tasks to ensure higher productivity. Information needs to be relayed and conveyed accurately to make sure there are no hiccups along the way. Effective communication can flourish when leaders know their employees well, so it's important to understand everyone's strengths and weaknesses. This comes in handy during communication, specifically when there is a language barrier, a gap in knowledge, or a fear that hinders productivity. All these factors, if not taken into account during communication, can cause obstacles with task-completion and productivity when working as a team. These varieties in communication need to be practiced effectively to ensure that all team members involved understand what is expected of them and feel understood, appreciated, and involved in the workplace.

With that being said, adopting this type of leadership requires the development of mentor-mentee relationships. So, positive feedback needs to be given to employees on a consistent basis. This creates a culture of understanding and learning within the organization, which generates a positive environment that allows people to truly thrive and reach new horizons.

When dealing with issues in the workplace, Coach Archetypes prioritize their team members, as they consider the organization to function much like a family. These leaders believe in nurturing their relationships with others, at all costs, and in resolving any possible conflicts that may occur. As such, Coaches do not accept dysfunctional relationships within the workplace. They consider it important to separate the problem from the person, rather than focusing on the problem itself. They also refrain from attributing any issues to possible deficiencies the person may have, as they consider that anything personal should be dealt with separately and delicately.

Moreover, for Coaches, it's important to be descriptive rather than evaluative. This allows the person who has committed the error to move past being accused of wrong-doing and understand why a mistake has been made in the first place. This speeds up the process of finding a solution and allows people to learn from their mistakes more readily and positively. Furthermore, when tackling work-related problems or difficulties, it is also important for leaders to listen supportively. This type of communication is important because it varies from one-way message delivery that more often results in negative consequences; such as affected workplace relationships and a lower likelihood for someone to improve their faults.

At the end of the day, adopting this culture requires leaders to make employees and peers feel welcome, accepted, and worthy enough to be present in the organization. Supportive communication is at the core of this type of leadership. Employees are important to the organization, and everyone's well-being should be a top priority to ensure that, moving forward, everyone feels mentally and emotionally capable of taking on any task at hand.

When assigning tasks within the context of teamwork, Coaches make sure to take everyone's capabilities into consideration. This is also the case when Coaches delegate tasks, as they think about the entire team's qualifications and skillsets. Furthermore, leaders strongly encourage teamwork, as it helps connections grow in a workplace and makes it easy for peers and subordinates to learn from one another. Finally, collective work helps team members discover new potential, learn new skills from others, and bring their strengths to the table.

What Skills Should Coaches Have?

Leaders looking to develop their Coach archetype leadership skills should do as follows:

For Team-Building

- o Establish and consistently maintain clear goals and a unified vision, with specific targets and objectives, for the team to work towards. This is done in order to make sure that team members work towards common goals and objectives at all times.
- o Hold either more informal team meetings or more company retreats. This allows team members to establish stronger bonds with each other and become more familiar with the company's vision.
- o Understand the different stages of team members' personal development (early, mid, late) and give them the corresponding guidance and attention.
- o Give team members the opportunity to teach and learn from one another by rewarding expanded knowledge, expert skill, and information dissemination.
- o Try not to form teams that are too large or too small to ensure that tasks and work-balance can be allocated evenly and that working as a team can be done efficiently.
- o Ensure that all team members are aware of their tasks and that information flows smoothly. This ensures that everyone is kept up-to-date and that constant exchange of ideas and participation occurs amongst all team members.
- o Pay close attention to the team's strengths and weaknesses and assign the roles and tasks accordingly.
- o Hold regular sprint team meetings to emphasize coherent teamwork. When doing so, facilitate efficient team meetings and avoid actions that may inhibit effective team meetings.

- ○ Seek feedback and ask for it from team members on a regular basis.
- ○ Ensure communicational free flow and idea-exchange.
- ○ Sponsor team members who don't participate regularly, while seeking input from every single team member.
- ○ Prevent any single team member or perspective from dominating team meetings.
- ○ Act as cheerleaders for teams.

For Managing Interpersonal Relationships

- ○ Ensure that giving praise and expressing appreciation occur habitually within the team, particularly when directed from team leaders to team members.
- ○ Make an effort to communicate feelings and demonstrate care at a personal level—for example: remember birthdays, special occasions, family-related events, etc...
- ○ Ensure that everyone on the team always feels important, valuable, and appreciated.
- ○ Be accessible to employees and team members at all times.
- ○ Foster an environment where employees can open up and where they feel comfortable sharing problems, concerns, or successes.
- ○ Approach people in a direct manner when problems occur and hold open and candid discussions.
- ○ Listen carefully when others speak.
- ○ Rely on descriptive communication instead of evaluative communication when faced with disagreements.

For Communication

- ○ Give subordinates regular feedback about their work performance and share recommendations for improvement when needed.
- ○ Communicate well when giving feedback and always check in with team members to make sure the feedback is enough.
- ○ Understand individual and collective strengths and weaknesses and get to know every team better on a personal level.

- Support individual members in reaching their goals and are role models for team members.
- Facilitate employees' success, recognize their accomplishments, treat the team like extended family, and speak of them with high praise when talking to outsiders.

Express confidence in the team's capabilities. When ability or skill problems exist, provide the necessary coaching.

ORGANIZATION CULTURE ARCHETYPE NUDGING HANDBOOK

INTRODUCTION

This book is intended to be a companion to the Paradoxical Management Assessment System book, and the Leadership Archetype Nudging handbook. For nudging to work and ultimately achieve its objectives, it needs to be applied to the organization both as a whole and on a smaller, more individual level—that of leadership.

To recap, the Organizational Culture Archetypes mentioned in the PMAS toolset stem from the concept of a paradoxical mindset. This way of thinking indicates the extent to which individuals embrace tensions, leverage them, and utilize them for creative output purposes. However, even though most people have a preference for one direction over the other, they still end up being dragged in two different directions which results in cognitive tension and stress. Yet, counter-intuitive research suggests that these conflicts can often work in a person's favor. Several studies conducted by psychologists and organizational researchers on the topic of paradoxical thinking found that people who learn to embrace, rather than reject, opposing sides of a paradox are more creative, more flexible, and more productive.

The organizational culture is driven by its leaders, managers, employees, and even its customers. It differs according to the organization's Leadership Style and the means by which employees pursue productivity, whether this involves more teamwork, more delegation, or more market-driven behavior. Moreover, workplace culture varies according to each organization. Interestingly, workplace culture can shift within organizations themselves depending on internal and external circumstances—ex. a change in the stock market, an unexpected global event, a surge of new competitors on the rise, a change of company location, etc. This is why it's important to note that workplace culture is not set in stone, but is rather a group effort that can be amended according to the organization's needs and preferences.

There are certain cultural attributes that are common across a wide range of experiences, dynamics, and spaces:

- Culture can be developed and changed over time with the conscious effort of its leaders, managers and employees. New skills and behaviors can be learned and practiced ensuring a higher level of knowledge that is involved in cultural creation and maintenance.
- Culture is a group effort and that requires the active input of all organizational members to ensure its coherence and maintenance over time.
- Culture is meant to help drive an organization towards its goals, rather than hinder or prolong the process. Within an organizational culture, team members collectively work towards an ultimate vision, which is necessary for developing structure and success.

The Culture Archetype Assessment design follows a structure that presents values in opposing axes across two key dimensions, Agility and Orientation, which are further broken down into six subcategories. These subcategories are grouped into three paradoxical pairs along the two main axes as shown below. Accordingly, the six Culture Archetypes are as follows:

A. **Entrepreneurial**: The Entrepreneurial Culture Archetype is characterized by innovation and trendsetting activities. The work environment is dynamic and agile, and creativity, risk-taking, and innovation are encouraged and rewarded. Employees take pride in their unique work execution, and they are typically driven by ulterior motives, such as a desire to positively change the world and/or disrupt the markets that they serve.

B. **Customer-Centric**: The Customer-Centric Culture Archetype is characterized by its focus on customers, as they weigh in heavily on organizational decisions and influence the organization's strategic direction. The work environment encourages incremental innovation and creative problem-solving, and employees are typically driven by the desire to please customers and provide products/services that exceed customers' expectations.

302

C. **Competitive**: The Competitive Culture Archetype is one that is driven by marketplace competitors. Its work environment practices meritocracy encourages high achievements and rewards performance. Competition, benchmarks, and market trends drive the organization's strategic direction. Employees continuously monitor their markets and are motivated by the desire to achieve excellence and to consistently beat their competitors.

D. **Process**: The Process Culture Archetype is one that is driven by clearly-defined processes and procedures, in an environment that is organized, hierarchical and structured. Stability, consistency, and quality drive the organization's day-to-day operations. Employees know exactly what's expected of them, and they are motivated by job security and by their ability to perform and deliver exactly what's expected of them.

E. **Empowerment**: The Empowerment Culture Archetype is one that is driven by empowerment and accountability, in a work environment that emphasizes inclusivity and accountability. A "laissez-faire" approach characterized by the delegation of authority is what drives the organization's management. Employees have a sense of purpose and always feel included in key decisions. Two factors motivate the employees of such a culture: an acceptance of responsibility and autonomous management of their work.

F. **Teamwork**: The Teamwork Culture Archetype is one that is based on active participation and openness. Two factors drive the organization forward: a teamwork-based approach and individual team members' collective involvement in the workplace. Such an environment is very people-friendly, and its members feel like an extended family. Employees know that they are able to achieve greatness by means of having their individual capabilities leveraged equally with those of everyone else, so they are motivated when working as a unit.

As discussed in the PMAS book, organizational culture develops over time and results from an accumulation of factors that shape the business into what it is today. For example, an organization that is initially established as a startup with a small team of founders and new-hires is likely to have an entrepreneurial culture—one that is lean, agile, and flexible. As this organization develops and survives each stage of growth, its internal and external circumstances change. As such, the organization's original entrepreneurial culture would not be sustained in the long-term, which leads to cultural shifts that would occur within the business in order to ensure sustainable growth. This is partially because new hires import previous cultures into their new units, and a new dominant culture emerges and sets the current-day status quo.

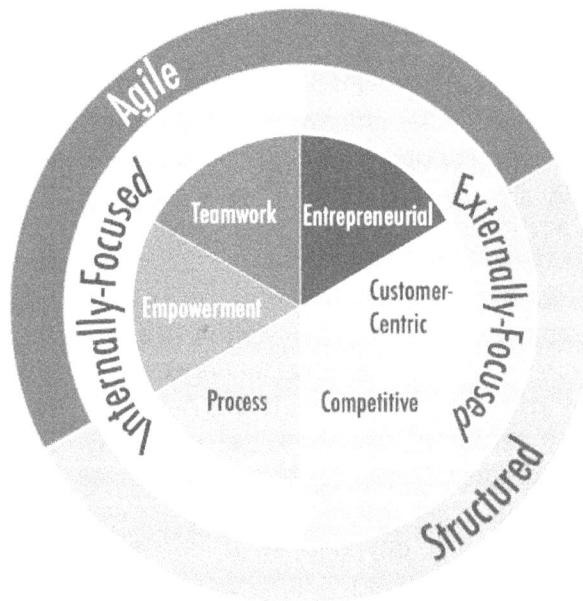

This book aids its readers in nudging individual and group values within organizations by providing techniques necessary for rapid change and transformation across a multitude of organizational cultures. By using this Nudging Workbook, you should be able to better understand what traits, skills and knowledge you need to be able to properly and sustainably situate yourself within your organization's culture.

HOW TO USE THIS GUIDE

This book provides brief descriptions of each Culture Archetype; for a more detailed explanation, please refer to the Organizational Culture Archetype Assessment Workbook. The main purpose of each section is to provide readers with the necessary tools and actions to nudge organizational culture towards a particular Archetype within that section. Therefore, whether you are bridging the gap between a status quo state and a target state, or whether you are ensuring the maintenance of a status quo state while nudging towards a particular archetype, you will want to include the initiatives from the section of that particular Archetype in your transformation program.

The Culture-related initiatives are added to the leadership to form a comprehensive transformation program that achieves the nudges required for change to occur.

The selection process follows the Value mapping process discussed in the PMAS book. The Critical Gap Analysis Map and the Transformation Program Plan requirements are used simultaneously when selecting initiatives from each of the below Culture Archetypes.

The initiatives are combined with the leader's initiatives to develop a comprehensive nudging that include one or more of the following initiatives.

1. Management tools
2. Leadership development initiatives
3. Cultural nudges and initiatives
4. Incentive design

IMPORTANT: The culture nudges and initiatives proposed in this handbook take the form of suggestions designed to nudge your organization in the direction of a particular archetype. The list is by no means exhaustive or comprehensive and will ultimately depend on your situation, your industry, and your specific context. We tried to make the list as general as possible and developed key starters to help you generate more initiatives and KPIs that are applicable to your situation.

On a final note, it's important to apply these initiatives to the formal and informal organization described in the PMAS.

In every section below, we start with a brief description of the organization culture archetype and its key values. For a more detailed description of each archetype, you can refer to the Assessment Workbook.

A. THE ENTREPRENEURIAL CULTURE

Entrepreneurial Culture encourages the creation of entrepreneurial spaces (if you are not already a startup) where teams can come together to co-create and be as innovative as possible. To maintain this culture and reinforce it, the organization, as a whole, must be willing to remain agile at all times and keep up with the accelerated pace of innovation within the business world. Everyone in the organization should be encouraged to pioneer forward and take risks by utilizing futuristic ideas, disruptive innovation, and trendsetting products and services.

Examples of such a culture can be found in the early days of startups, as well as in corporate ventures where environments exist as semi-controlled or managed entities. Beyond startups, entrepreneurial culture cannot co-exist as a dominant archetype alongside large enterprise culture. This is because larger organizations require more discipline and a more rigid structure to function cohesively. However, hi-tech companies and innovative corporations have been known to promote such work environments outside the usual day-to-day structure (or even by granting and encouraging that a day in the week, for example, is provided in this manner) to help foster and maintain continuous innovation. We have seen many examples of large enterprises that ended up killing otherwise successful venture startups by overreaching, interfering, and/or implementing controlling measures too soon.

The culture within this organization needs to foster a mindset targeted towards innovation. Everyone in this organization needs to be trained on the kind of innovation the organization is seeking, whether it relates to products and services or to organizational functioning.

Alongside innovation is the necessity for collective agility, as these two attributes define the Entrepreneurial Culture Archetype.

307

Entrepreneurial Culture thrives amidst unpredictable circumstances, and its participants are expected to adapt to their environments, practice flexibility, and maintain innovation and agility.

When it comes to decision-making, it is important to understand and respect the functioning of power and responsibility within Entrepreneurial culture. Rather than having completely centralized power or an authoritative figure, it is recommended for power to go to whoever is assessing problems at the time. This emphasizes individuality and allows for innovation to flow freely throughout the organization. Each project should be treated independently, and its plans should be temporary and specific to each task in order for adaptability and agility to be present at all times. This helps make room for innovation and co-creation. Moreover, roles and responsibilities are assigned differently, as they vary according to the task at hand.

In general, this culture may seem difficult for some to adopt and adapt to given its turbulent and unstructured nature. However, once it is followed through and maintained well, entrepreneurial culture forges innovation in unexpected ways and allows its members to explore creative potential they didn't know they had. This type of culture requires a leader who is willing to be flexible and adaptable, and who reinforces this behavior across the whole organization.

Below is a long list of initiatives that can be adopted to ensure an Entrepreneurial Culture endures and thrives within an organization:

Innovation:

- Ensure that you have an organizational vision that inspires and impacts the future and the world.
- Run monthly hackathons and design sprint workshops.
- Run structured week-long design sprints and hackathons on a quarterly basis.
- Include external perspectives in workshops by inviting attendees from outside the organization.

- Perform continuous reviews and revisions of visions and mission statements to adapt to market trends and external market conditions.
- Develop systems to encourage, measure, and reward innovative behavior across all levels.
- Set up training programs that encourage and promote creative thinking and cutting-edge methods. Also, emphasize the importance of knowing basic principles of organizational innovation.
- Keep up with teams and provide them with the information necessary for them to be comfortable using new technology in order to create innovative alternatives to pre-existing, stream-line methods.
- Create annual internal exhibitions that allow employees to show off their experimental ideas and learn those of their colleagues.
- Develop tangible rewards that recognize the creativity and innovation displayed by employees, teams, and units. Recognize not only good ideas but also those that support the development and adoption of new methods.

Risk-Taking:

- Celebrate trial-and-error learning, as employees should be encouraged to take on unfamiliar challenges that don't always have a guaranteed outcome.
- Encourage continuous improvement and experimentation and maintain an optionality pipeline.
- Set up a mechanism to continuously prototype, test, and validate concepts and optionalities with potential users.

Agility:

- Move from a hierarchical to a flexible structure that emphasizes speed and agility.
- Involve wider ranges of participants in workshops, sprints, and meetings within the following departments: marketing, finance, customer service, technology, product, human resources, purchasing, engineering, etc.

309

- Hold demo meetings and invite the entire organization to showcase its talents for sprint outcome reviews.
- Hold meetings to discuss differences between transformational and transitional leadership, and explore each leadership style's contributions towards potential change within respective units.
- Assess the organization's overall behavior and don't be afraid to get an outsider's perspective when it comes to potential changes in functioning, goals, targets, tasks and projects.
- Make work visible and maintain a progress board (e.g., Burn-down Chart, Scrum Board).
- Maintain and update regular sprint schedules.
- Maintain a core team of no less than three people who have all the necessary skills to turn visions into realities.
- Maintain and continuously update prioritized product/service backlog lists of necessary requirements for organizational success.
- Run daily (15-minute) stand-up meetings to find out the previous day's accomplishments, the current day's accomplishments, and possible obstacles hindering individuals and/or teams from participating and achieving their goals.

In addition to what was mentioned above, the following Management Tools can aid employees and leaders with the implementation of initiatives:

- Agile Management
- Complexity Reduction
- Internet of Things
- Digital Transformation
- Strategic Alliances
- Zero-based Budgeting

Please refer to the Management Tools Section below for descriptions of the recommended tools.

B. THE CUSTOMER-CENTRIC CULTURE

Customer-Centric ("CC") Culture prioritizes customers at all times. If you wish to incorporate CC Culture into your organization, you need to believe that "the customer is always right," and encourage your team members to adopt this mantra. Taking on a customer-centric approach requires your organization to exhibit a variety of key traits and attitudes.

Placing your customers first means you have to prioritize them in all organizational decisions, including those that have to do with the creation of products and services for them. CC Culture encourages the use of creative approaches when it comes to satisfying customer needs. Consequently, organization members must try to consistently achieve incremental improvement, as customer demands, needs, and wishes are constantly changing. If your organization's culture is not the type that readily adapts to change, this will be a struggle. You need to keep up with customer demands and be ready to deliver high-quality goods and services when necessary.

As a whole, the organization needs to set targets, goals, and objectives to make sure its members don't fall short in anticipating and tackling customer's needs. Also, team meetings need to be held and new projects need to be taken on. Both should be centered around what customers are missing, what needs to be improved on, and if anything needs to be discontinued. This should be done consistently and creatively to make sure it never misses the mark.

The market is constantly changing as are its needs and technological advances. Therefore, in taking on a customer-centric attitude, one needs to be up-to-date with these changes in order to adapt and change their vision, strategies, goals, and products accordingly. As previously mentioned, it's important to centralize customers when making any kind of decision. Accordingly, customer feedback needs to be taken into consideration when products and/or services are released to the public. At the end of the day, anything given out to customers needs to be exactly what they want and need; you need to satisfy their personal demands instead of those of the organization.

Overall, maintaining open communication with your customers is the only way to truly understand and anticipate their needs, and this is where feedback comes in. Organizations should aim to satisfy customer demands using original, unprecedented methods.

As such, the following initiatives can aid you in developing and/or maintaining a Customer-Centric workplace:

Customer-Led Incremental Improvement:

- Make sure that your customers are always well-represented and that any decisions being made are well-coordinated with the customer in mind.
- Involve all departments to make sure customers' needs are at the forefront during the design process.
- Establish a formal customer board that reviews new products before they get approved into the development stage, and provide feedback on existing products and services.
- Consider your customers your allies, develop partnership programs with them, and make sure their input is well-considered in every step forward.
- Regularly assess current loyalty levels through surveys and behavioral data and ask frontline employees whether or not they believe the organization deserves their loyalty.
- Increase the sense of integrity that customers see in your organization.
- Develop a customer education system to help customers make informed choices when it comes to the products and services you provide.
- Consider your customers' feedback evaluations when planning future practices.
- Maintain and update your customer journey map and ensure it is visible to everyone.
- Combine data about each customer interaction with information about its impact on customer satisfaction, loyalty, and business economics.

- Track customer behavior on an ongoing basis and use the data to compile an advanced customer experience dashboard.
- Consider inviting loyal customers to participate in hackathons and design sprints.
- Make sure customer lifetime value is a key performance metric among standard customer-related performance indicators.
- Coordinate information flows dynamically between sales/marketing staff and customer support representatives.

Customer Relationship and Feedback Management:

- Anticipate your customers' needs and find ways to exceed their expectations.
- Have the team be up to date about what's new in the market to ensure continuous improvement.
- Re-examine or re-invent processes associated with customer contacts and customer-to-organization information flow.
- Manage businesses around customer episodes and interactions rather than around internal organizational silos.
- Make sure customer service, marketing, and sales departments consistently prioritize customer feedback and conduct ongoing surveys to assess customer satisfaction.
- Gain insights into which sequence of events leads a customer to a positive result or an unsatisfactory one, and reduce customer complaints and turnover rates.
- Assess your employees' courtesy, competence, and concern levels.
- Hold focus group interviews with customers to understand their current expectations and levels of satisfaction with products and services and, subsequently, hold meetings discussing how to exceed customer expectations.
- Make it easy for customers to make requests and reach out to the company with any concerns.
- Monitor how long it takes for customers to receive products and services, and aim to provide them more quickly while maintaining the same quality.

313

- Analyze the physical location of all units and compare it with an analysis of internal customer relationships. Review what changes might be possible to facilitate better coordination among internal customers.

Creative Problem Solving:

- Make a conscious effort to move from giving customers what they need to giving customers what they would like, to pleasantly surprising customers with products and services that solve problems they didn't expect to be solved.
- Consider the needs of special segments within the customer population. Find new ways to respond to them.
- Highlight problems impacting customer satisfaction and loyalty; provide subsequent solutions that could lead to superior financial rewards and competitive advantage, and determine what kind of creative solutions and initiatives could fix these issues.
- Encourage employees to tackle problem-solving more creatively and invest more time in it by recognizing, defining, and breaking down problems. Also, consider the relationship between problems' hierarchy and root causes before attempting to solve certain issues.

In addition to the above, the following Management Tools can help employees and leaders enforce, monitor, and measure progress towards the attainment of desired results:

- Advanced Analytics
- Balanced Scorecard
- Complexity Reduction
- Customer Journey Analysis
- Customer Segmentation
- Customer Relationship Management
- Customer Satisfaction System
- Internet of Things
- Price Optimization

Please refer to the Management Tools Section below for descriptions of the recommended tools.

C. THE COMPETITIVE CULTURE

Competitive Culture occurs within a competitive, fast-paced, high-intensity work environment. This culture encourages competition both internally and externally, as the organization strives to beat its opponents, and workers aim to come out on top within the company. Moreover, your team, leaders, and managers need to be well-aware of the market they want to dominate in order to set up internal goals and targets that can help them achieve external success.

This culture fosters an environment that keeps everyone on their toes and drives employees to be high-achieving. Also, competitive organizations should aim to both keep up with market changes, emerging trends, new competitors, disruptive innovations, and disruptive market forces. Within an organization adopting Competitive Culture, maintaining market leadership, and ensuring profitability should be two of the company's primary objectives.

If your organization seeks to foster or maintain such a culture, there needs to be an ongoing commitment to excellence, high achievement, and goal-accomplishment, in order for all employees to push their limits. To achieve this, employees need to be energized at all times, and the environment needs to encourage moving forward without focusing on issues that may hinder progress.

The organization, as a whole, needs to be well-aware of its market and how to dominate it. Moreover, predefined performance achievement metrics along with a transparent, unbiased, merit-based reward system should be what determines tangible and intangible benefits and rewards such as pay raises, promotions, and bonus payouts. This is often combined with an "up-or-out" policy that governs promotions and staff retention.

In order to work fairly, it is important to have clearly-defined goals and targets in place at all times to ensure each person is aware of what they need to achieve. Moreover, within Competitive culture, there is little room for anyone to fall short, as goals are strictly aligned with tasks. Finally, this culture encourages its members to explore niche markets and maintain their reputation of being overachievers through hard work.

The following initiatives can help teams foster and reinforce Competitive Culture:

Market-Led Strategy:

- Maintain a strong intelligence system about competitors and internal market trends.
- Dedicate a team to conceptualize new strategies for expanding markets and developing new businesses.
- Make focus groups your go-to in order to keep up with the evolution of the market.
- Ensure proper allocation of direct and indirect costs to all units and emphasize the performance responsibility of every unit, including staff units, while ensuring transparency regarding each unit's performance contribution to the organization's bottom line.
- Build a team to identify areas of growth and to focus on better understanding the market.
- Maintain a visible dashboard and benchmarks against competitors.
- Foster a culture of continuous improvement and reinvention and take on aggressive challenges while maneuvering appropriate changes.
- Examine your current time-to-market response times, and compare them with those of key competitors.

Benchmarking and Overachievement:

- Make achievements and/v.s. target KPIs visible to everyone at all times by emphasizing leaderboards, and recognizing and rewarding high-achievers.

- Identify methods that aid inconsistently gaining a competitive edge, and reward high-achievers that adopt such methods.
- Study competitor best-practices and achievements and share them with employees.
- Implement an assessment framework that evaluates unit contributions to overall corporate competitiveness. Based on the evaluations (feedback loop), establish systems whereby every unit can better contribute to overall competitiveness.
- Use competitive benchmarking in your change efforts and analyze data to identify improvement opportunities. Keep your people aware of the best practices going on elsewhere.
- Choose relevant internal areas and external companies to benchmark.
- Identify extreme targets and goals that require previously-unachieved performance.
- Invest in internal capabilities and compare them with those of other companies to determine the specific skills producing unique capabilities and differentiation.

Recognition and Meritocracy:

- Clarify management priorities to employees and review the current vision, values, goals, objectives, and measures as often as needed.
- Conduct regular anonymous employee surveys to identify motivators, values, and rewards having the highest impact on employee work. Accordingly, translate results into rewards and incentive mechanisms to drive performance, recognition, and meritocracy.
- Analyze the organization's competencies and assess them against anticipated future demands. Develop a competency acquisition program.
- Ensure goals and objectives cascade up and down in abstraction and make sure every KPI drives a specific goal and target measure for both unit and individual levels.
- Set frequent targets, continuously monitor both individual and unit-level KPIs, ensure rewards, recognition, and awards are granted, and continuously celebrate both individual and unit achievements as needed.

317

- Collect and analyze individual and unit performance data regularly and compare actual results with desired performance to take action towards resolving unfavorable gaps.
- Elevate performance evaluation standards and let go of poor performers, or put them on notice.

In addition to the above, the following Management Tools can be used alongside the aforementioned initiatives in order to help employees and leaders enforce, monitor, and measure progress towards the attainment of desired results:

- Advanced Analytics
- Core Competencies
- Customer Segmentation
- Balanced Scorecard
- Benchmarking
- Price Optimization Models
- Internet of Things
- Mergers and Acquisitions
- Strategic Planning

Please refer to the Management Tools Section below for descriptions of the recommended tools.

D. THE PROCESS CULTURE

Process Culture is built around structure, hierarchy, and standardized processes and procedures that ensure consistency, security, quality assurance, and uniformity. The organization practices situational engineering to ensure the order is always in-store and to provide employees with clear job descriptions, and clearly defined roles, responsibilities, and tasks. In such organizations, members feel comfortable in stable and controlled work environments.

Examples of such cultures can be found in different types of franchises: fast-food restaurants, hotel chains, public sector organizations, military units, utility companies, and manufacturing plants that generate products and services according to predetermined standards. Other examples include payroll and accounting departments/units and any process-driven departments within any type of organization. In this case, creative thinking and strategizing are done entirely in hub/command centers—e.g. corporate headquarters or strategy departments.

When it comes to participating in this culture, employees need to work cohesively and be actively aware of the organization's goals and future plans. This means that everyone needs to be sure of what is expected of them and what their specific tasks are. Moreover, the team needs to be comfortable with being monitored, and organization members must ensure consistency in standards. Creativity and outside-the-box thinking are not encouraged and could be detrimental to the organization, especially when everything already runs according to very specific, predefined standards.

Given the fact that the business world can be unstructured and ambiguous, Process Culture tries to ensure a controlled environment by uniformly and consistently monitoring, evaluating, and structuring organization performance. Within this culture, processes and procedures are constantly revised and updated according to the goals and targets set by the organization to ensure collective cohesion.

Overall, long-term goals aim to maintain stability and order, and they ensure that performance targets always meet the required standards. These targets also maintain predictability and ensure all processes are running smoothly and efficiently.

To foster a Process Culture, initiatives are implemented on a top-down, basis and compliance and incremental changes are prioritized. Initiatives meant to strengthen this culture archetype include:

Structure, Stability, Consistency, and Uniformity:

- Adopt the use of technology and/or ERP to reduce paperwork and transition towards a paperless organization.
- Establish, automate, and maintain authority matrices covering every organizational function and level.
- Conduct an initial baseline to determine which processes can be standardized and automated, and which need standardization and automation.
- Implement a total quality management system to ensure the organization has clear processes, procedures, and standards to abide by.
- Acquire relevant management certificates, where applicable, to hold internal processes accountable and have something to measure them against and evaluate them with.
- Assess the disruptions that can affect your organization and set a plan for crisis prevention and response.
- Reduce work fragmentation and establish clear process ownership where employees can gain responsibility and can be held accountable for their performance.
- Maintain and update possible scenarios and options for crisis management and disaster recovery continuously, and prepare action plans in order to immediately resolve possible taxing issues.

- Manage the supply chain holistically rather than fragmentally while leveraging player core competencies and automating information exchange.

Measure, Monitor, and Evaluate:

- Adopt continuous process improvement audits and benchmark them against industry standards.
- Develop your financial, operational, human capital, and customer KPIs at all levels of the organization, based on your vision, mission statement, short-term goals, and long-term objectives.
- Maintain continuously updated internal and external benchmarks, best practices, and industry standards in order to compare and measure performance.
- Set targets and KPI measurement frequencies based on the above, and update targets dynamically.
- Implement a real-time, dynamically adjustable balanced scorecard visible dashboard to measure, monitor, and evaluate your KPIs.
- Monitor, run, and test various "what-if" scenarios in order to prepare for both the expected and unexpected.

Efficiency and Continuous Improvement:

- Ensure you have an internal improvement program that keeps your structure, processes, and procedures up-to-date.
- Redesign core processes and rethink basic organizational and individual issues to improve efficiency and business processes across the organization.
- Rethink and reduce cycle time by eliminating unproductive processes and activities.
- Evaluate and reduce complexity within the organization by reevaluating decision making, decision rights, business processes, procedures, and spans and layers.
- Work on improving quality and scrap reduction where appropriate.
- Understand sources of complexity within the organization and examine trade-offs between operations and customer variety.

Identify opportunities to simplify products, organization structures, business processes, and information systems, all while strengthening core capabilities.

- Track employee time usage, eliminate unproductive meetings and make time-discipline an organization-wide practice.
- Evaluate the organizational structure and process flow in order to drive productivity at both the employee level and that of the organization as a whole.
- Eliminate unproductive activities, improve forecasting, and reduce inventory levels while cutting supply chain management cycle times.
- Implement a total quality management system that ensures continuous improvement and high-quality assurance.

In addition to the above, the following Management Tools can be used alongside the aforementioned initiatives in order to help employees and leaders enforce, monitor, and measure progress towards the attainment of desired results:

- Balanced Scorecard
- Benchmarking
- Complexity Reduction
- Scenario and Contingency Planning
- Business Process Reengineering
- Organizational Time Management
- Supply Chain Management
- Total Quality Management
- Digital Transformation

Please refer to the Management Tools Section below for descriptions of the recommended tools.

E. THE EMPOWERMENT CULTURE

This culture revolves around the empowerment of units, teams, and individuals and provides these entities with the autonomy to operate reliably and efficiently. Employees are comfortable and ready to handle responsibilities by taking on tasks and actively involving themselves in the organization. Leaders, managers, and employees that work together empower one another, as empowerment culture includes everyone in key decisions. Efficient delegation is a key factor of success, so leaders should be able to comfortably assign tasks according to a unit, team, or individual capabilities. Also, employees should be willing to take on these tasks with the goal of completing them to the best of their abilities.

This culture also encourages cross-functional coordination, communication, collaboration and information flow. This enables inclusivity and transparency, allowing collective involvement in and awareness of key organizational aspects. Decision-making in such organizations flows bottom-up and is usually decentralized, with key decisions and authority skewed towards the bottom and left to individuals and employees. This fosters a strong sense of inclusion, as managers and leaders do not simply force decisions onto others, but rather encourage collaborative agreements and collective participation.

Examples of such organizational collaborations include the following: holding companies and their subsidiaries, venture or equity funds and their portfolio companies, federal entities and their state entities, and multinational corporations and their high-level national presence. At lower levels, such examples can be seen in decentralized units such as human resources, and accounting and payroll. This specifically occurs in newly setup functions and departments within growing startups, in corporate headquarters.

An "all hands on deck" approach is the way to go within empowerment culture, as all employees can experience confidence and autonomy. Both of these factors allow team members to further

323

their skills and discover the new potential that could help the organization reach its goals. The team should be well-aware of its capabilities as well as its limitations, even when an individual and/or unit-based overcoming of obstacles is encouraged.

Because internal and external work environments are unstable and unpredictable, Empowerment Culture encourages adapting to the environment. This is why it's important to have accurate, concise, and relevant information move throughout the organization.

In order to foster such a culture, it is necessary for the following initiatives and prerequisites to exist:

Inclusivity:

- Establish a performance improvement program where employees are required to suggest items leading directly to increased profitability, productivity, quality, or responsiveness.
- Involve as many employees as possible in all organizational processes including strategic planning, performance appraisals, pay raises, promotions, incentives design, goals, objectives, vision, mission, resource allocation, management priorities, value proposition, and budget-setting.
- Ensure performance results are dynamically collected, continuously communicated, and visible to all levels of management.
- Make 360 performance appraisal part of the regular performance assessment and KPIs for all unit or team leaders in the organization.
- Make employee engagement a top priority for managers, leaders, and employees. Adopt reliable systems for quickly responding to feedback and developing solutions to key issues.
- Evaluate visions, missions, and aspirations statements to ensure continuous alignment across all levels of the organization.

Autonomy:

- Decentralize authority from central corporate bodies so that each unit or plant director has control of all budgets within the unit.
- Provide high-level strategic guidance and strategic direction and maintain regular communication of shareholder expectations.
- Assist in continuously and actively measuring and reporting results. Then, make information on unit performance against targets available concisely and transparently.
- Consider transitioning to an all-out or a hybrid zero-based budgeting.
- Simplify, evaluate, and increase autonomy by continuously reducing complexity and increasing delegation when it comes to decision making, decision rights, business processes, procedures, and spans and layers.
- Ensure that current incentive schemes are designed to make unit managers feel more empowered.
- Provide a formal review of recommended major ideas generated and proposed by employees or teams. Assist in seeking formal approval from broader governing entities.

Coordination:

- Hold regular retreats with all executives and managers and combine reviews and improvement proposals with measurement and result-reporting sessions.
- Establish standing committees with clearly-defined scopes of engagement for auditing, compensation, board representation, and finance.
- Institute an internal communications program that more effectively informs people of events, activities, and programs.
- Use information about organization ideas and engagement in order to run continuous employee polls and surveys and generate useful, concise, and simple reports.
- Establish a best-practices knowledge base from relevant organizations and make it available to all units of the organization.

- Assist in collecting and sharing information on benchmarks, competition, tools, and performance across departments and units.
- Design a top-level career development program that emphasizes interunit mobility and contributes to cross-functional communication.
- Maintain a log of intergroup conflicts and analyze them in order to generate a systematic set of interventions to resolve these issues.
- Hold regular and coordinated strategic agenda workshops with different cross-sectional groups, and identify problems and collect suggestions for better cross-functional coordination.
- Establish internal support groups and appoint facilitators to help each support group identify its strengths and weaknesses when it comes to providing support and assistance. Hold sessions for the groups in order for members to better explore their relationship and develop a new set of expectations for working together.

In addition to the above, the following Management Tools can be used alongside the aforementioned initiatives in order to help employees and leaders enforce, monitor, and measure progress towards the attainment of desired results:

- Scenario and Contingency Planning
- Strategic Planning
- Benchmarking
- Business Process Reengineering
- Digital Transformation
- Internet of Things
- Employee Engagement Systems
- Complexity Reduction
- Strategic Alliances
- Mergers and Acquisitions
- Zero-Based Budgeting

Please refer to the Management Tools Section below for descriptions of the recommended tools.

F. THE TEAMWORK CULTURE

Teamwork Culture emerges within family-type organizations. As such, it is important to keep in mind certain key traits and attributes that all members should adopt to enrich this culture and maintain it.

The main attributes of Teamwork Culture are shared values and goals, workplace cohesion, togetherness and belonging. All these factors emphasize the need to have supportive and open communication in the workplace. Members of teamwork-centered organizations need to understand the importance of being open and honest when it comes to communication, as it contributes to mental and emotional well-being. This helps create a positive and nurturing environment where all team members feel comfortable sharing their thoughts and feelings. When teams exist in spaces where they feel safe and comfortable, everyone is more likely to put their best foot forward and be consistently productive.

Moreover, when such a coherent and well-established culture is created, teamwork becomes easier and smoother. As such, this culture considers teamwork-driven environments to be necessary. Collective work is considered key when establishing and maintaining such a culture, as organization members can learn from one another and discover new potential they can further, more comfortably, explore within supportive and encouraging spaces. The organization does not only function as an economic entity; it also represents an extended family unit. As such, Teamwork Culture stands out when compared to cultures that are oriented towards processes, organization, and profit. The company as a whole has a commitment to its employees and places them first at all times. It thrives on semi-autonomous work, so while managers/leaders supervise organizational tasks, it is actually employees who are responsible for themselves.

Alongside teamwork comes the added value of developing mentor-mentee relationships. Colleagues, leaders, and managers should strive to develop and nurture such bonds as they speed up the learning process and allow peers to forge through difficult circumstances—whether it be work-related or personal matters.

In general, work relationships should be given importance, and bonds between colleagues should be considered vital when trying to sustain a teamwork culture. When it comes to voicing suggestions, rewarding accomplishments and critiquing setbacks, each of these situations should be handled carefully in order to ensure no relationship is jeopardized and the culture remains well-intact. Employee loyalty, participation, and commitment are considered the major goals for management teams to accomplish. As such, these ambitions should be prioritized when trying to adopt such a collaborative culture.

Examples of this culture could be found within any department across any level and throughout any stage of development. Teamwork Culture does not depend on organizational size, but it's important to note that this culture is not likely to exist as a dominant archetype alongside competitive culture.

Overall, this culture creates a friendly environment that is open to those who wish to work as a happy collective. Such a culture also encourages healthy and educational mentor-mentee relationships. Moreover, tradition and loyalty are key to ensuring everyone works together willingly and cohesively. Finally, participation and consensus are key attributes that should be consistently developed and maintained.

Fostering and promoting Teamwork Culture across organizations requires the following initiatives:

Team-Building:

- Provide regular team-building exercises—either as project segments or as extra-curricular activities—to help promote and refine team-building skills.
- Prioritize budget provision to ensure the celebration of team accomplishments and achievements.

- Conduct social activities that promote teamwork and team-building exercises.
- Include teamwork evaluation and team-related KPIs in performance assessments.
- Ensure employees are actively involved in the planning and execution of team-building activities.
- Implement awareness campaigns designed to make line managers and team leaders better understand the organization's strategic imperatives.
- Implement awareness campaigns highlighting the importance of line manager and team leader roles in relation to company performance.
- Reduce gaps between subordinates and superiors by including performance assessments that allow employees to evaluate their respective higher-ups.

Supportive Communication:

- Consider having a counseling office within the organization to assist employees and to offer free and confidential assessments, short-term counseling, referrals, and follow-up services to employees who have personal and/or work-related problems.
- Conduct effective employee feedback surveys on an ongoing basis to allow for a systematic gathering of employee ideas.
- Re-assess and improve the processes associated with employee diversity.
- Implement a program with generous benefits allowing employees to select their desired levels of medical, dental, life, and disability insurance coverage.

Employee Nurturing:

- Ensure effective succession plans along with collective awareness of these plans.
- Make employee vacations mandatory and consider adding days above industry standards.
- Analyze spans and layers, and consider revisiting/reducing layers and increasing control span.

- Reduce organization complexity.
- Make employee suggestion systems more effective. Accordingly, benchmark the best systems in other organizations in order to upgrade your own.

Training and Development:

- Establish dedicated committees to oversee the continuous education and development of employees.
- Establish orientation programs and a formal training curriculum for all new employees. Similarly, develop extensive (1-2 year) rotational programs for entry-level employees enabling their proper placement upon graduation.
- Continuously assess training needs in each unit in order to evaluate priorities and necessary program revisions.
- Ensure mandatory training attendance to make employees understand that training is part of their jobs.
- Ensure ongoing coaching and mentoring training not only for leaders but also for team members. Also, assert that these programs are meant to foster open communication.
- Allocate a budget for training and development/consider establishing an internal training facility that allows organizations to reflect on employee development.
- Invest in a 360-degree performance evaluation process to assess leadership practices across all management levels.
- Conduct annual performance review meetings involving mostly senior organization members and ensure all cases are reviewed fairly and objectively.

In addition, employees and leaders can benefit from the following Management Tools:

- Employee Engagement Systems
- Balanced Scorecards
- Complexity Reduction

Please refer to the Management Tools Section below for descriptions of the recommended tools.

MANAGEMENT TOOLS DESCRIPTION

As mentioned above and in the PMAS toolset book, without adequate management tools, companies might not be able to achieve targets and goals, and they may also not be able to maintain monitor, or track initiative progress. Therefore, in order to achieve cultural changes and cultural nudges, adopting an integrated approach with the right management tools is essential.

As a side note, no matter the size of the culture gap, two main tools should always exist, and this is why we did not add them at every level. The first management tool is Vision and Mission Statements. Whether at an organizational unit level or at an enterprise-level, having a **"Congruent"** vision and mission statement is essential to establishing your goals, objectives, and, ultimately, your target state. Whether you already have one in place or not, in almost every single engagement we had, we found that not all stakeholders and organization leaders agreed to or understood their organizational visions and missions. If you don't have that as a well-established base, you will lack direction and alignment, and you will face many disagreements throughout your journey of organizational culture change. The second management tool is Change Management. Although it does not need to exist in the long run, the reason we recommend having change management is that it is an essential first step towards building a culture of adaptability. In the PMAS book, we argue why this is more important than nudging towards a specific culture: adapting to external factors (e.g., pandemic, global shocks and events, disruptive technologies, terrorist attacks, recessions, etc.) may require a fast cultural shift and cannot endure a long-term transformation program.

The table below summarizes the management tools that are recommended for each culture type. However, no matter the type of nudges you're trying to implement, you will need to take the entire system into consideration when adopting an integrated approach towards the implementation of these tools. Please refer to the

Balanced Scorecard book that you received as part of this package. Moreover, the list below is by no means exhaustive and should be used as indicative; there are subsets of tools and other nomenclatures adopted to refer to the same or a combination of tools. All in all, this list covers more than 80% of what most successful companies use as management tools that help them make business decisions that lead to enhanced processes, products, and services—as well as deliver superior performance and profits. Successful adoption of these tools requires an understanding of the pros and cons of each one, as well as an ability to creatively and "**<u>systematically</u>**" integrate the right tools in the right way at the right time. Choosing management tools on the basis of hype makes adopting such tools a wasteful and risky undertaking.

	A	B	C	D	E	F
	Entrepreneur	Customer-Centric	Competitive	Process	Empower-ment	Teamwork
Vision/Mission Statements	✓	✓	✓	✓	✓	✓
Change Management	✓	✓	✓	✓	✓	✓
Advanced Analytics		✓	✓	✓		
Agile Management	✓					
Balanced Scorecard		✓	✓	✓	✓	✓
Benchmarking			✓	✓	✓	
Business Process Re-engineering				✓	✓	
Complexity Reduction	✓	✓		✓	✓	✓
Customer Journey Analysis		✓				
Customer Relationship Management		✓				
Customer Satisfaction Systems		✓				
Customer Segmentation		✓	✓			
Digital Transformation	✓			✓	✓	
Employee Engagement Systems					✓	✓
Internet of Things	✓	✓	✓		✓	
Organizational Time Management				✓		
Mergers and Acquisitions			✓		✓	

	A	B	C	D	E	F
	Entrepreneur	Customer-Centric	Competitive	Process	Empower-ment	Teamwork
Price Optimization Models		✓	✓			
Scenario & Contingency Planning				✓	✓	
Strategic Alliances	✓				✓	
Strategic Planning			✓		✓	
Supply Chain Management				✓		
Total Quality Management						
Zero-Based Budgeting	✓				✓	

Herebelow is a brief description of each management deployment. However, we will not be going into much detail, as each tool warrants a book of its own.

Vision and Mission Statements

A Vision/Mission Statement is what guides your company and allows it to reach its desired goals and objectives. This statement provides your company with a path to follow and helps the business define its purpose. This statement is more meaningful and should not be neglected, as a well-thought-out mission/vision statement highlights the company's purpose, goals, and values.

The Vision/Mission Statement is usually established and agreed upon by top-level managers who expect its implementation by lower-level management and employees. Shorter, more precise, statements are produced across various departments.

The development process requires managers to:

- Have a clear idea of the culture, values, and strategy within the organization.
- Address and align its vision and mission to key stakeholders.

334

- Ensure that objectives are measurable, approaches are actionable, visions are achievable.
- Communicate the message using clear, simple and precise language.
- Develop buy-in and support throughout the organization.

Mission and Vision Statements are commonly used to:

- Guide management thinking on strategic issues, especially during times of significant change.
- Define performance standards and help develop a written-out protocol for the organization to follow.
- Inspire employees to work more productively by providing focus and common goals.
- Guide employee decision-making.
- Help establish a framework for ethical behavior.

Adopting this management tool across every nudging initiative is key for congruency and alignment. Without a vision or mission statement in place, your target state can't be set. In fact, if you develop and/or update this statement on a regular basis through an inclusive process, you can align the organization with your mission. In advance, it helps you accelerate the change management program by allowing your organization to skip the step involving collective alignment with Target State (refer to the PMAS book for details).

Change Management

Change Management is a program facilitating the implementation of new processes that guide the organization towards the greater output. Such programs include the exploration and possible implementation of change initiatives, the generation of organizational buy-ins, and the creation and establishment of models ensuring continuous future success. This management tool helps leaders and managers understand and highlight possible weak points and, subsequently, establish strategies that can mitigate risks and monitor progress for eventual success.

The development process requires managers to:

- Set clear goals and design incentives to ensure reaching these goals is done as efficiently as possible and attain desired results.
- Identify change risk and work towards predicting, measuring, and managing its contributing factors.
- Ensure communication is always clear and concise during times of change to make sure employees are aligned and motivated.
- Delve into the most important decisions that need to be made.

- Monitor progress at all times, especially when taking no-change initiatives.

Change Management is commonly used to:

- Establish stable strategic initiatives to adapt to market changes, customer preferences, and strategic company plans.
- Align the organization and stay on track when major change is taking place.
- Implement new processes and new initiatives.

As such, Change Management should be part of any program that involves culture change or the maintenance of cultural adaptability. Whether Change Management takes the form of a major initiative or a minor tactic, its techniques should be part of all culture-related nudge initiatives.

Advanced Analytics

Advanced Analytics is a strategy that allows for the rapid extraction, transformation, loading, search, analysis, and sharing of massive data. This method aims to quickly identify previously unnoticed correlations in order to perform efficient data analysis. Data is processed easily via the following means:

- Expand the volume of data processed.
- Increase the speed at which the data is processed.
- Improve on the type of data processed.
- Have a wider range of data to process.

Applying this management tool helps managers better measure and manage critical functions within their organization as well as with customers and competitors. The implementation process requires managers to:

- Identify significant business opportunities that could benefit from superior data, then determine if Advanced Analytics solutions are needed.
- Develop hardware, software, and talent needed to implement the management tool.
- Incorporate data scientists who better understand how to implement this tool into the organization.
- Identify specific decisions and actions that can be improved.
- Establish guiding principles such as data privacy and security policies.
- Expand management tools to other business areas.

In the context of culture-nudging, we recommend that the following archetypes consider adopting Advanced Analytics

- Customer-Centric Culture

- Competitive Culture
- Process Culture

Agile Management

Agile Management is all about bringing the most noteworthy innovations to light and introducing them to the market at a faster pace to improve team engagement and customer satisfaction. Some common Agile Management approaches include Scrum, Kanban, Lean Development, and Lean Startup.

The development process requires managers to:

- Identify opportunities for agile innovation.
- Assemble a small, multidisciplinary, self-governing team to tackle important opportunities.
- Have a 'Head of Initiatives' to help the team with establishing a vision, developing a list of initiatives, and planning on how to tackle those opportunities and their expected results.
- Have the team create a roadmap of all possible problems and their subsequent solutions. Produce and test prototypes before committing to a new idea; adapt the next step forward depending on feedback received.
- Have the team continuously identify opportunities to improve effectiveness.

In the context of culture-nudging, we recommend that Entrepreneurship Culture Archetypes consider adopting Agile Management.

Balanced Scorecard

A Balanced Scorecard defines an organization's performance and measures how well and how accurately it achieves its desired results. This management tool accompanies Mission and Vision Statements well, as it translates them into more solid objectives and goals that can be quantified, measured, and evaluated. There are five main categories of performance that are measured:

A. Financial performance (revenues, earnings, return on capital, cash flow)
B. Customer value performance (market share, customer satisfaction measures, customer loyalty)
C. Internal business process performance (productivity rates, quality measures, timeliness)
D. Innovation performance (percentage of revenue from new products, employee suggestions, rate of improvement index)
E. Employee performance (morale, knowledge, turnover, use of best-demonstrated practices)

The development process requires managers to:

- Understand and establish a coherent vision and strategy for the business.
- Understand which performance category would best suit the organization's vision.
- Establish objectives best-suited to the organization's end goal.
- Develop effective measures and standards, to quantitatively evaluate the organization's performance.
- Check-in with the organization to make sure everyone is on board when it comes to feasible measures and standards.
- Introduce budgeting, tracking, communication, and appraisal systems.
- Compare actual results with desired levels of performance.
- Close unwanted gaps.

In the context of culture-nudging, we recommend that the following archetypes consider using the Balanced Scorecard:

- Teamwork Culture
- Customer-Centric Culture
- Competitive Culture
- Process Culture
- Empowerment Culture

Benchmarking

Benchmarking has one main objective: improving the performance of organizations. This is usually done by identifying and applying well-known, successful practices to operations and sales. Managers adopt this tool to compare their performances with those of competitors and best-in-class companies, and to understand what practices drive higher performance so that they can determine how competitive they are in the marketplace, and so they can identify areas of weaknesses that require improvements. Successful companies adopt this tool to improve and incorporate the aforementioned operations into company processes by using them as inspiration, not imitation.

The development process requires managers to:

- Select a product, service, or process to benchmark.
- Identify KPIs.
- Use other companies or internal areas as benchmarks.
- Collect data and measure performances.
- Analyze the data and identify areas that need improvement.
- Adapt and implement the best practices while keeping in mind that reasonable goals should be set and that all organization members should be discussing their opinions of this tool.

338

In the context of culture-nudging, we recommend that the following archetypes consider using Benchmarking:

- Competitive Culture
- Process Culture
- Empowerment Culture

Business Process Re-engineering

Business Process Re-engineering is an exhaustive redesign of the business core process. The goal of this tool is to improve productivity and quality. Companies usually re-design what already exists to bring more value to their customers or to eliminate redundancies such as low productivity.

The development process requires managers to:

- Refocus on what customers need and desire.
- Redesign core processes while keeping up with the best-used technology for improvement.
- Assemble teams that coordinate and align processes.
- Improve processes across the organization as a whole.

Business Process Re-Engineering is commonly used to:

- Reduce costs and cycle times by eliminating redundancies, ensuring overall employee productivity and smooth information flow, and accounting for and dealing with errors.
- Improve the quality of products and services by measuring performance and establishing responsibility for outputs produced.

Complexity Reduction

Complexity Reduction is a management tool that helps organizations simplify their strategy processes and outputs and reduce organizational clutter. Usually, the more intricately an organization runs, the higher its risk of experiencing unnecessary complications leading to higher costs, poor returns, and less growth. By trying to intersect customers' needs with low cost, organizations are able to simplify their processes while maintaining quality and services at the lowest cost possible.

The development process requires managers to:

- Identify and understand what are the current complicated processes in the organization.
- Identify any opportunities that could help simplify certain processes.

- Simplify decision-making and ensure consistent coordination and communication when taking on this tool.

In the context of culture-nudging, we recommend that the following archetypes consider using Complexity Reduction:

- Teamwork Culture
- Entrepreneurship Culture
- Customer-Centric Culture
- Process Culture
- Empowerment Culture

Customer Journey Analysis

Customer Journey Analysis provides companies with an inside look into customer perspectives. As such, organizations are better able to understand their customers' experiences with the companies. Organizations can then use this information to better map out future strategies, eliminate redundancies, and achieve objectives.

Everything from start to finish is noted, whether it's an online service, delivery experience, or a chat with customer service. As such, this data should be used to close any gaps for future improvement.

This management tool usually uses Big Data to identify complex patterns in customer behavior and trends so that immediate action can be taken against potential issues.

The development process requires managers to:

- Analyze and monitor every step of their customers' experiences.
- Present data on customer satisfaction for further improvement.
- Collect performance information detailing how customer experiences should be, from start to finish.
- Have a better understanding of what customers value.
- Identify a possible waste in company resources and/or customer time.

In the context of culture-nudging, we recommend that the Customer-Centric Culture archetype consider adopting Customer Journey Analysis.

Customer Relationship Management

Customer Relationship Management (CRM) is a tool used to better understand customers and respond to changes in their needs and desires as quickly as possible. This technology allows organizations to collect data and put it to use for strategic purposes. As such, the data collected helps organizations solve their customers' problems more quickly and effectively, which allows organizations to better target products towards their clientele. Ideally, this information should aid in generating solutions to problems occurring outside of organizations' marketing functions.

The development process requires managers to:

- Identify their customers' 'pain points' to better understand what causes them dissatisfaction and what standards the organization is unable to meet.
- Evaluate whether or not adopted CRM can help bridge the aforementioned gaps.
- Calculate the cost of adopting and implementing the program.
- Assess the pros and cons of adopting the program.
- Design an incentives program ensuring employee participation, since targeting customers has proven most successful when adopting this management tool.
- Measure the tools' progress and impact, and monitor employee participation.
- Share all the data collected about the success or failure of the program with the whole organization so that everyone understands the need for improvement.

In the context of culture-nudging, we recommend that companies adopting the Customer-Centric Culture archetype consider using Customer Relationship Management. Customer Satisfaction Systems.

Customer Satisfaction Systems help the business increase its revenues and profits by improving retention among its customers, employees, and investors. This tool helps companies recognize the importance of loyalty programs and implement them, so it's easier to understand the root cause of dissatisfaction. This, ultimately, helps companies improve and strengthen ties with their customers. Furthermore, this tool quantifies financial results and helps companies benefit from any small shifts in performance or growth.

The development process requires managers to:

- Assess, on a regular basis, current loyalty levels by collecting data and understanding the difference between satisfaction and loyalty. Customers, employees, and investors should be taken into consideration when collecting this information.
- Study and benchmark this information with that of competitors.
- Track important performance dimensions according to information provided by customers.
- Conduct regular feedback surveys.
- Set targets in order to build loyalty and decrease retention. These targets would need to be incentivized, planned, and well-budgeted.

341

- Revise currently applicable policies that provide customers with short-term results such as discounts or service feeds.
- Understand why certain groups are loyal to the organization.

In the context of culture-nudging, we recommend that individuals adopting the Customer-Centric Culture archetype consider using Customer Satisfaction.

Customer Segmentation

Customer Segmentation is a subdivision of marketing whereby customers with similar interests are grouped together in order to improve and enhance their experiences and target their specific needs. This provides the organization with a competitive advantage, as members are better able to understand the niche groups within the customer market. This management tool aids the organization by providing its customers with tailoring offers, discounts, products, and services to suit their needs. This will also aid in campaigns and pricing strategies and will help improve resource allocation and product development.

The development process requires managers to:

- Divide the market into respective segments according to customer needs, past behaviors, and demographics.
- Identify which segment could be most profitable and which could be the most costly.
- Use cost-profit analysis to establish a system that highlights segments that can be targeted and segments that are not feasible.
- Allocate resources for production, service, marketing, and distribution so that each target segment's needs are met.
- Measure and monitor individual segment performance and improve approaches over time.

In the context of culture-nudging, we recommend that the following archetypes considering adopting Customer Segmentation:

- Customer-Centric Culture
- Competitive Culture

Digital Transformation

This management tool brings together the use of digital technologies into organizational strategies and operations. This helps the organization focus on the best opportunities to take when it comes to merging the digital and physical worlds. This transformation prioritizes customers, as their experiences are directly tied to the path the organization chooses to take. This tool should help improve competitive advantage and increase profits.

The development process requires managers to:

- Determine whether to apply Digital Disruption—a complete transformation from a physical business to a digital one—or Digital Transformation—a merger between the physical and digital worlds that creates entirely new sources of value.
- Understand the extent of digitization and assess any future threats.
- Develop means of engaging customers and gaining their loyalty throughout periods of significant change.
- Improve customer experiences by studying digitization's best sources of values.
- Orient the organization towards more innovation.

In the context of culture-nudging, we recommend that the following archetypes consider adopting Digital Transformation:

- Entrepreneurship Culture
- Process Culture
- Empowerment Culture

Employee Engagement Systems

This management tool is used to measure how involved and satisfied employees are with their work and with the organization. This ensures that the employee's well-being is always up to standard and that customer loyalty and business performance are constantly improving. Furthermore, this survey is a good indicator of how attached employees are to their jobs, colleagues, and organizations, and it aids in determining employees who are willing to go beyond their basic job duties. This also helps determine what factors will reduce employee retention and improve employee satisfaction and loyalty. This is very similar to customer engagement and is usually measured in the same way.

The development process requires managers to:

- Understand what drives employee engagement, by using various sources including surveys, suggestion boxes, and discussions.
- Understand that surveys need to be respectful of employee time, all while retaining as much information as possible.
- Conduct surveys frequently so information is more accurate and reliable.
- Value employees and prioritize them when it comes to developing solutions to key issues.

In the context of culture-nudging, we recommend that the following archetypes consider adopting Employee Engagement:

- Teamwork Culture

343

- Empowerment Culture

Internet of Things

This management tool is an expansive network of connected sensors, smart devices, and advanced analytics used to retrieve vital information for monitoring and evaluating services.

The development process requires managers to:

- Incorporate sensors and devices into consumer goods and industrial equipment in order to gain more information and feedback.

In the context of culture-nudging, we recommend considering that the following archetypes consider adopting the Internet of Things:

- Entrepreneurship Culture
- Customer-Centric Culture
- Competitive Culture
- Empowerment Culture

Mergers and Acquisitions

M&As have become vastly popular over the past decade, as companies use corporate finance strategies to create competitive advantage and increase shareholder value. An acquisition is when a larger company takes over a smaller one, and merging is when the two forces join equally. Usually, these are friendly business encounters—unless the board of a company is completely taken over, then this is considered more hostile. The key success factors depend on competition reduction thereafter and on the speed of shareholder value increase. This is why it's important to assess and understand businesses well before such a commitment is made.

The development process requires managers to:

- Prioritize the merger's strategic rationale and goals.
- Communicate vision transparently with merger leaders.
- Design new organization and operating plans.
- Address the specific challenges that need to be overcome as a result of business negotiations as immediately as possible.
- Implement the integration plan aggressively, with little room for failure or setbacks.

In the context of culture-nudging, we recommend that the following archetypes consider adopting Mergers and Acquisitions:

- Competitive Culture
- Empowerment Culture

Organizational Time Management

By adopting this management tool, organizations will start viewing time as a scarce resource that needs to be invested ineffectively—as is done with finance. It will then be more possible to track levels of engagement and time spent on tasks. This can help in managing budgets, reducing pressure on executives, and lowering costs, all while boosting productivity.

The development process requires managers to:

- Prioritize time when completing tasks.
- Use time management tracking tools to help increase productivity and improve time management.
- Combine these tools with analytical tools, such as productivity benchmarking, to improve performance.
- Eliminate low-value tasks that take up too` much time.
- Delegate authority when it comes to time-consuming tasks.
- Standardize the decision process.
- Make time discipline an important factor in daily work life.
- Use feedback to help manage workloads.

In the context of culture-nudging, we recommend that the Process Culture archetype considers adopting Organizational Time Management.

Price Optimization Models

Price Optimization Models are mathematical programs that calculate demand variation across different price levels in order to collect data necessary for regulating prices and increasing profits. This highlights price as an important profit lever and tailors prices to customer segments. Furthermore, this also helps with forecasting demand, developing pricing strategies, improving promotion strategies, and controlling inventory levels, all while improving customer satisfaction.

The development process requires managers to:

- Determine the desired outputs and required inputs.
- Collect data on their prices, promotions, competitor prices, economic conditions, product availability, and various costs.
- Set rules to help guide the modeling process.
- Run the model and pay attention to feedback.

345

- Monitor results and improve data input to enhance process accuracy.

In the context of culture-nudging, we recommend that the following archetypes consider adopting Price Optimization Models:

- Customer-Centric Culture
- Competitive Culture

Scenario and Contingency Planning

This management tool allows executives to explore and prepare for several alternative futures. It helps examine expected outcomes under various economic conditions. This tool also helps assess any sudden market changes or business disruptions that may occur. It allows managers to practice a "what-if" mindset in order to expect the worst and prepare for it. Finally, it creates a hypothetical environment that forces companies to prepare a course of action, no matter what comes ahead.

The development process requires managers to:

- Choose time frames to explore.
- Create and explore different scenarios that could occur.
- Test the impact of each scenario.
- Develop an action plan for the best solution.
- Monitor events and keep track of what is going according to plan and what isn't.
- Make any changes necessary, after evaluation.

In the context of-culture nudging, we recommend that the following archetypes consider adopting Scenario and Contingency Planning:

- Process Culture
- Empowerment Culture

Strategic Alliances

Strategic Alliances are agreements between different firms in which they decide on a common path to take, projects to complete, and/or challenges to take on. Alliances can include any group of people—customers, suppliers, competitors, or even the government. This helps both parties gain a competitive advantage, enter new markets, and/or share the risk of a current crisis they may both be facing.

The development process requires managers to:

- Understand their business visions and strategies so that when they align with their alliances, their objectives are well understood and they can fit in together harmoniously.
- Choose potential alliances depending on how well they can benefit the organization.
- Develop a strong working relationship and understand that all parties involved are doing so for their own benefit.
- Monitor alliance performance.

In the context of culture-nudging, we recommend that the following archetypes consider adopting Strategic Alliances:

- Entrepreneurship Culture
- Empowerment Culture

Strategic Planning

Strategic Planning is a process used to determine where the business is at present, where it should be, and what needs to be done in order to reach its desired state. The business' objectives should be directly linked to its goals, and resources should be allocated in order to achieve those goals.

The development process requires managers to:

- Understand the organization's mission, vision, and fundamental values.
- Recognize the strengths, weaknesses, threats, and opportunities present.
- Set current and future priorities.
- Improve and focus on competitor intelligence and actions.
- Identify and evaluate alternative strategies.
- Establish clear and concise objectives.
- Allocate resources to achieve these objectives.
- Plan for any strategy-related changes that may occur.
- Monitor performance.

In the context of culture-nudging, we recommend that the following archetypes consider adopting Strategic Planning:

- Competitive Culture
- Empowerment Culture

Supply Chain Management

Supply Chain Management aligns the efforts of suppliers, manufacturers, distributors, dealers and customers to meet customers' demands. This usually involves a technological approach, for purposes of increased efficiency. This helps customers feel more valued in the business and helps create stronger relationships between all involved parties. Furthermore, this enhances and maintains both communication and trust because all parties have a common aim—achieving total customer satisfaction.

The development process requires managers to:

- Increase trust and improve existing supply chain relationships.
- Improve the quality and quantity of information exchanged, so everyone can be up-to-date and performance can be steadily improved.
- Combine processes in the supply chain to avoid having too many loose chains and independent processes.
- Transform the supply chain completely in order to exceed customer expectations.

In the context of culture-nudging, we recommend companies following the Process Culture archetype to consider adopting Supply Chain Management.

Zero-Based Budgeting

This management tool is typically adopted to help with resource planning and resource allocation. It forces managers to deal head-on with current finance allocation and use. This tool also demands that leaders justify actions they have taken in terms of expenses. Such a task should be performed through streamlining, standardization, outsourcing, offshoring, or automation. This process helps align resource allocation with strategic goals.

The development process requires managers to:

- Re-examine current resource allocation and consider what should be kept and what should be abandoned.
- Build an ideal future plan.
- Decide on what activities should be performed.
- Start from scratch with budgets, planning, and implementation.

In the context of culture-nudging, we recommend that the following archetypes consider adopting Zero-Based Budgeting:

- Entrepreneurship Culture
- Empowerment Culture

•

BIBLIOGRAPHY

Introduction

Benatar, D. (2009). Better to have never been. Oxford University Press, Oxford University, Oxford.

Bright, D. et al. (2019). Principles of management. Openstax College, Rice University, Ann Arbor, MI.

Debevoise, N. D. (n.d.). The Third Critical Step In Problem Solving That Einstein Missed. Forbes. Retrieved February 13, 2023, from https://www.forbes.com/sites/nelldebevoise/2021/01/26/the-third-critical-step-in-problem-solving-that-einstein-missed/?sh=9b6b77438079

Dobrescu, R., & Purcarea, V. (2011). Emergence, self–organization and morphogenesis in biological structures. Journal of Medicine and Life, 4(1), 82–90. https://www.ncbi.nlm.nih.gov/pmc/articles/PMC3056426/

Godwin, D. K., Boyle, D. M., & Higgs, M. A. (2021). Chapter 14: Organizational Culture. Mtsu.pressbooks.pub. https://mtsu.pressbooks.pub/usingteamsfororgdev/chapter/chapter-14-organizational-culture/

Haack, S. (2009). Evidence and inquiry. Prometheus Press, Amherst.

Hayek, F. (1996). Individualism and economic order. University of Chicago Press, University of Chicago, Chicago.

Hoopes, J. (1993). Peirce on signs. University of North Carolina Press, University of North Carolina, Chapel Hill.

Yang, X.-S. (2021). Genetic Algorithm — an overview | ScienceDirect Topics. Www.sciencedirect.com. https://www.sciencedirect.com/topics/engineering/genetic-algorithm

Background

Amissah, M., Gannon, T., & Monat, J. (2020). What is Systems Thinking? Expert Perspectives from the WPI Systems Thinking Colloquium of 2 October 2019. Systems, 8(1), 6. https://doi.org/10.3390/systems8010006

Grohs, J. R., Kirk, G. R., Soledad, M. M., & Knight, D. B. (2018). Assessing systems thinking: A tool to measure complex reasoning through ill-structured problems. Thinking Skills and Creativity, 28, 110–130. https://doi.org/10.1016/j.tsc.2018.03.003

Harding, D., Vorobyov, A., Kumar, S., & Galligan, S. (2022, February 8). State of the M&A Market. Bain. https://www.bain.com/insights/state-of-the-market-m-and-a-report-2022/

Kengelbach, J., Utzerath, D., Kaserer, C., & Schatt, S. (2010, March 27). How Successful M&A Deals Split the Synergies. BCG Global.

https://www.bcg.com/publications/2013/mergers-acquisitions-postmerger-integration-divide-conquer-deals-split-synergies

Martin, R. L. (2016, June). M&A: The One Thing You Need to Get Right. Harvard Business Review. https://hbr.org/2016/06/ma-the-one-thing-you-need-to-get-right

Miles, L., Borchert, A., & Ramanathan, A. E. (2014, August 13). Why Some Merging Companies Become Synergy Overachievers. Bain & Company. https://www.bain.com/insights/why-some-merging-companies-become-synergy-overachievers

Morey, T., Forbath, T., & Schoop, A. (2015, October 11). Customer Data: Designing for Transparency and Trust. Harvard Business Review. https://hbr.org/2015/05/customer-data-designing-for-transparency-and-trust

Schad, J., M.W. Raicsch, S. & Smith, W. K. (2016). Paradox Research in Management Science: Looking Back to Move Forward. Academy of Management Annals, 10(1), pp. 5-64. doi:10.1080/19416520.2016.1162422

Systems Thinking — Rethink Everything. (2022, January 13). Systems Innovation. https://www.systemsinnovation.io/post/systems-thinking-rethink-everything

Thompson, E. K., & Kim, C. (2020). Post-M&A Performance and Failure: Implications of Time until Deal Completion. Sustainability, 12(7), 2999. https://doi.org/10.3390/su12072999

Wang, Z., & Wang, Y. (2020). Prospect theory-based group decision-making with stochastic uncertainty and 2-tuple aspirations under linguistic assessments. Information Fusion, 56, 81–92. https://doi.org/10.1016/j.inffus.2019.10.001

Definitions and Applications

Clauset, A., Shalizi, C. R., & Newman, M. E. J. (2009). Power-Law Distributions in Empirical Data*. SIAM Review. https://pdodds.w3.uvm.edu/research/papers/others/2009/clauset2009b.pdf

Warusawitharana, M. (2016). Time-varying Volatility and the Power Law Distribution of Stock Returns. https://www.federalreserve.gov/econres/feds/time-varying-volatility-and-the-power-law-distribution-of-stock-returns.htm

Organizational Structures and Design. (n.d.). Canvas.wayne.edu. Retrieved July 11, 2022, from https://canvas.wayne.edu/courses/1/modules/items/1879707

Gitman, L. J., McDaniel, C., Amit Shah, Reece, M., Koffel, L., Talsma, B., & Hyatt, J. C. (2018, September 18). The Informal Organization. Opentextbc.ca; OpenStax Introduction to Business. https://opentextbc.ca/businessopenstax/chapter/the-informal-organization/

Andriani, Pierpaolo and McKelvey, Bill, Beyond Gaussian Averages: Redirecting Management Research Toward Extreme Events and Power Laws (July 2006). http://dx.doi.org/10.2139/ssrn.983084

Godwin, D. K., Boyle, D. M., & Higgs, M. A. (2021). Chapter 14: Organizational Culture. Mtsu.pressbooks.pub. https://mtsu.pressbooks.pub/usingteamsfororgdev/chapter/chapter-14-organizational-culture/

Informal Organization: Definition, Structure & Examples — Video & Lesson Transcript | Study.com. (2016). Study.com. https://study.com/academy/lesson/informal-organization-definition-structure-examples.html

Kahneman, D., & Tversky, A. (1979). Prospect Theory: An Analysis of Decision Under Risk. Econometrica, 47(2), 263–292. https://doi.org/10.2307/1914185

Kahneman, D. (2011). Thinking, Fast and Slow. Farrar, Straus and Giroux.

Linkov, I., & Trump, B. D. (2019). Applications of Network Science and Systems Thinking. The Science and Practice of Resilience, 167–179. https://doi.org/10.1007/978-3-030-04565-4_9

Reynolds, C. (n.d.). Boids (Flocks, Herds, and Schools: a Distributed Behavioral Model). Red3d.com. http://www.red3d.com/cwr/boids/

Reynolds, C. W. (1987). Flocks, herds and schools: A distributed behavioral model. ACM SIGGRAPH Computer Graphics, 21(4), 25–34. https://doi.org/10.1145/37402.37406

Starlings Coordinate Movements Within a Flock — Biological Strategy — AskNature. (2020). Asknature. https://asknature.org/strategy/starlings-coordinate-movements-within-a-flock/

Lundstedt, S. (1972). Consequences of Reductionism in Organization Theory. Public Administration Review, 32(4), 328. https://doi.org/10.2307/974993

Moe, N. B., Šmite, D., Paasivaara, M., & Lassenius, C. (2021). Finding the sweet spot for organizational control and team autonomy in large-scale agile software development. Empirical Software Engineering, 26(5). https://doi.org/10.1007/s10664-021-09967-

Organizational Structures and Design. (n.d.). Canvas.wayne.edu. Retrieved July 11, 2022, from https://canvas.wayne.edu/courses/1/modules/items/1879707

Ståhle, P., & Åberg, L. (2015). Organizations in a Non-Linear, Unpredictable World. Business and Management Studies, 1(1). https://doi.org/10.11114/bms.v1i1.667

Stanford 125. (2016, June 14). Lessons from ants: Deborah Gordon. Stanford 125. https://125.stanford.edu/lessons-from-ants-deborah-gordon/

Theurer, C. P., Tumasjan, A., & Welpe, I. M. (2018). Contextual work design and employee innovative work behavior: When does autonomy matter? PLOS ONE, 13(10), e0204089. https://doi.org/10.1371/journal.pone.0204089

Warusawithrana, Missaka (2016). "Time-varying Volatility and the Power Law Distribution of Stock Returns," Finance and Economics Discussion Series 2016-022. Washington: Board of Govenors of the Federal Reserve System, http://dxdoi.org/10.17016/FEDS.2016.022

WATCHDOG HOW-TOS. (n.d.). https://www.ucsusa.org/sites/default/files/attach/2018/07/SN_Toolkit_Power_Mapping_Your_Way_to_Success.pdf

Zamaleo, F. (2012). Peirce's Logic of Continuity. Boston: Docent Press.

The PMAS

Andriani, P., & McKelvey, B. (2006, July 1). Beyond Gaussian Averages: Redirecting Management Research Toward Extreme Events and Power Laws. Papers.ssrn.com. https://papers.ssrn.com/sol3/papers.cfm?abstract_id=983084

Fox, A., McCormick, R., Procter, R., & Carmichael, P. (2007). The design and use of a mapping tool as a baseline means of identifying an organization's active networks1. International Journal of Research & Method in Education, 30(2), 127–147. https://doi.org/10.1080/17437270701383271

Goleman, D., Boyatzis, R. E., McKee, A., & Finkelstein, S. (2017). Everyday Emotional Intelligence: Big Ideas and Practical Advice on How to Be Human at Work. In Google Books. Harvard Business Review - Press.

Jennings, M. D. (2000). Gap analysis: concepts, methods, and recent results. Landscape Ecology, 15(1), 5–20. https://doi.org/10.1023/a:1008184408300

Kermally, S. (2021). Gurus on People Management. Thorogood.

McLean, S., Read, G. J. M., Hulme, A., Dodd, K., Gorman, A. D., Solomon, C., & Salmon, P. M. (2019). Beyond the Tip of the Iceberg: Using Systems Archetypes to Understand Common and Recurring Issues in Sports Coaching. Frontiers in Sports and Active Living, 1. https://doi.org/10.3389/fspor.2019.00049

Mandelbrot, B. & Hudson, R. L. (2007). The (mis)behavior of markets: A fractal view of financial turbulence. Basic Books.

Nadler, D. A., Tushman, M. L. (1989). Organizational Frame Bending: Principles for Managing Reorientation. Academy of Management Executive, 3(3), pp. 194-204

Nordstrom, C., Choi, G.E., Lloach, C. (2012). The Organizational Life Cycle Stages and Effectiveness. Jonkoping International Business School.

Owen, G. (2013). Game Theory. In Google Books. Emerald Group Publishing.

Quinn, R. E., Cameron, K. (1983). Organizational Life Cycles and Shifting Criteria of Effectiveness: Some Preliminary Evidence. Management Science, 29(1), pp. 33-51

Taleb, N. N. (2012). Antifragile: Things that gain from disorder. Random House.

Chase, M. A. (2010). Should Coaches Believe in Innate Ability? The Importance of Leadership Mindset. Quest, 62(3), 296–307. https://doi.org/10.1080/00336297.2010.10483650

Schiffer, E. (2007). The Power Mapping Tool: A Method for the Empirical Research of Power Relations. In AgEcon Search. https://ageconsearch.umn.edu/record/42410/

Laffont, J-J., Martimort, D., (2002). The Theory of Incentives: The Principal-Agent Model. Princeton University Press. https://doi.org/10.1515/9781400829453